Boots and Pedals

Four Challenging UK Journeys

By

Bob Higgs

Simon wishing you a speedy and complete recovery

Bob

Published in 2020 by FeedARead.com Publishing

Copyright © Robert Higgs

First Edition

The author has asserted their moral right under the
Copyright, Designs and Patents Act, 1988, to be identified
as the author of this work.

All Rights reserved. No part of this publication may be
reproduced, copied, stored in a retrieval system, or transmitted,
in any form or by any means, without the prior written consent of
the copyright holder, nor be otherwise circulated in any form of
binding or cover other than that in which it is published and
without a similar condition being imposed on the subsequent
purchaser.

A CIP catalogue record for this title is available from the British
Library.

All artwork copyright Jane Cope

Acknowledgements

To my wife Ali, for her love, support and encouragement, without which none of these trips would have been possible.

To Tom Coleman, Vernon Hamson, Martin Stansell and Dave Minty, my regular walking companions throughout the 90's. Without the experience gained walking with them for hundreds of miles on misty moors and mountains I would not have had the confidence to tackle Scotland's wildest country on my own.

To the wonderful 'Pilots 4', Peter and Adrian Wynn, Mark Hodgson and Ian Beadle. Their tandem skills, support and companionship combined to give me a truly incredible 'trip of a lifetime'.

To Dr. Min Wild for her constructive and encouraging review of the manuscript. Her helpful advice and suggestions have served to create a more cohesive narrative.

To Jane Cope for her artistic and digital skills in the creation of the maps and cover designs.

To Ian Jay for his willing and invaluable help at the start of the ride, transporting Ali, Peter and I together with the Beast, to the windswept carpark at Cape Cornwall.

Synopsis

Boots and Pedals is a fascinating account of four journeys. Three on foot and one on two wheels. Between 2000 and 2004 Bob Higgs made three solo backpacking trips to the Scottish Highlands. In 2017 to mark his 70th year he made a 2410km UK end to end cycle trip, from S.W. Cornwall to Northern Scotland.

This is a book that will appeal not only to experienced walkers and cyclists but also to anyone who can enjoy reading of the beauty, diversity and challenges of both weather and terrain that Great Britain has to offer.

The first adventure in 2000 was a five day expedition to the Cairngorms, 86km and 6 of the highest mountains in the UK. Next, in 2003 a coast to coast route across Scotland from Inverie on the west coast to Montrose, twelve days and 281km. In 2004 the Cape Wrath Trail, from Fort William to Cape Wrath, thirteen days and 329km.

By 2015 a degenerative eye condition had brought about the premature end to both his hill walking and solo cycling. In 2016 he purchased 'The Beast', a splendid bright yellow tandem. In 2017 with four amazing friends to pilot the tandem in turn, he completed a unique journey from Cornwall to Inverness. The 2410km route took him through the West Country, around the Cotswolds to the Peak District, N. Yorkshire Moors, the Lake District, Galloway, Isle of Arran, Kintyre, Western Highlands, Isle of Skye, Outer Hebrides, N.W. Highlands, Durness and the north coast to Dunnet Head, the most northerly point of mainland UK. Then south through the Flow Country and the Black Isle to Inverness. 29 days cycling and 11 ferry crossings.

The narratives are in the form of daily logs recounting each day's journey, and pondering, sometimes, the knowledge that the day's experiences have given him. His writing displays the passion and enthusiasm with which he undertook these adventures, and his observations and gentle humour are a constant incentive to continue travelling the roads, tracks and hills beside him.

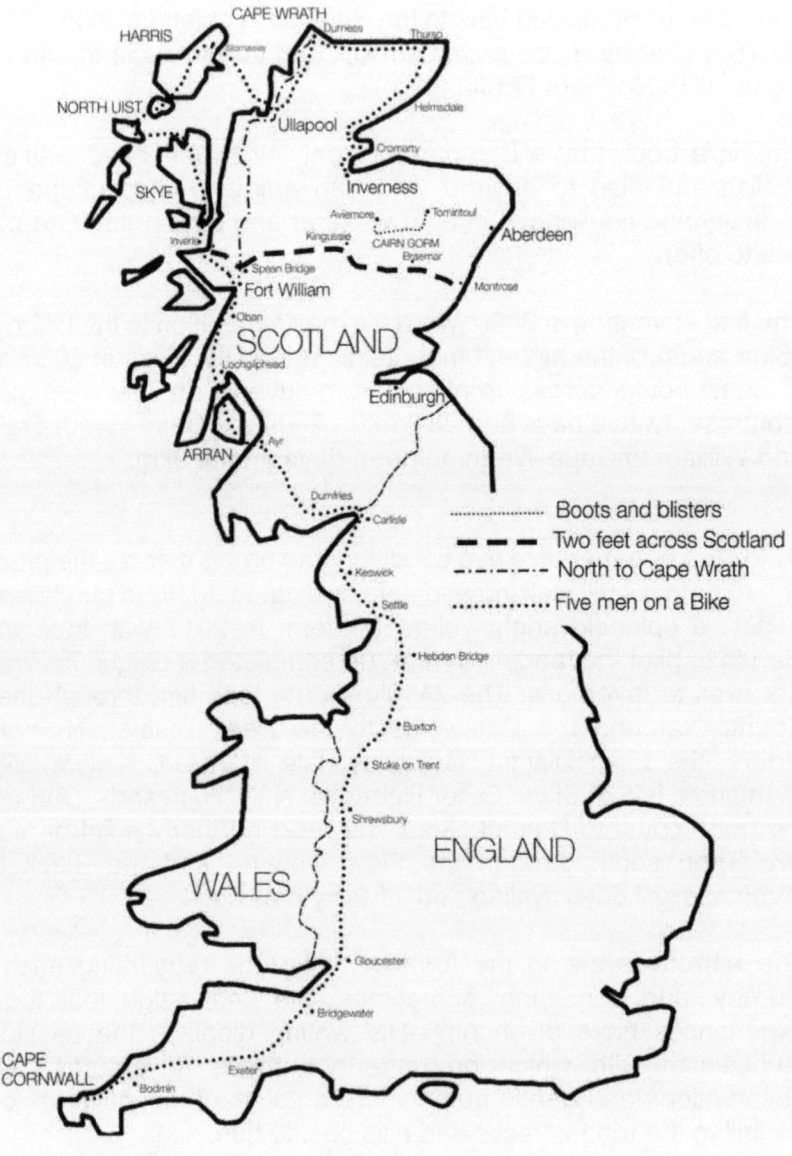

Boots and Pedals

By Bob Higgs

Contents

1. Highs and lows
2. Introduction
3. Boots and Blisters - 5 days in the Cairngorms
    Part 1 The idea
    Part 2 The walk
4. Two feet across Scotland - Scotland coast to coast
    Part 1 The idea
    Part 2 An unexpected delay
    Part 3 The walk
5. North to Cape Wrath - The Cape Wrath Trail
    Part 1 The idea
    Part 2 Preparation
    Part 3 The walk
6. The intervening years
7. Five men on a bike - A tandem tale
    Part 1 The back story
    Part 2 The Beast
    Part 3 The plan
    Part 4 The ride
8. Appendix

1. Highs and Lows in the life of an intrepid traveller.

....It was Day 2 and nothing had prepared me for my first sight of the Cairngorm plateau. I stood on the summit of Beinn a' Bhuird, at 1196m the tenth highest mountain in the UK. Under a cloudless blue sky the plateau spread out in front of me, sloping away gently to the middle distance. The winter snow cover had partially receded , exposing the unique sub-Arctic terrain. Beyond this a black and white panorama - the crags, peaks and snowfields of the distant mountains. It was a truly breathtaking sight that has imprinted itself in my mind...........

....LOCATION —- somewhere in Assynt N. Scotland .... low cloud was swirling across the lonely hill top. My rucksack had landed on the boggy ground with a dull thud and now lay about 3m away from me. The problem being that an extremely sturdy, recently constructed 2m high deer fence stood between me and all I needed to survive in this hostile environment, tent, sleeping bag, stove, food. Looking in both directions along the fence, it extended unbroken till swallowed into the cloud. What on earth would I do if I could not retrieve my bag?..........

....Even the rain that had been falling for the last hour could not detract from the majestic wild beauty of this place. The dark waters of the river flowed silently and determinedly in their haste to be free of the mountains bruising grip. Beyond the river mighty Caledonian pine trees standing amidst a sward of close cropped grass, one of the few remaining stands of these ancient trees that once covered so much of Scotland. They had stood here since the days when rebellion was in the air. The vertiginous crags that rose up behind them offered some limited protection from the destructive forces of the winds that roar through the confines of the glen; in summer tearing at their foliage, in winter coating them with ice and snow. ......

......LOCATION - Clive and Sarah's garage, Settle N. Yorkshire......9.00am I stood there feeling utterly helpless and incapable of offering any useful assistance, as Adrian slowly deconstructed the rear wheel of the tandem. Eleven days and 885km since leaving Cape Cornwall had brought us this far, but there were still another 18 days and 1530km to go. Yet the problem of breaking spokes that had dogged us since day 3 threatened to disrupt or even curtail the whole wonderful trip. Adrian was very able in the cycle repair department and had taught himself the dark secrets of wheel building, probably the most skilled and difficult of all aspects of cycle repair and maintenance. He was to re-build the wheel using the set of new spokes sent to us from the tandem manufacturer, the next twelve hours or so would determine whether his skills could keep our show on the road............

So what was the path that lead me into these situations?

2. INTRODUCTION

'People like us don't have adventures'. I'm sure my father never spoke those words to me, but that was the subliminal message I took from his mantra, oft repeated during my teenage years. 'You must have a career and a steady job, then you can marry and raise a family'. As I matured I did understand his concerns and had immense respect for what he had achieved in his early life. Growing up the eldest of three children in a poor family, he left school at 13 during the first World War. In the immediate post war years he worked as a clerk and studied at night, taking a correspondence course in accountancy. In time becoming a qualified chartered accountant and Fellow in the R.I.C.A. By the 60's when I was in my teens he struggled to come to terms with the way society was developing. Young people's attitudes were changing, with ever increasing opportunities for travel and 'adventure'. There never seemed to be any place left for 'fun' in his template for life. I did in due course succeed on 2 out of his 4 requirements for a successful life. I always had a steady job but not what one would call a career, I married my life long partner Ali in 1968 but we never had a family. It was this latter factor which later on gave me a bit more freedom to have my own adventures. Mine were not in the same vein as those of Francis Chichester or Chris Bonnington, Ranulph Fiennes or Pen Hadow but nevertheless wonderful experiences that lavishly demonstrated the beauty, variety of landscape and supreme challenges of weather and terrain that our incredible country has to offer.

Throughout my boyhood years I loved hearing or reading of 'adventures'. I would imagine myself exploring frozen wastes or steaming jungles; sailing uncharted seas or struggling across arid deserts. By my mid-teens in the early 60's any such thoughts had been driven from my mind by the soft brain-washing of a grammar school education and a very conventional upbringing. I did not appreciate at that young age that 'adventures' come in many different shapes and sizes. Ali and I moved to Devon in 1972 where we have lived ever since and enjoyed a varied and fulfilling life. During the next 15 years or so we regularly walked on Dartmoor and had many walking holidays in different mountainous locations in the UK and Europe. Towards the end of the 80's though Ali's knees were troubling her and she was no longer able to cope with steep ascents and descents. So for several years I had little opportunity for mountain walking.

By 1999 the opportunity for the first of my adventures was rapidly approaching, although I did not realise it at the time. For the previous 8 years I had been walking with a group of friends; regularly exploring Dartmoor, our local wilderness and once a year venturing north to the Lake District and then the Scottish Highlands. We had walked in Glencoe, The Mamores, the Isle of Skye and Torridon but The Cairngorms remained on our 'to do' list. In early 1999 we decided that should be our next challenge. Due to the less accessible nature of the Cairngorms for 'day walks' it was decided the best option would be to camp. Train travel was booked for the first week of May and prudence suggested that a trial back-packing trip was necessary. So it was that over a weekend in early April the five of us set off for Minehead. The plan being to walk, over two days, to Combe Martin. A challenging 60km route along the south-west coast path. It proved to be a pretty disastrous trip. The first casualty we left at Porlock, only a couple of hours into the walk. His grumbling hernia unable to cope with the heavy rucksack. The rest of us carried on, enduring a debilitating selection of impediments, blisters, creaky hips and dodgy knees. The first thing we did on our return was to cancel the train tickets! Not for the first time, I had suffered with very painful blisters on both heels.

The others had no stomach to fulfil the plan to visit the Cairngorms. However I did not give up the idea. Shortly afterwards I read a book of mountain walks by Cameron McNeish, seeds were sown in the fertile soil of my mind and an idea grew rapidly.

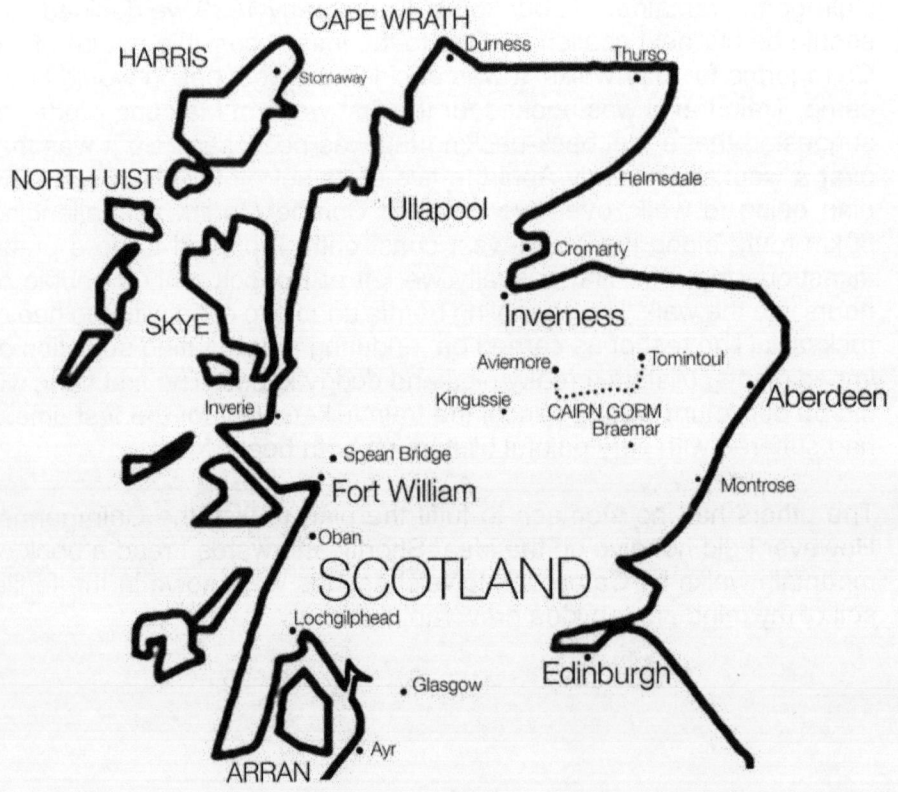

Boots and blisters

3. Boots and Blisters
Five Days in The Cairngorms May 2000

Part 1 The Idea

One of the walks Cameron McNeish described is introduced as:

A long distance high mountain walk taking in the six highest summits in the Cairngorms, Ben Avon, Beinn a Bhuird, Cairngorm, Ben Macdui, Carn Toul and Braeriach. A long remote high mountain walk that is extremely strenuous and serious, there are no technical difficulties.
Distance 73km ascent 2830m
Duration 4 days

The route starts in Tomintoul to the NE of the mountains and finishes in Glen Feshie to the west.

I read his description then read it again with the map for reference and was hooked, determined to make this my introduction to the Cairngorms. Interestingly I found his timings were quite realistic. I could not interest any of my friends, memories of the SW coast path were still too painful for them, so I began planning my first adventure.

The Minehead trip had revealed a few shortcomings in the kit department. Although I had most of the basics, I did equip myself with a multi-fuel stove, stainless steel cooking pans and a Thermarest mattress. I planned the trip from 7th-11th May 2000 and booked my rail tickets accordingly. Around mid-April a late return to winter brought a heavy snowfall to the Scottish highlands. I phoned the outdoor centre near Aviemore and was told that it had resulted in 100% snow cover down to low level. Following the weather reports closely I was relieved to see by the end of the month that there had been 10 days or so of warm spring weather. I spoke to my contact at Glenmore Lodge again and he told me that nearly all snow below 800m had cleared, above that a considerable amount remained on the tops but many slopes were clear. I decided that was a good basis to continue, so set off on May 6th as planned, complete with ice axe and crampons.

Before setting off from Aviemore a couple of conversations regarding the snow conditions led me to the decision to leave ice axe and crampons at the B&B. I booked a taxi to take me to Tomintoul, the start point of the walk, on the following morning, the 7th May all was set for the beginning of my first back packing adventure.

Part 2 The Walk

DAY 1 Sunday May 7th
Tomintoul to Lochbuilg Lodge
Camped at NJ187027
17km

The day dawned bright and sunny and what was even better, settled 'high pressure' weather was forecast for the next few days. An inauspicious start in Tomintoul due to my not checking the map correctly; saw me walk for 200m or so down the wrong road, before realising I needed to be on the other road that I could see across a field! I left the village for the second time in 15 minutes, on a minor road that led steeply downhill towards the River Avon. Just before the river I turned left on to a track leading south into the hills up the east bank of the river. After the slight trauma of finding the way out of Tomintoul, I settled in to the day. The track was good and the walking easy, I began to take in my surroundings; Glen Avon is a good example of a glaciated U-shaped valley. Steep slopes rising up on both sides and the valley floor wide enough to allow the river to wind a sinuous course through fertile looking pastures. Within 4 or 5km the view down to the river was much less pastoral; although the altitude had not risen by very much, the valley was becoming wilder. I suspect accessibility and fertility were contributing factors. There were several small conifer plantations in this lower section of Glen Avon, but within a further 2 or 3km most signs of

Man's intervention had gone and the overwhelming presence of the mountains was becoming more dominant.

I was feeling an ever increasing excitement at the prospect of exploring these mountains. However my mood was slightly tempered by the realisation that even after just a few kilometres I was beginning to feel that familiar sensitivity in my heels that warned of impending blisters. I had hoped that a winter of 'breaking-in' had tamed the killer Zamberlan boots and this did not bode well. The track was still good and views were ever more dramatic. The river Avon turns west after 10km and my route continued south, following the Builg Burn to my first camping site at the southern end of Loch Builg by the ruins of the old lodge which must have seen so much fishing and shooting activity in the 19th and early 20th centuries. Just south of the confluence of the Avon and Builg Burn the track crossed and re-crossed the river. Since there was no such luxury as foot bridges, boots and socks were removed and I waded the river having donned my sandals. A further 5km or so brought me to the ruined lodge and I quickly set up camp on the smooth sward adjacent to the ruins.

I went down to the edge of the loch, stripped off and splashed around in the shallow water. Feeling much refreshed I sat looking north down the loch, then surveyed my damaged heels. It was not a pretty sight, blisters on both heels had rubbed off and were now a gory mess. I was flooded by conflicting emotions, on one hand really disappointed that the foot problem would at best make the rest of the trip a painful endurance test and at worst curtail my adventure; yet the excitement of being in this lonely beautiful place was overpowering. The late afternoon sunshine suffused the glen, loch and distant hills with a soft clear light; accompanied by an endless symphony created by the hundreds of red grouse and black-headed gulls that nested in the moorland around the many lochans just south of the old lodge.

After clearing up my evening meal I sat in the still evening and pondered my situation. The two items of footwear available were sandals, which while comfortable and easy on my heels, could not be considered serious contenders for the 'footwear of choice' award. Boots on the other hand were intent on inflicting pain at every step. I inspected the offending boots and while there did not seem to be any prominent seam in the inner lining, there clearly was a pressure issue there. Having mused on the problem for some time I took the decision to remove part of the leather lining with my trusty (sharp) Swiss Army knife. I cut a section about 40mms square from the lining. This revealed a further layer of white dense foam which was sandwiched between the inner and outer leathers. I was pleased with the neatness of my handiwork, however when trying out the boots although easier I could still feel the pressure on my sore heels. I decided to 'sleep on the problem' and think about it again in the morning.

Before I turned in I walked up on to the higher area above my camp site, towards the nesting grounds of the gulls and grouse. I looked north across the loch and over the days route. To the south lay the hills and moors of the Grampian Mountains, for I was on the edge of the Cairngorms which are the 'hardcore' centre of the Grampians.

I retired to my tent and was pleasantly surprised at the effectiveness of the Thermarest sleeping mat. I slept fitfully, the argumentative chatter of the black-headed gulls continued unabated; complemented by the calls of the grouse and occasional snuffling of deer.

DAY 2 Monday May 8th
Lochbuilg Lodge to Loch Avon
Camped at NJ025032
23km

Some time after 5.00am as the half light of night gave way to the strengthening light of dawn, I got up, put some water on for tea then went to the loch for a splash wash. While having my first cuppa I looked at the boots again and decided there was nothing to lose by cutting out the foam layer that had been exposed by my ministrations of the previous evening. I carefully cut out the foam which proved to be about 2mms thick. I donned socks and boots and went for a short walk up the hill. The improvement was immense, with no pressure on the heels the boots were transformed and I felt comfortable and confident with every step. Indeed for the rest of the expedition I barely gave them another thought.

I was now impatient to start, the weather was fine and sunny and all was well with the world! The 1:25000 map shews a path leading up the hill from Lochbuilg Lodge but petering out after about 3km. True to the map the path did disappear, where it went there was no telling. That has always puzzled me, how a well defined path can just fizzle out. Where did the people go who had trodden that path? Did they all give up at the same point and return the way they had come? Or did they all at a given point fan out in all directions, leaving no further impressions? I mused on these rhetorical questions as I made my way upwards.

From the lodge to the summit of Ben Avon is a climb of around 570m, a steady climb over high moorland terrain. I found it quite difficult to be precisely clear of my exact position. It is a convex slope and sufficiently steep as to give no long views ahead. Very often in terrain like this what appear to be considerable outcrops from below, turn into insignificant pimples close to. As I climbed higher I could not ascertain my position on the map but my instinct told me I had come too far south. I headed north for about 300m and soon was able to pinpoint my position. Soon after the gradient eased as I approached the plateau. I passed Clach Choutsaich 1112m and contoured round to the summit Leabaidh an Dainh Bhuidhe 1171m.

I knew that the Cairngorms are different to any other range of mountains in the UK, but I was not really prepared for the sight that was now unfolding before me. These high level plateaux are designated as sub-Arctic terrain, they appear to be barren but they do support a unique flora. The main summit and the surrounding tops were little more than outcrops standing only metres above the plateau; similar to the granite tors of Dartmoor. The sun dazzled off the vast snow fields that still remained, although there was a very considerable amount of bare ground. To the north and west the edge of the plateau curved its way above the corries and massive deep valley that formed part of the Forest of Glen Avon. The completely snow clad plateau of Beinn A Bhuird lay more or less due west, about 3.5km away. Being just 20m or so higher than Ben Avon it concealed the view further west. To the south there was a glaciated sculpture of interconnecting valleys. In the middle distance were the lower hills that bounded the greener lowlands of Argyll.

From the summit I followed the edge of the plateau south-west towards The Sneck NJ117010 this is the rather mystical name given to the bealach (col) between Ben Avon and Beinn A Bhuird. It is a huge cleft nearly 300metres deep. Fortunately the steeper slope I was about to descend was relatively clear of snow but the east facing slope of Beinn A Bhuird was about 80% covered. This was a thrilling but rather time consuming section, great care had to be taken descending as it was steep and in parts quite craggy. I was able to make part of the ascent on bare ground but then had no option but to cross the snow field. The snow was of a good consistency but it was slow going, often having to kick steps.

As the slope began to ease on the approach to the North Top to my left the South Top came into view. The plateau here was completely snow covered and the fearsome east facing cliffs of the South Top appeared black against the dazzling snow. As I climbed the last few metres on to the North Top, the view west unfolded, for me it will forever remain the most dramatic, beautiful and awe inspiring memory of all my trips to mountainous parts. The North Top of Beinn a Bhuird stands at 1179m, the tenth highest peak in Great Britain, to the west the plateau, still partially snow covered, dropped away for 5km before plunging into the lesser of the two huge passes that traverse north to south, the Cairngorms. The pass - Glen Derry leading into The Lairig an Laoigh, was unseen from this distance, but the crags and snow fields of the mountains on its western side created a breathtaking black and white panorama. Carn Crom, Derry Cairngorm, Sgurr an Lochan Uaine, Stob Coire Etchachan, with the peaks of Cairngorm, Ben Macdui and Carn Toul peeping over their tops. The barren plateau with the early afternoon sun reflecting off the watery remains of the recent thaw.

I set my sights on Stob Coire Etchachan as that seemed to be about where I would descend into the Lairig an Laoigh. On the way I stopped and sat on a convenient outcrop and while having some refreshment and a relax, I happened to lean back and found the rock supported my rucksack at such an angle that I felt as comfortable as if I had been sitting in a deckchair. The warmth of the sun quickly lulled me to sleep. Wonderfully refreshed I awoke about 20 minutes later all set for the final section of the days walk.

The descent into Lairig an Laoigh was extremely steep and I was heartily thankful for my walking pole. Once on the floor of the pass I headed north for 2km or so, to the last challenge of the day, The Fords of Avon NJ042031. I knew that of the expedition's 6 or 7 river crossings, this crossing of the River Avon would be the most demanding. As there had been no recent rain the river would not be in full spate. However, the melt water from the hundreds of acres of snow fields in its catchment area would mean that there would still be a fair amount of flow. The apprehension turned to a rather sick feeling in the pit of my stomach, as I stood on the bank and surveyed the 'Fords of Avon'. The flow immediately up and downstream of the ford was pretty frightening, but the ford itself was not going to be a cakewalk. The river was about

10-12m wide and although the riverbed at this point was reasonably level it was very swift flowing.

I set about removing boots and socks, unzipped the legs of my trousers and stepped into a quiet pool on the edge of the cataract. Completely unprepared for what was to follow, I took one step into the current. I did not have a secure anchorage for the walking pole and the force of the water nearly unbalanced me. Fortunately my weight was such that two frantic steps backwards, falling as I went I landed in a very undignified way back on the rock from which I had just stepped. The second time was fine, ensuring that at each step one leg and the pole were securely placed I crossed with no further mishap. Having dried feet and donned boots I set off up the right bank of the river for about 2km to find a camp spot on the banks of Loch Avon.

It is difficult to imagine there could be a more dramatic place to spend a night. The vista from the outfall of the loch was majestic, towering cliffs on all sides plunging straight into the loch with the evening sun creating great shadows at the head of the loch, where the incredibly steep headwall rises over 400m on to the main Cairngorm plateau. Everything was so peaceful but little imagination was needed to realise how hostile this could be under different weather conditions.

The weather remained benign and after my meal a last wander, marvelling again at the beauty of this wild place.

DAY 3 Tuesday May 9th
Loch Avon to An Gharbh
Camped at NN959986
13km

Another fine and sunny day. The early morning sun illuminated the far end of Loch Avon with the Shelter Stone clearly defined on the southern side.

Excited at the prospect of the day ahead I breakfasted and packed without delay. From my camp spot the path lead around the north side of the loch and angled up the steep south facing slope to The Saddle, the unimaginatively named bealach, which is in fact the entrance to a rather spectacular hanging valley, Strath Nethy. This is a deep glaciated valley running north south immediately to the east of Cairngorm which in the Ice Age was truncated by the huge glacier that left the high plateau and ground its way down the course of what is now Glen Avon.

I paused for a while in The Saddle, although less than 100m above the loch, the view was already very dramatic, an unbroken view of Glen Avon, the loch and the plateau. I turned and headed north up Strath Nethy for no more than a kilometre. To reach the summit of Cairngorm I had to make a direct assault on its steep eastern flank, between the two areas of crags. The slope was very steep, rising about 500m in less than 1.5km, this represents an average gradient of about 1:3 and as the lower section was considerably steeper than the last half a kilometre to the summit; it is not unreasonable to suggest that initially the gradient is about 1:2.

There was still a great deal of snow on this slope but the steepest part was clear and I encountered no difficulty. As I climbed the views south and east opened out. In the distant haze I could pick out Beinn a Bhuird and other landmarks of the previous day's walk. All of a sudden I was on the summit plateau. Close by was the rather ugly communications mast and its aluminium hut of equipment with its surrounding protective stone defences, crowning the summit with a giant pylon topped cairn.

I spent some time taking in the view. Immediately to the west and south the fearsome black crags and cliffs of the north facing corries stood out in stark relief against the snow. Although there was probably only about 40-50% snow cover on the plateau the effect in the dazzling sunshine was overpowering and made me realise the importance of sun glasses! About 5km away to the SSW was Ben Macdui appearing to be only slightly higher than the surrounding slopes. Rather understated considering it is the second highest peak in the U.K. Further away again to the west Carn Toul and Braeriach with some of the connecting horseshoe ridge were clearly visible. A rather thrilling insight into the next day's walk.

The route to Ben Macdui was easy walking, a mixture of snow fields and bare scree. I did not hurry, just drinking in the stupendous views and the thrill of being in this unique environment. It took me nearly 3 hours, following a rather serpentine route trying not to lose too much height over the plateau's undulations. I rested a while, chatting to a couple who were sat in the open summit shelter.

My immediate destination for the day now lay due west about 3km away. To reach this goal entailed a 700m descent into the Lairig Ghru, across the River Dee then another steep climb into An Garbh Choire and another river crossing. I anticipated that both rivers would not be entirely straightforward to cross. I left the summit of Ben Macdui and headed north-west to find the Allt a Choire Moire at about NN985993, a stream that rises near the summit of Ben Macdui then plunges steeply down the side of Lairig Ghru. I soon reached the top of the watercourse. This proved to be a descent to savour and remember, incredibly steep but no real technical difficulty, just demanding of a cool head, good balance and sure feet.

The view from the floor of the Lairig Ghru was pretty awesome, the valley is a huge glaciated trench that carves through the centre of the Cairngorm mountains. Looking south, to the right, the unmistakeable pointed summit of Devil's Point; while on the left the more rounded profile of Carn a Mhaim. My concerns regarding the first river crossing were well founded, a considerable flow and not enough rocks meant boots off and wade across. Once re-shod I contoured round on the west side of the Lairig Ghru then began climbing. I came to the river - Allt an Garbh Choire and followed its north bank up into An Garbh Choire. This is a valley set above the Lairig Ghru enclosed on three sides by the Braeriach - Carn Toul horseshoe ridge, which must rank as one of the most spectacular ridges in the U.K. The wall of the valley was deeply scalloped by four clearly defined corries hanging beneath the towering crags of the ridge. Altogether a very impressive and slightly intimidating place. To put the size of these mountains into some sort of context, the floor of the valley where I pitched my tent, is at an altitude of over 700m; this is higher than many of the mountains in the Lake District, Snowdonia and the Pennines. The summits of Carn Toul and Braeriach are 500m higher again, at over 1200m.

My route the following day was to climb Carn Toul, so I needed to be on the south bank of the river. Just over a kilometre into this vast amphitheatre there is a stone shelter built on the side of the river. I could see that the ground around it was fairly level and decided to camp there, as it was ideally placed for the next morning's climb. My concerns over the second crossing were also correct and for the second time in under an hour boots were removed. I was soon pitching my tent on a little grassy area that I suspect had been used by many climbers and backpackers over the years. The evening sun gave a certain warmth to my immediate surroundings, contrasting starkly with the cold light reflecting off the rocks and scree high above me. The rim of the valley seemed to be a continuous band of snow, like a wintery fringe accentuating the black crags beneath and the great tongues of snow curving over the edge, licking the rock faces of the corries.

A fabulous day in the mountains rounded off by a good supper and a restful night's sleep.

DAY 4 Wednesday May 10th
An Gharbh Choire to Glen Feshie
Camped at NN850985
20km

The 'head out of the fly sheet' routine revealed nothing. My world had shrunk to a few square metres of boggy grass with me at its centre; the high corries of An Gharbh Choire and the towering cliffs of Braeriach were just a memory from the previous evening, now completely hidden in cloud. As the mist billowed and eddied, dark ghostly shadows and shapes appeared then melted away again; the only suggestion of solidity in a mist wrapped world. The hour was still early and by the time I had washed, dressed, breakfasted and drunk my second mug of tea the situation had improved somewhat. The light overhead was brighter, a hopeful indication that not too far above the mantle of cloud clear sky and the morning sun were ready and waiting to take over weather duty from the unwelcome cloud.

An Gharbh Choire was once again displaying a misty majesty by the time I was ready to set off. The plateau beyond Lairig Ghru was more or less clear, but cloud maintained its reluctance to loosen its grip on the summit of Ben Macdui. Looking down into the Lairig Ghru it appeared to be a ghostly glacier of cloud.

My immediate objective was Carn Toul. The corrie containing Lochan Uaine was immediately above my camp site. The evening before I had sat looking up trying to plot a route through the crags that lay higher up towards the rim of the corrie. It was one of those immensely satisfying climbs, steep and challenging so one had to pick and plan several moves at a time, which meant a good rhythm could be maintained, with a very satisfying rate of height gain. I climbed over the rim of the corrie adjacent to the outfall stream and stood to take in my new surroundings. An utterly awesome sight, the still, cold lochan was set in a vast amphitheatre, its rocky wall rising up several hundred metres on three sides and crowned with a pelmet of fearsome crags.

An eerie creamy blue light emanated from a large floe of ice just under the surface at the 'shallow-end' of the lochan, nearest to the outfall: I concluded this was the remnant of the winter's ice. While the top of the ice had melted in the recent warm weather, the remainder was still locked to the bed of the lochan, thus defying the normal laws of physics.

The climb up to the summit of Carn Toul was superb, a wonderful prolonged scramble up the north ridge, with a vertiginous slope to my left, dropping 600m to the floor of Lairig Ghru. There was no real technical difficulty, tremendous views across and along Lairig Ghru. To the south the formidable pinnacle of Devil's Point, seeming to almost defy gravity, so steeply does it rise from the bottom of Lairig Ghru. The sky above was bright with the suggestion that blue skies were not far away, but down below the glacier of thick mist still flowed.

Mist swirled about me as I stood at the summit. The time was about 10.00am and I had hoped that by then the mist would have made a concerted effort to disperse, but it was shewing a distinct reluctance to give way to sunshine. I took advantage of a rather weak phone signal, to call Ali, while we talked a collie dog emerged out of the mist, to be closely followed by its master. We chatted for a time and he told me of an outdoor centre by Loch Insh, which served a mean breakfast. As I would be walking out near there the following morning I mentally filed that nugget of information. By the time I set off again I had good views of the magnificent horseshoe ridge, which would take me around the rim of An Garbh Choire to Braeraich. The Angel's Peak - Sgor an Lochain Uaine, lay just a kilometre and a half around the ridge, the second of the twin peaks that overlooked the corrie of Lochan Uaine. It was easy walking and I made good progress. The next high point on the ridge, more of a rounded lump at the head of the horseshoe, was Carn na Criche, beyond which was the Wells of Dee, a few rather inauspicious shallow pools which were the source of the River Dee. I could see that a considerable snowfield extended from the rim of An Gharbh Choire towards the Wells of Dee, more or less covering the infant river until about 20m back from the rim, where it issued from a snow tunnel, more like a full bloodied teenager than an infant. Then throwing itself over the edge with abandon in a spectacular waterfall. My initial awe of the view was soon replaced by anxiety of its implications. I had to cross the snowfield and clearly any attempt to cross too close to the edge ran the risk of falling through the roof of the tunnel and plunging into the icy torrent. I diverted well over 100m towards the Wells of Dee and it was still with great relief that I safely completed the crossing.

The views I had enjoyed since Carn Toul had been fabulous, the curving ridge around what seemed like a huge bite out of the plateau. There was a great contrast between the snow, bare soil and rock of the ridge against the dark almost black rock faces and crags of the corries below. All with the backdrop of the Ben Macdui plateau and glimpses of the mist filled Lairig Ghru. But by the time I reached the summit of Braeraich, the mist that had been swirling round for the previous 30 minutes or so had now consolidated once again into cloud. I now had very limited visibility in more or less a white out situation. Meaningful visibility was limited to about 15-20m. I was a little concerned that I now faced a challenging task, to find my way across Moine Mhor - The Great Moss and descend safely into Glen Feshie. but part of me thrilled at the prospect of employing my compass, at least it would give a bit of spice to what so far had been a wonderful trip in beautiful benign weather conditions. I took a bearing from the map to Loch an Cnapan NN917961 this took me past Einich Cairn and above the crags over the corries of Loch Eanaich and well clear of the Dee snowfield. The terrain was very uneven and at times impossible to maintain a straight line course but I came on the outfall stream about 100m from Loch an Cnapan. Under the circumstances I thought that was reasonably creditable navigating. At the top end of the loch I took another bearing, on the start of a track that would take me to Glen Feshie. This time I was spot on, admittedly it was only about 750m away!

I set off along the track and after about a kilometre turned right on to a path that lead NW towards Carn Ban Mor, the cloud had lifted allowing me to appreciate what a bleak place is Moine Mhor. I began losing height and after a while the path lead through areas of fairly young conifer plantations. In less than 2km I was at Auchlean in Glen Feshie. This is the most remote farm in a remote glen, 8km up the no through road from Feshiebridge, it takes a particular type of farmer to cope with these sorts of conditions. I was to find out in the morning what type of person that was! I turned right and headed down the road, very tired and anxious to find somewhere to camp.

The road was fenced on both sides but in less than 2km an unfenced area on the edge of a plantation offered all I needed except running water. I did feel rather guilty that I had to climb over 2 wire fences in order to fill my water container in the River Feshie but when needs must......

The only other incident of note that day was allowing my supper to boil over. I was forced to spend about 20 minutes cleaning my multi-fuel stove, pricking pasta residue from the burner, before I could complete the cooking.

DAY 5 Thursday May 11th
Glen Feshie to Loch Insh
13km

An early morning call of nature was rudely interrupted by the appearance of a battered pickup truck from the direction of the farm. An unpleasant discussion with the farmer who clearly held entrenched and definite views on wild campers, left me no option other than to effect an expeditious departure, while my rustic adversary watched me from the cab of his truck parked 100m away.

Half an hour later I set off down the road, smiling what I hoped was a cheery smile as I passed the truck. I felt wrongly affronted but I was pleased I had not reacted to his rudeness, which probably indicated that he had on occasions just cause to be upset with campers for their thoughtless actions. Within a short time all rancour ebbed away and the still beauty of the early morning overcame me. As I looked over a gate into one of the riverside meadows two hares were gambolling in the sunshine. By the time I reached Feshiebridge hunger was making its presence felt. Remembering the conversation the previous morning I turned left and headed for Loch Insh. It was about 9.45 as I entered the gates, passing several dozen youngsters already preparing dinghies, sail boards, canoes etc.,. for their day's activities. I found the dining area more or less deserted, a young woman was just finishing standing the chairs on the tables, an ominous sign I thought! Catching sight of me she said in a cheerful Australian accent 'Hiya,! Would you like some brekkie?'

There followed a wonderful ample breakfast, willingly and cheerfully prepared. There were three young women, all Aussies and as they bustled back and forth with jugs of orange juice, pots of tea, piles of toast and an enormous double everything fried breakfast, wanted to hear all about my trip.

A fitting end to what had been a demanding, challenging but incredibly fulfilling and exciting expedition.

An hour or so later I made my way back to the road and phoned the taxi man who had taken me to Tomintoul. Within the hour I was back in the hustle and bustle of Aviemore. A slightly unreal feeling that less than 24 hours earlier I had been making my way by compass across the Cairngorm plateau.

CONCLUSION

I remained in a sort of euphoric state for some days, the experience had been so intense. Even though I had been lucky to have had good weather, my senses had been at a heightened level for the whole walk. A very different experience than that of walking with a group, when one can consciously or sub-consciously rely on others in the group for some of the decision making.

More than anything though I was so grateful to Ali for making no objections to taking myself off into the wild. Although she was confident of my ability it was only natural to worry about the unforeseen incidents that can happen no matter what level of experience one has.

I think it true to say that even on the journey home I was beginning to think about my next adventure.

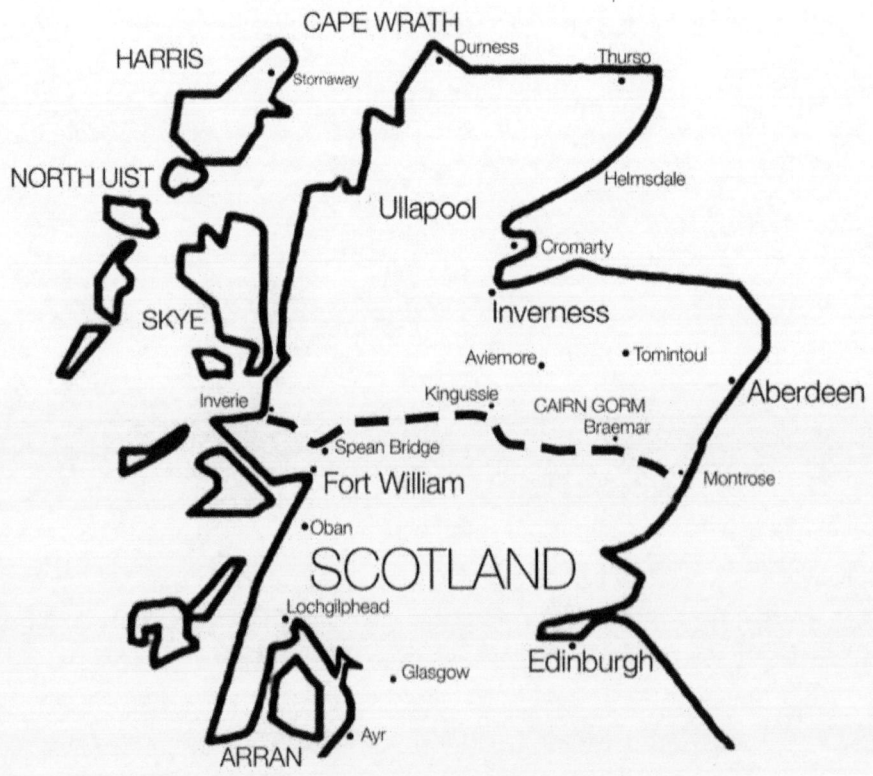

Two feet across Scotland - - -

4. Two Feet Across Scotland
Coast to Coast walk - May 2003

Part 1 The Idea

In the early 90's I had read about the Ultimate Challenge. An organised but un-supported coast to coast walk across Scotland. At the time I did not have the experience to attempt such a challenge, but the concept had lit a slow fuse of interest in my mind. In the summer of 2000, fuelled by the Cairngorm trip that fuse began to crackle and fizz. Ali and I talked it over and she agreed that as long as she had full details of my route and I reported in as regularly as mobile phone signals and public phones allowed then she would be happy (ish!)

Many happy evenings during the winter of 2000/01 were spent surrounded by maps and guide books, planning a route. An invaluable addition to my way-finding arsenal was the SRWS handbook (Scottish Rights of Way Society). A wonderful publication describing 332 rights of way in Scotland and including a brilliant detailed map.

By the late winter I had set a route that was a mixture of mountain, glens, roads and open moorland, with a couple of options for high level diversions, should weather conditions and energy reserves allow. My route started at Inverie in Knoydart on the west coast and finished at Montrose on the east coast. A walk of about 330km which I thought would take me 13 or 14 days.

Shops would be few and far between and anyway unlikely to stock the high energy low bulk foods that I needed. I was to be unsupported and it is impossible (or unrealistic) to carry food for two weeks. So my only practical option was to rely on collecting supply parcels from post offices en route, using the Post Restante service. With thanks to successive cut backs there was not an over abundance of sub-post offices in that area of the Scottish Highlands. The only viable choices were Kingussie and Braemar, rather too close together but still workable. The finalising of dates would have to take into account opening hours and any early closing/closed days of the post offices.

Part 2. An Unexpected Delay

Through the late winter early spring of 2001 I sorted the finer details of my projected next trip and was keenly anticipating setting off in the first week of May. However the spring of 2001 brought the horrors of Foot and Mouth and I soon realised that my trip would not happen that year.

At short notice I booked a two week holiday trekking in the Atlas Mountains in Morocco. It was a wonderful experience, but I could not think of it as a true 'adventure' because I had not organised it and was just one in a group of a dozen or so.

Unfortunately I returned bringing with me more than just good memories. I had suffered a sickness/tummy upset at the end of the trip. Later that summer while walking the West Highland Way another similar bout prompted me to seek medical advice. This revealed that I was suffering from giardiasis, a particularly nasty parasitic micro-organism that once established in the gut can be quite difficult to eliminate. This indeed proved to be the case and it was not until the autumn of 2002, after 12 months of poor health that I really began to feel that I may have beaten the little devils.

By the beginning of 2003 I was confidently planning to start the coast to coast in early May.

At last after a two year delay I set off by train to Fort William on May 1st 2003. All the preparations had been made, copy maps, routes and grid references made out for Ali; food parcels despatched and a change of clothes forwarded to a B and B in Montrose, for the homeward journey.

Part 3. The Walk

Day 1 Friday May 2nd
Inverie to Loch Mhaim
Camped at NM903946
Est 19km

I caught the early train to Mallaig, where I joined an excited group of walkers and climbers on the quayside waiting for the little ferry to take us across Loch Nevis to Inverie.

We disembarked in a flurry of rucksacks, walking boots, coils of rope and all sorts of other camping paraphernalia. I stood on the little jetty in a fuddle of mixed emotions, excitement and apprehension. I asked one of my fellow passengers to take a photo and checking the map walked out of the village in a bit of a daze.

My objective was to follow SRWS route 238 which passes through the heart of the remote mountains that form the southern border of Knoydart. It is a 27km path from Inverie to Strathan, at the western end of Loch Arkaig. The handbook describes it as one of the best cross country routes in the Western Highlands. The route is shown on Roy's map of 1755 and on a large scale OS map of 1876 it is classified as a second class road. It is a measure of the remoteness of this part of the west coast, to realise that for centuries these coastal communities had only rough tracks through the mountains to connect them with the rest of Scotland. In the early 19th century Thomas Telford built a single track road from Fort William to Mallaig which was not fully widened until 2009! The railway came towards the end of the 19th century.

A short distance out of Inverie the path crossed the river and climbed steadily to a height of 550m at Mam Meadall where it then dropped back to sea level. There was then a rather boggy section across a stream and along the shoreline of Loch Nevis before another climb up to 310m.

The weather forecast had not been good but the rain had held off until 16.00 at the start of the second climb. I carried on until 17.30 in heavy rain but when a suitable camp site presented itself by a lochan I decided to call it a day. One of the problems of backpacking and wet weather is keeping the inside of the tent dry. In fact it is more a case of keeping the ingress of water to a minimum. I have always been averse to lighting a stove in the tent so I had to wait and hope that the rain would ease and allow me to cook dinner. The rain did not ease and in due course I fired up the multi-fuel stove outside and prepared the first of the expedition freeze dried meals. These were a bit of a luxury, quite expensive but well worth the money, so quick, just add the relevant amount of boiling water and leave for five minutes. I also had a starter in the form of powdered tomato soup to which I added some Smash, the resulting glutinous red slurry was really tasty and filling. It has to be said though that one's nasal protuberance would definitely have pointed skywards if that had been served up at home.

I was particularly pleased with my Paramo coat and trousers, really comfortable and very waterproof. My rucksack was causing a bit of shoulder ache but I hoped I could adjust the straps in order to eliminate that. Feet were a bit sore and I fully expected a return of the blister problem.

Day 2 Saturday May 3rd
Lochan Mhaim to
Campsite at NN187835
Est 38km

I awoke early and before 06.00 was up and about, encouraged to see some early morning sunshine. My horizons were restricted by the surrounding mountains and it soon became clear that there was rather too much cloud and this did nothing to instil confidence of a dry day ahead. Breakfast consisted of lumpy porridge and chocolate.

I broke camp and set off just after 08.00, the eastern end of the path down to Strathan was more boggy and followed a tortuous course, winding this way and that. The slow progress was frustrating so early in what I knew would be a long day. In the first hour I covered a straight line distance of only 2km. It was 11.20 by the time I reached the western end of Loch Arkaig. The rain had started about 09.00 and persisted on and off all morning, more on than off. This did little to aid my progress, but at least now I had a tarmac road rather than a boggy path. Loch Arkaig must be a contender for the Premier League of Scottish lochs. An impressive 19km long it has a more or less east-west alignment. The whole area of Knoydart has no road access from any direction, although there are a number of estate tracks which give limited access to some fringes of the wilderness. Unlike many remote parts of the Highlands which have tracks suitable for 4-wheel drive vehicles which penetrate for miles from public roads. Even the most cursory study of a 1:50k OS map will reveal the reason for this lack of access. This area of the Western Highlands is a mass of mountains which interlock and dovetail together, barely leaving any room between, what room there is has to accommodate a multitude of rivers and lochs.

Having reached the relative luxury of a straight road I could only wonder at the determination and fortitude of the inhabitants of former times who regularly traversed this path taking horses laden with barrels of salted herrings etc.,. to market. I had noticed some evidence along the way of the original surface which must have extended for a good part of its way. Closely laid stone, rather reminiscent of the stone sets that are now used on some maintained estate paths.

After the first few kilometres coming westwards there is no habitation along this glen, so traffic was not an issue. As I drew away from Knoydart the views back became more and more dramatic. The heavy squally rain showers were being hustled along by a stiff westerly wind, thus giving another reason for rearward glances. For the next couple of hours frequent heavy squalls obliterated the mountains as they swept down the loch. Rain rattled on my back, the strong wind whipping rain drops from my hood. As the wind eased and the last dribbles of rain were being squeezed from the heavens a backward glance revealed the mountains again, very often lit with that crystal clear light that comes after rain. After 9 or 10km, looking ahead, I began to see parts of the massive ridge that lies between Loch Lochy and Glen Gloy and further in the distance the top of Creag Meagaidh. My route would take me up Glen Gloy the following day and past Creag Meagaidh the next day. There was a contingency plan to divert and climb Creag Meagaidh if weather and energy levels allowed.

I tried to discipline myself to stop every couple of hours for 10 - 15 minutes just to take on some food and get a break from the pack. I had a hydration system which enabled me to drink whenever I wanted. This trip's selection of energy snacks for daytime consumption was dried fruit and nuts, 70% Green and Black chocolate, beef jerky, dry roasted pumpkin and soya seeds and sesame seed snack biscuits. All very high calorific content but very often I just longed for a ham and tomato roll. The jerky was mostly quite tasty but needed a lot of energy to eat, being a bit like chewing the strap of my old school satchel. The pumpkin seeds were excellent but I found the soya seeds very dry and not ideal when I was a bit dehydrated anyway.

The weather had improved, the last of the squalls having passed through in early afternoon. For a few hours the sun shone off and on and all was well with the world.

As the afternoon wore on my mind turned to thoughts of finding a camp spot. The OS map showed a campsite at Gairlochy which is about 8 or 9km beyond the end of Loch Arkaig, so I was pretty sure that if I could not find a wild camp spot towards the eastern end of the loch I would have to go on to the campsite. For some considerable distance before the bottom end of the loch all suitable flat areas were sectioned off and marked with plot numbers. I assumed whoever managed this rented out these sites for caravans. I plodded on in the hope I would come across something more suitable, but alas no such luck. To make matters worse it began to rain again, not the vicious squalls of earlier but just a steady rain. Around 18.00 I found a public telephone and called Ali. This did a lot to restore my humour and I headed off again for Gairlochy. In the little village I was about to pass a house and saw a B&B sign outside. I was so tired that in a moment of weakness I pressed the doorbell. A very polite lady told me there was no room, so I plodded on, with the distinct impression that had I arrived in a respectable saloon car she would have found a vacant room.

The man at the campsite was very obliging and pleasant, showed me where to pitch my tent and said there were two showers which fed on 20p coins. I struck camp and went off with my wash bag. There was not a dribble of hot water to be found so 15 minutes later and 40p worse off I prepared to have my evening meal. A steady rain forced me to carry out this operation in the partial shelter of the washing up zone, with an uncompromising wind to make life more uncomfortable.

I was so tired and by the time I had retired to the tent a foot inspection revealed blisters on both heels, another job for Compeed Man! I slept the Sleep of the Just and treated myself to a lie-in the following morning.

Day 3 Sunday May 4th
Gairlochy to Glen Gloy
Camped at NN301932
Est 18km

A fine morning and a leisurely start to the day. There was still too much cloud around for comfort but at least for the time being it was bright and clear. I was prepared for possible problems in the first section of the day's route, my immediate objective was Glenfintaig on the A82 at the bottom end of Glen Gloy; only about 5 or 6km away as the eagle flies but with main roads and forestry to negotiate. The OS map showed two possible paths that would offer an off-road option all or part of the way. I set off at 10.15 and within 30 minutes had found my only option was the road. The first choice, a path along the bottom edge of some forestry more or less on the shoreline of Loch Lochy would have taken me to Glenfintaig. Part way along the track a car stopped and I was told in a polite but extremely firm way that 'no there was definitely no right of way here'. Back on the road near the campsite the second option, a path through the forest boasted a pair of substantial steel gates set in an equally unwelcoming high deer fence.

I set off up the B8004 to the Commando Monument on the A82. This was a fairly quiet road with stunning views to the south; where The Aonachs and The Mamores formed a stunning mountain panorama, with Ben Nevis crowned with its cloudy shroud, a looming presence behind. Further along I saw two birds of prey, slightly smaller than buzzards, they seemed to be worrying a sheep. I did wonder whether they were goshawks who were rather too interested in a new-born lamb; but with no binoculars they were just too far away to be certain.

At the Monument I stopped for a few minutes, joining a throng of bikers and sightseers. I then gritted my teeth and set off up the A82. This was extremely busy and by far the most uncomfortable 5km of the whole trip. The sun was shining and views north and west were beautiful, but I was hardly able to really enjoy them. Cars, lorries and coaches whizzed by at great speed, most of the way I had to walk on the road as the verge was non-existent or too uneven. Part way along something at the side of the road caught my attention and the image has stayed with me ever since, somehow representing how nature can survive even in the face of all the pressures that 21st century life exerts upon it. A squarish hole about half a metre cube had been hewn out of the rock to take surface water from the side of the road into a culvert that ran under the road. The south-west facing side of the hole had been colonised by a primrose plant; the warm micro-climate allowing it to flourish in the sheltered environment. A solid yellow drift of flowers extended round the hole and right down into it, to the point where depth excluded direct sunlight. I stopped for some minutes, rather overcome by such beauty in such close conjunction with the ghastly traffic. The other lesson it brought home to me was how much people miss when rushing from one place to another. I doubted whether anybody driving along the A82 had been aware of that spectacular display.

It was with huge relief that I turned off the main road at Glenfintaig on to the minor road that lead to the upper reaches of Glen Gloy. The road dropped steeply down, past Glenfintaig Lodge, over a magnificent stone bridge, then steeply uphill to the 'big house' and thence on up the glen. I sat at the side of the river, contemplating and admiring the magnificent General Wade bridge as I chewed my fruit and nuts.

....

A Brief Diversion into History

In the early part of the 18th century, following the Jacobite Rebellion of 1715 the British Government perceived the necessity of making the Highlands of Scotland more accessible. Many books have been written on this subject and I do not intend to add myself to that collection of learned historians. However a few salient points are worth mentioning, they being particularly pertinent to the area I was now approaching.

In 1724 General George Wade was sent to Scotland, having been commissioned to undertake a programme of road building to aid the movement of troops from the Lowlands to the Highlands. The purpose of this was to facilitate the subjugation of the Clans whose activities were causing increased consternation further south. General Wade's plan was for building four roads and a series of forts and fortified barracks; thus creating a communication network and the means of defending it. At regular intervals he constructed what became known as King's Houses, which served to provide shelter and sustenance for the hundreds of soldiers involved in the project. A few of these still survive today, probably the most famous being Kings House Hotel on the edge of Rannoch Moor at the top of Glencoe.

One of the four roads went from Dalwhinnie to Laggan on Speyside to Fort Augustus in the Great Glen via the Corrieyairack Pass. Spur roads went N.E. to Ruthven Barracks near Kingussie and S.W. to Glen Gloy to Gairlochy in the Great Glen and thence to Fort William.

General Wade built his roads 16 feet wide, narrowing to 10 feet where physical constraints demanded. He used highly skilled masons and carpenters in the construction of the many bridges that he built. So many of these having received regular maintenance over the intervening 280 years or so are still in use today. Their unique design being clearly identifiable.

After the 1745 Jacobite uprising the British Government realised the pressing need for a detailed map of the Highlands. In 1747 Lt. Col. David Watson was appointed to fulfil this task. A young surveyor, William Roy although still a civilian was seconded to Watson and it was his work using innovative surveying techniques and equipment that ultimately lead to the publication of what is referred to as The Duke of Cumberland's Map in 1755. Roy went on to join the Military where his unique skills resulted in steady promotion. He became one of the most notable surveyors and cartographers of his time. For many years he championed the cause of having a national Ordnance Survey, but it was not until some years after his death in 1790 that the Government found the considerable sum of money required to undertake this project.

An interesting footnote to this is that after the 7 year war with France, in the latter part of the 18th century, Major William Caulfeild was appointed to carry on the work of constructing Military Roads. He continued to use the same methods and designs as General Wade; ultimately building over four times the distance of roads than General Wade; yet his name is almost forgotten. For whatever reason the O.S. refers to General Wade's roads by name but those built by Major Caulfeild are just referred to as Old Military Roads.

....

Back in Glen Gloy

Glen Gloy is bounded on its N.W. side by the huge straight ridge I had seen the previous day. This ridge is part of The Great Glen, a massive glacial trench that extends for well over 100km from Inverness to Fort William. Having crossed the General Wade bridge and climbed past

Glenfintaig House, the view opened out. Stretching ahead a classic U-shaped valley, conifer plantations covering a lot of the steep sides. The sunshine had disappeared and it was not long before a light rain started. The heavy rain clouds realising what fun they were having soon increased the rate of discharge. I walked on for a couple of hours but by 17.00 was tired of that game and began looking for a camp spot. I was in a fairly dense plantation that seemed to offer little in way of level swards. Eventually to my left there was a smallish area of grass at the confluence of two streams. I was not convinced by it but gave it a go. Having quickly pitched the tent I scrambled inside to escape the downpour and immediately found the slope was too much. However I managed to wedge myself and very quickly dozed off. I awoke at 18.45, the rain had stopped, so I unravelled myself and decided to reconnoitre, hoping to find a better site. Sure enough, no more than 100m further on, a wide flat area between the forest and a stream. Half an hour later I had relocated and was much happier, confident of a good night's sleep. A review of weather conditions did not reveal much, only misty tops, broken cloud and watery blueish patches so no grounds for undue confidence. I retreated to my sleeping bag shortly after 21.00.

Day 4. Monday May 5th
Glen Gloy to Melgarve
Camped at NN468960
Est 21km

I awoke some time after dawn and dozed till 07.00, I enjoyed the luxury of a lie-in, even more as the whisper of early morning rain on the tent did nothing to lure me from the embryonic warmth of my sleeping bag. When eventually I emerged from the tent, the rather limited horizons of my forest camp site reduced my weather assessing. Looking east up the glen a reluctant sun peered shyly through pressing low clouds and westward the view was even less encouraging, but at least the rain had more or less stopped. As usual the breakfasting and packing up routine took about two hours and I duly set off just after 09.00. I was entering the area that could be regarded as the 'bottom left-hand corner' of the Monadhliath Mountains; a mountainous region covering hundreds of square kilometres. It is not so high or spectacular as its near neighbour, the Cairngorms, but nevertheless a seriously remote and wild tract of land. Mostly lying at an altitude of between 600 and 900m, uncrossed by any public roads, with only a handful of tracks daring to penetrate its interior.

Within a kilometre I reached the top of the glen. The forestry did not extend beyond the watershed so I was soon out on the open rather bleak moorland. Keeping to the left bank of the stream that flowed east from the bealach I contoured round the hill and across the moor towards Glen Turret and dropped down to the bridge. Glen Turret is a small glen coming from the north to join Glen Roy. I turned south on a track that took me to Turret Bridge in Glen Roy. Views were now opening out and I could see my route to the east up the glen. Standing at the confluence of the rivers Turret and Roy is Brae Roy Lodge a well kept farm. The fields around the farm looked surprisingly fertile considering their remote location. Glen Roy is a rather dramatic glen, very narrow in places, especially the lower section. From the farm to the main A86 at Roybridge is about 12km. Glen Roy must be a delight to glaciologists because of the extensive range of moraines deposited here during the last Ice Age. The constrictions in the glen created choke points during the period when glaciers were melting which lead to the excessive deposition. Lateral moraines extend along the sides of the glen, marked on OS maps as 'parallel roads', on the floor of the valley are many other dumps of glacial material, providing a vast reserve of hardcore for upkeep of the tracks.

The rain was holding off and conditions were reasonably bright but there were low clouds over the hilltops and I felt that rain was never too far away. The decision not to go 'off piste' and climb Creag Meagaidh had been easy. It would have been a longer and harder day's walk and only really worth doing if the weather insured a grand day on the top. The walk up the glen was a good substitute though, a craggy path up the left bank of the river, with good views along the glen. As I walked through the small plantation about 5km on from Turret Bridge I had a strange rather unnerving confrontation with three sheep. They were very large and mean looking, with massive curly horns and heads that appeared so solid they could have been used to demolish stone walls. They were standing on the track in line abreast blocking my way. As I approached they showed no inclination to give way. I stopped and we eyed each other up. I felt quite intimidated, their whole demeanour suggesting they may resort to violence if I tried to pass. The stand-off ended peacefully when they ambled at a very leisurely and condescending pace off to the side and I carried on my way.

About 8km of gradual climb brought me to the col where having passed through the watershed I began the easy descent into the valley of the River Spey. The path continues on the north bank of the river and crosses several streams feeding into the Spey from the hills above. Just before Melgarve the path passes a conifer plantation, on the far side of which stands a Wade bridge spanning the Allt Yairack and Melgarve. This is an historic area for it is here that in 1731 General Wade commenced the construction of the road to Fort Augustus. An extremely ambitious undertaking that would link the road he had finished some years before, from Dalwhinnie to Lochaber via Laggan and Glen Roy, to Fort Augustus and Inverness. A high level route over the mountains through what is now known as the Corrieyairack Pass. Historians suggest that this proved to be of less use to the British army and was probably more of a help to the Jacobites, allowing them speedier, undetected passage through that wild area. A fine but steady rain started as I approached Melgarve and just a short way further on by the edge of another plantation I decided to look for a camp spot.

This was a mature plantation, a long deceased deer fence lay along the edge, rusting and useless, bound to the ground by grass and heather. The trees were so spaced that a grassy sward extended underneath, creating a sheltered and peaceful impression. I left my rucksack and set off into the trees to explore. To my great delight about 200m into the wood I came across another Wade bridge crossing a small but energetic stream. I was so impressed to read on a plaque on the bridge stating that it had been restored by a group of volunteers in 1984. I retrieved my sack and erected my tent on the flat approach to the bridge. As I lay in the tent later I fancied that as well as the murmuring of the stream I could hear the muffled footsteps and subdued talk of soldiers long passed.

To improve my humour even more, the rain had stopped and I spent a relaxed few hours sorting kit, writing my log and eating. I reviewed my progress, after four days; the new Paramo jacket was performing brilliantly, no problems on the clothing front. Body was standing up to the strain very well, apart from blistered feet and aching shoulders. Food was ok especially the Expedition meals; it is never possible to carry enough to fully satisfy appetite increased by such activity, I found the secret was to eat enough of the right things that at least conned the body into thinking it was having a sufficiency. My spirits were still high even though too often dampened.

Day 5 Tuesday May 6th
Melgarve to NN718962 (Nr Kingussie)
Camped at NN725961
Est 33km

A good night's sleep and a reasonable start, on the track by 9.30. The weather was still not promising but through the day I got away with just a few showers; it was evident from the more distant views that the higher hills were attracting some very heavy showers.

About 5km from Melgarve the old military road crosses the River Spey at Garva Bridge and a short way further on I passed Garvamore which is the site of the former barracks and an inn. Views east down Speyside were opening out as were distant glimpses of the high Cairngorms to the south; I could see the hills of Glen Feshie and the snowy west facing corries of Braeraich. Just beyond Glenshero Lodge the track passes over an aquaduct that links two lochans. The rugged wildness of Glen Roy and the upper part of Glen Spey, had gone, there were now areas of grassland where nesting curlew kept up their territorial calling. Just before the village of Laggan I had a brief sighting of an eagle as it flew low over the fields then disappeared from view. At Laggan I called Ali from a telephone box and stood outside holding the receiver at arms length so she could hear the curlew's liquid call.

A couple of kilometres along the A889 to Catlodge a cafe provided an excuse for a rest and very welcome refreshment. Then back on to a minor road that took me through a wooded area to a very smart memorial at The Mains of Glentruim. This commemorated Ewan Macpherson 'Colonel of The Badenoch Men' who was one of the leaders of a Jacobite uprising in the middle of the 18th century. Feeling rather chastened and needing to apologise for being English I crept away. The path turned sharply back on itself, contouring round the base of a hill. Very shortly I came to The Falls of Truim, where the constriction in the glen squeezes the river, the A9 main road and the railway line, into a fine conduit of communication. I followed the main road for a short way then a zig-zag to the right brought me to Etteridge and I was back on General Wade's road again. It was 17.30 and I was getting pretty tired but it was to be another two hours before I found a suitable camp spot. The track took a fairly level course along the side of the glen, passing through several small wooded sections. I passed many good spots to pitch a tent but none had any access to water. Eventually in a rather exposed area of open moor I came across another Wade bridge with an adjacent grassy sward and running water. Another long day, pretty dry on the whole and now time to relax. Yet again I struggled to foretell the weather, the sky being a mixture of blue and dark grey!

Day 6 Wednesday May 7th
Nr Kingussie to Inshriach Forest
Camped at NN831982
Est 15km

I woke to the calls of curlew and lapwing and the sun was shining, what a pleasant change! An early skat of rain cleared as quickly as it had appeared and the sun continued to shine. I sat in the tent and wrote a few postcards which I would be able to post later, then finally got going at 07.45. There was quite a drying breeze so I spread out sleeping mat and sleeping bag to dry and air.

My first objective was Kingussie where I could collect the supply parcel I had posted a couple of weeks previously. The 5km walk into the village was uneventful. I reclaimed my parcel from the general stores cum sub post office and treated myself to some fresh fruit and a large bag of hot chilli crisps. Having stowed the supplies and consumed the fruit I retraced my footsteps, passed under the A9 yet again and headed for pastures new. I turned left on to the road that went past Ruthven Barracks. This is an extremely sombre looking but well preserved building. It is built on a promontory, adjacent to the river. Its elevated position giving good views up and down the glen. Another factor that would have discouraged any offensive intent was that in the 18th century the flood plain of the river would have been much wetter than it is nowadays, thus reducing the risk of attack from different directions.

The weather had been quite sunny and bright during the morning but by midday clouds were appearing, high and hazy at first but becoming dark and ominous. After a day and a half of minor roads and occasional habitations I felt very much now that I was heading back into the mountains. Glen Spey is the NW edge of the Grampian Mountains which extend eastwards for over 100km; a huge area of high mountains, great glens and remote high moorland. I passed by a few small woods and reached Tromie Bridge where the road turned sharply to follow the river, after a short distance it turned right on to a minor road to Drumguish. It was along this little road that I had two interesting sightings. Firstly I saw a red squirrel, then as I sat quietly on the grass verge a group of about 10 ducklings emerged from the undergrowth on the opposite side of the road and waddled purposefully towards me. They minded me very much of naughty boys being lead astray by their gang leader. I sat perfectly still and they were so engaged with their adventure that they did not notice me. They stopped on the road just a few metres away from me, milling around for a while, then all stood in a little circle facing each other; it was just as if one of the less adventurous had said "now look fellas we have had a great time but I really think we ought to be getting back to Mum" and with that they turned round and waddled back whence they came.

The minor road became a track that crossed an open area then I entered the Inshriach Forest. After 3km the track emerged from the forest again, crossed a river then another section of open moor before re-entering the forest.

I now faced a bit of a quandary, the time was only 16.00 and I had at best only covered about 15km; if I carried on then I would drop down into Glen Feshie. Remembering my experience three years earlier, I was apprehensive about camping in the realm of my farmer 'friend'. If I stayed put I had a choice of suitable camp spots. The wind had strengthened and the sky was looking rather ominous. I pitched the tent in the lee of a ridge and as I was not ready to eat settled down for a doze. I awoke some time later, the tent flapping violently. Yet again my choice of camp spot had been found wanting. I set off along the track to see if I could find a more sheltered spot. Sure enough about 100m from the forest an old stone sheep fold whose walls were at least 1.5m high offered protection from the wind. I decamped and felt a lot happier about the prospects of the night ahead. To make life even more uncomfortable it was now raining. I managed to prepare my meal in spite of the wet. I had been really impressed with the multi-fuel stove, it would light up even when being rained on. I turned in early and lay for a long while listening to the wind till eventually I fell into a fitful sleep.

Footnote:
My blistered feet had continued to be a discomfort, before I set off this morning I sterilised a pin and burst blisters on both feet. Walking today has been a lot less painful.

Day 7 Thursday May 8th
Inshriach Forest to Nr White Bridge
Camped at NO008873
Est 27km

All things considered I had a reasonable few hours sleep but woke around 04.00 and lay for an hour or so listening to the wind. Compared to when I first pitched camp in the sheep fold, the wind had very considerably increased in ferocity and by 05.00 I was convinced that things were getting worse. Heavy rain had continued into the night but at least now it was holding off. At 05.15 I decided that I must decamp to eliminate the risk of damage to the tent. I crawled out of the tent and was rather taken aback by the ominous sky; at this time of day heavy storm clouds can appear almost brown, the patches of lighter sky accentuating their threatening aspect. Breaking camp was no easy feat as I had to avoid leaving the tent open for any length of time. I did manage a life giving cup of tea and by 06.30 was ready to start walking.

The day proved to be one of the most difficult and challenging walks I had ever done, but in many ways enjoyable and very fulfilling. In just a short distance I entered the forest and soon the track began to drop down into Glen Feshie. Rounding a bend I saw a herd of deer ahead, I walked on slowly until I was only about 40-50m away when they saw me and just ambled off the track and into the trees. It was probably only a minute or so later that I reached that spot and was amazed that they had just disappeared, the trees had swallowed them up.

I reached the river directly opposite Auchlean where I had descended at the end of my walk three years earlier. I turned right on to the riverside track and headed south up the glen. It was now that I began to realise that the weather was colder than previous days. Since the start of the walk I had worn the Paramo trousers and my new lightweight Paramo jacket, which had been 100% waterproof and quite warm enough. Now I was thinking maybe the big Paramo jacket would be more comfortable. The decision was made shortly afterwards when the rain began. Heavy rain and the gale force winds were too much for the thin jacket. I found some shelter and quickly unpacked the big jacket, together with my fleece hat and gore-tex gloves. I immediately felt the benefit of donning warm clothes, I ate some chocolate, nuts and dried fruit and carried on my way with raised spirits. The importance of good quality waterproof clothing and footwear cannot be overstated; the effect on mind and body of being wet and cold can be debilitating, yet to be out in really bad conditions and remain warm and dry is exhilarating.

This route is route 180 of the SRWS and is described in their handbook as 'one of the great long Cairngorm rights of way'. It takes a path round the south-west perimeter of the mountains yet is nevertheless a remote path with many challenges on the way. After about 4km I crossed over to the east bank of the river. This section of the glen has a number of conifer plantations on both sides of the glen. However these give way to stands of majestic Scots pine trees which are the remnants of the ancient Caledonian Forests that once covered so much of Scotland. The trees stand widely spaced which allows grass to grow under their feet. I continued up the glen through the rain but still able to enjoy the magnificent scenery. The glen turned eastwards through 90degrees and narrowed with steep crags rising up above me and on the west side too. The rain continued more or less unabated; sometimes reducing to a dribble but mostly heavy squalls with hail mixed in for a bit of variety.

The path crossed many streams, the majority of which would present no problem in dry conditions but with the persistent rain by the afternoon some were very challenging and hazardous to cross. In the early afternoon three guys carrying mountain bikes appeared over the rocks as I approached one of the streams. We had a short hurried conversation and they were off, leaving me to muse on the additional hazards of carrying a bike while crossing a cataract of white water. My track crossed the River Eidart, fortunately by a bridge, just beyond the River Feshie twists south and west, I carried on east through the watershed over a particularly boggy section and soon the Geldie Burn materialised in the glen to my right. The walking was relatively easy, slightly downhill on a reasonable path, although there were still many streams crossing the track, all full up with water collected from the southern slopes of the Cairngorms and rushing to deliver it to the Geldie Burn.

As I carried on eastwards the rain did ease somewhat but the wind remained as fierce as it had been for many hours. I was tired, having covered over 20km since early morning with no proper stops, just standing in the rain for a few minutes to eat some hard rations. The glen was wide and open, offering no possibility of a sheltered camp spot. I knew I just had to carry on, but I did find my ideal place. Just a short distance before White Bridge the ruins of a house stand on a level area of grass, protected to the west and north by the mature conifer trees of a small plantation. By the time I had erected the tent the clouds were breaking and a watery sun showed itself. I was well protected from the worst efforts of the wind but there was still enough to dry the washing I had done the previous day in Kingussie. I brewed myself a mug of tea and by the time I had eaten my spirits were in great shape again. I was tucked into my sleeping bag by about 20.30 and slept the sleep of the Just.

Day 8 Friday May 9th
Nr White Bridge to
Campsite at NO153909
Est 16km

Nearly 12 hours later I emerged to be greeted by a slightly brighter sky but skats of rain, the wind was still present but not so intrusive as it was yesterday. I took my time over breakfast and packing up and was walking by 10.20. On my way to White Bridge a weasel scurried across the track. I was grateful for this little bit of wildlife to present itself to me as I often feel that with all the pressure of navigation and treading a safe path I do not always have nature watching at the forefront of my mind, generally only seeing birds or animals if they are thoughtful enough to come into my line of vision.

At White Bridge the track crosses the River Dee just before its confluence with the Geldie Burn. I stood on the bridge looking at the Dee, now a mature river strong and muscular, well able to elbow its way through and round all the rocky obstacles in its path. I reflected on how three years earlier I had admired the Infant Dee, showing off at an elevation of 1240m by throwing itself over the lip of the ridge below the Wells of Dee. A spectacular waterfall at the head of An Garbh Choire in the heart of the Cairngorms.

On my way onwards to The Linn of Dee it started to rain, heavy rain that persisted for the next 4 or 5 hours. Occasionally reducing to a grudging drizzle but mostly aggressively heavy with a few vindictive squalls thrown in for good measure.

The Linn of Dee is a well frequented beauty spot, about 10km out from Braemar along a no through road. The river is wide and very active as it tumbles over a series of rocky wrinkles in its bed. I stopped long enough to take a photo but the weather did not encourage any further delay.

The 10km walk to Braemar was fairly uneventful, the minor road followed the River Dee east. Traffic was very intermittent so I did not have to think about jumping on to the verge every few metres. Just below the Linn of Dee the river is further reinforced by Lui Water, a powerful river that flows down from the north. 5km further downstream is the confluence with Quoich Water which takes its waters from the big mountains of the eastern Cairngorms. The River Dee has become one of Scotland's great rivers and by the time it flows through Braemar is responsible for draining a considerable proportion of the 1107 square kilometres of the Cairngorms.

On a better day this would have been a very pleasant walk and a welcome break from more challenging terrain. A levellish road winding through the trees down a beautiful glen, with occasional stunning views of the Cairngorm's high tops. As it was the road was still levellish but the trees dripped endlessly and the occasional views were of misty lumps with cloudy headdresses; but I did have a good view of a red squirrel, which was great.

By the time I reached Braemar the rain had at last relented. I found the sub post office and collected my parcel. I found a public phone and had a long chat with Ali, very good to hear her and all the news from home. All set now till the end of the road! I found the excellent Caravan Club camp site and experienced the luxury of pitching my tent on a perfectly flat area of smooth cut grass. Further treats followed, a hot shower and the facility to wash clothes properly and comfortably.

I now felt well set up for the last few days of the journey.

Day 9 Saturday May 10th
Braemar to upper Glen Clova
Camped at NO283768
Est 23km

I was excited about this day's walk, it promised to be one of the more demanding days of the expedition; crossing the high plateau of the S.E. Cairngorms reaching an elevation of 8-900m and an opportunity to 'bag a Monroe' (a mountain over 917m). I was to follow the SRWS route 175, of which the handbook says '....*one of the most serious walks described in this book....accurate route-finding in bad weather will require considerable skill.'*

Bearing in mind the weather I had endured so far I was slightly apprehensive over what the day would bring. I emerged from the warmth of my sleeping bag at 06.00, there had been no overnight rain and a lively wind had made a grand job of drying the tent, but it was very cold.

A combination of the cold and my anxiety to get going saw me on the road by 07.50. My route out of Braemar was south along the A93 for 3km, then at Auchallater I turned left on to a track that lead me up a narrow steep sided glen following Callater Burn. For about 5km the track climbed, a rather serpentine path that brought me to Lochcallater Lodge overlooking the expanse of Loch Callater. Before I reached the lodge the rain started and for the next five hours or so I was battered by a succession of huge squalls, sometimes almost horizontal rain and later high up on the plateau these came as hail. Life was made even more uncomfortable because for the first time really since leaving Knoydart the wind had swung right round and it mostly came as a headwind. Loch Callater is a sizeable loch aligned NW-SE nearly 2km long, wedged into the steep confines of the glen. My path lead along the NE side of the loch and looking forward the awesome majesty of the place revealed itself. The glen narrowed and the sides became higher and steeper. For about 2.5km beyond the top end of the loch the floor of the glen climbed gradually. Towering above the head of the glen was the summit of Tolmount, standing at 958m like a huge sentinel guarding the corries below. As the glen became like a vast amphitheatre the head wall climbed vertiginously rising well over 300m in about 800m to the summit of Tolmount. Over to the right was a spur valley, Coire Loch Kander, smaller but equally impressive. The rims of both corries are lined with massive crags.

As the path steepened up the headwall of Glen Callater it swung east and I reached the plateau in the bealach (col) between Tolmount and Knaps of Fafernie. The weather was still very confrontational, there were some brief clearer spells between squalls and on one occasion looking back I had a dramatic view of the snowy slopes of (probably) Ben Macdui but before I could take a photo and confirm its identity the clouds closed in again. A short time later on the plateau I could appreciate the volatility of the weather system. The 360 degree aspect revealed clouds racing across at great speed, squalls of rain or hail, sudden bursts of sunlight spotlighting part of the panorama, banks of lower cloud that rapidly swallowed me with an alarming outbreak of disorientation. In one of these 'now you see me, now you don't' sequences to the north clouds parted and a shaft of sunlight shone on Meikle Pap, an outlying peak on Lochnagar. No sooner had I realised what it was and it was gone again.

Although my path lead to the east and south of Tolmount NO210800, I felt it would be churlish of me not to divert and climb the extra 80m or so to its summit. Sat on the top in a complete white-out I had to change maps. The process of removing sheet 43 from the mapcase and replacing it with sheet 44 was tricky with the fierce wind threatening to tear them to shreds. I retraced my steps to pick up the path then took a compass bearing in case the clouds should come down again. I thought that the weather was changing a bit as most of the clouds did appear to be higher. The sting in the tail though was a prolonged squall of hail coming at me almost head-on. Once that had passed through the visibility was really good, showing the spectacular landscape in all its glory. This section of the route leading to and down Glen Doll is called 'Jock's Road'

In the latter part of the 19th century Duncan Macpherson, having made his fortune in Australia returned to Scotland and purchased the Glen Doll estate. He then attempted to ban people from crossing his land. John (Jock) Winter fought this decision. The Scottish Rights of Way and Access Society took up the case and fought it through every court in the land, on the basis that the path was an ancient drovers road that had been used for generations to move cattle through the mountains. Finally winning the day with a positive ruling in the House of Lords in 1888.

The scenery of Glen Doll and the adjacent Glen Clova was every bit as dramatic as the OS maps suggested. Tightly packed contours indicate the very steep sides to the narrow glens. Jock's Road gradually steepened as it descended into the head of Glen Doll, the views down the glen and across the plateau towards Glen Clova were stunning; as in Glen Callater massive crags lined the rims of the glen, a sharp contrast to the rounded glaciated surface of the plateau. Extensive conifer plantations extended across the lower part of the Glen. I did investigate the fringe of the forest as a possible camp spot, dropping off the track towards the river, but the wind was much too gusty so I decided to press on. My map showed a car park and campsite at the bottom of the glen near Glendoll Lodge at the end of the public road from Glen Clova. I reached the car park at 18.00, pretty tired and wind battered, having been walking for ten hours. A sign announced that the campsite no longer existed and helpfully advised the nearest sites were 19, 20 or 22 miles away. Backpackers could phone this number for more information. I cursed roundly telling the sign that with no public telephone and no hope of a mobile signal that nugget of information was as much use as a chocolate fireguard.

I was in a bit of a quandary, my onward route was SE down Glen Clova and from the map I suspected I may struggle to find a decent camp spot. While I was musing over my predicament a walker appeared from the track that came from the north. He told me that I may well find somewhere up that track, but not to go too far as the local gamekeeper lived at Moulzie about 2km up the track.

Sure enough about halfway to Moulzie on the left, between the track and the river a sheltered depression proved an ideal spot. I quickly erected the tent and was pleased that from the track it was almost invisible.

In spite of the inclement weather I had seen a snow hare, quite a number of ptarmigan and many black grouse as I came across from Tolmount. When the grouse are put up they almost explode from the undergrowth flying rapidly away veering from side to side very low to the ground.

The heavy rain showers had returned as evening developed but at least I managed to cook my meal in the dry.

Day 10 Sunday May 11th
Upper Glen Clova to Glen Mark
Camped at NO442807
Est 27km

The weather was marginally better. I suspected this was due to my continued easterly progression away from the high hills. I did have a few showers but nothing as dramatic as the violent squalls that still seemed, periodically, to envelope the hills behind me. It had been a cold night and I had been in no hurry to vacate the embryonic embrace of the sleeping bag. The walking day started with an easy 6 or 7km down Glen Clova, I phoned Ali from the public phone by the hotel, then walked back a short way to the very welcoming Brandy Burn Cafe. I stoked up on coffee and cheese and ham rolls, to give a bit of fuel for the steep climb to come.

The next stage of the day was SRWS Route 164, which would take me from Clova Hotel to Tarfside in Glen Esk. The immediate vicinity of the hotel was clearly land belonging to the hotel and it was not until I had gone some way up a track from the road that I came across the familiar SRWS sign indicating the path up the mountain. Both sides of the majestic Glen Clova seem to have similar uniformly steep gradients. A steady climb of about 400m brought me to Loch Brandy. The loch set in an almost perfect semicircular corrie could have come straight out of an illustrated geology text book. The path crossed the outfall stream from the loch and continued to climb up the righthand shoulder for another 250m to the summit of Green Hill. The views both into the corrie and across the glen were very dramatic, on one hand the almost claustrophobic character of the corrie and on the other the panorama of hills that lead away to the south-west.

To my surprise Green Hill was swarming with people who I guessed were on a weekend mountain skills exercise. I wanted to have a rest so I headed away from the crowd anticlockwise around the rim of the corrie to The Snub, the peak that was above the left hand shoulder of the corrie. A short shower that swept through at Green Hill soon cleared and I found a comfortable seat under The Snub and sat there for 45 minutes, drinking in what would be my last views of the eastern Cairngorms. The unmistakable outlines of Mount Keen, Meikle Pap and Lochnagar were easily identified to the north and west; then to the east and south the high hills of the eastern Grampian Mountains.

I retraced my steps towards Green Hill which now stood in fine solitude. The plateau here gradually lost height and further across was at least 200m lower than the area I crossed the previous day.

I headed east towards White Hill then north-east to the grandly named Muckle Cairn and Cairn Lick. From Cairn Lick at an altitude of 682m the path lead down east south-east for 2km along a narrow steep shoulder which goes with the magnificent name of The Shank of Inchgrundle. The final section zig-zags down very sharply to the tiny settlement of Inchgrundle at the head of Loch Lee.

It was now late afternoon and I realised I was in a similar quandary to the previous day with regard to finding a camp spot. The map gave no encouragement to finding anywhere along the loch and beyond that was the settlement of Kirkton and the public road that comes up Glen Esk.

Although my route for the next day lay eastwards down Glen Esk when I reached the car park at the end of the road, I turned the other way, up Glen Mark, because I guessed it would be easier to find a camp spot as I headed into the hills again rather than in the glen where there were farms and outlying houses. Sure enough in less than a kilometre I found a plantation of well spaced mature pine trees. As the wind was fairly light I felt the possibility of branches falling on me was quite remote so I pitched camp on the soft grass beneath the trees.

A nearby stream provided the liquid requirements and I was really comfortable. Later as I sat and wrote my log I was surprised at the variety of wildlife I had seen. The further east I had come the more I had seen or heard. The list for the day included two dotterel, cuckoo, oystercatchers, owl, curlew, doves and a number of song birds serenaded me as I sat there writing; I had also seen several snow hares on the higher ground earlier in the day.

As I sat in the tent that evening, musing on the day's progress and what was in store for the next day, I began to fully appreciate that the walk was nearly over. By the end of the next day I would be more or less clear of the mountains and glens, with only a relatively short walk through rural Angus remaining, before I reached the east coast.

Day 11 Monday May 12th
Glen Mark to Edzell
Est 26km

Another really cold night, I was up and doing by 07.00 and walking by 09.00. Shortly after setting off a Landrover stopped and the driver, who I took to be a local farmer, was keen to chat. During the course of the conversation he commented on the cold night and said there had been an overnight snowfall on Mount Keen, about 7km to the north.

The walking was easy on a quiet road. A 5km brisk walk in the chilly early morning brought me to Tarfside, a small village situated on the north side of the glen, at the confluence of the Burn of Clearach with the River Esk. I found a public telephone and called 'mission control', it was good to hear all of Ali's news. I told her that all being well I would be home the day after tomorrow. I also called a hotel in Montrose to confirm a room for the following night. I had made a provisional arrangement with them before starting the walk and they had agreed to take in a parcel for me. Ali had duly sent off a parcel containing a pair of trainers, jeans and a tee-shirt.

The road continued down the glen along the north side of the Esk and although there was not much traffic, I figured that the further down the glen I went the more traffic there would be. I could see on the map a track on the south side of the river, that should offer a more interesting walk than just staying on the road. A few kilometres on from Tarfside I left the road, crossed a bridge to join with this track. The walk was a delight and quite different to previous days; the glen less rugged and the surrounding hills considerably lower. In the meadows alongside the river sheep and lambs enjoyed the dry bright weather. Throughout the day I saw curlew, oystercatchers and lapwing; further down the glen riverside pastures gave way to incredibly fertile looking fields, some freshly sown with potatoes; the dark soil neatly ridged.

The track eventually comes of age, and becomes a proper road, a short distance before the splendidly named 'Rocks of Solitude'. This is a local beauty spot where the river is constricted at the point where it flows across the Highland Boundary fault in a series of spectacular waterfalls. There is a folklore legend that a local piper was once kidnapped by fairies as he played here and that his music can still be heard on occasions. Unfortunately I knew nothing of this at the time and walked on by, in happy ignorance. The further down the glen the more farms, everywhere looked so verdant. I was left with the impression that just under the bare soil of the fields frenzied activity was taking place and the new crops were preparing to burst forth.

I was approaching the village of Edzell and once again I had been contemplating my options (or lack of them) for a resting place. Opportunities for a wild camp were non-existent, the OS map showed a riverside campsite about 5km beyond Edzell. It had been another long day, having walked for about 9 hours, I was tired and thoughts of a pub meal and a soft bed were taking root in my mind. On the outskirts of the village I was impressed by a very pleasantly arranged park area with picnic tables, a really remarkable children's play area and comprehensive fitness trail. The village looked comfortably prosperous, with very wide streets and many of the older properties built of a local stone almost purple brown in colour. Ten minutes later I was ensconced in a friendly B & B.

One of the more notable features of the village is the Dalhousie Arch. A magnificent stone archway which spans the B966 at its southern approach to the village. This was erected in 1887 to commemorate the deaths of the 13th Earl of Dalhousie and his wife, both of whom rather strangely died on the same day.

Day 12 Tuesday May 13th
Edzell to Montrose
Est 18km

I had the luxury of a leisurely start, having been engaged in a lengthy conversation with mine host at the B & B. He told me the history of RAF Edzell, an airfield to the east of the village, about 2km away on the other side of the river. In 1960 the RAF vacated the site but leased it to the United States Navy, who occupied it until 1996. With their normal desire to be self contained, amongst other things they brought over a magnificent array of children's play equipment, including swings, slides, roundabouts etc.,. and erected them on the base. When the Americans moved out they donated all this playground equipment to the village. Installing it at its new location for good measure. An interesting explanation of my puzzlement the previous day, having never seen such equipment before.

The walk from Edzell to the coast through the quiet byways of Angus was memorable for just a couple of reasons. Firstly the wonderful sighting of an eagle, just cruising around circling and occasionally alighting on a tree; until eventually finding a friendly thermal and disappearing over the horizon, seemingly with no effort whatsoever. One normally associates eagles with wild areas but of course the reality is that even though they breed and very often roost in wild parts they will sometimes cover miles to find the easier pickings of fat rabbits etc.,.

in the rural lowland fields. The other reason was more depressing, for I was shocked at the amount of litter along the verges. Sandwich packets, sweet wrappers, fizzy drink bottles, cake packets; in profusion, all the detritus of modern snacking. The only conclusion I could reach was that this was rubbish jettisoned from cars on the school run, being driven by parents who not only were too lazy to feed their children properly but were also so unsocial and uncaring that they were happy to have their little darlings lob all this rubbish from their cars.

It was a tremendous thrill when I crested a small hill and there about 3km away, was the North Sea. With the benefit of hindsight I made the wrong call in my choice or route after crossing the A90 trunk road, a few km south of Edzell. A minor road does lead straight to Montrose; but my thinking was to aim for the coast immediately to the north of the town. The problem with this decision became apparent when I was forced into walking along this busy road and finding no way through the golf course to the sea.

I eventually reached the rather bleak promenade, the atmosphere not improved by the weather's obvious determination to revert to its bad habits of the last two weeks. The dry morning of high cloud had given way to big rain clouds not too far out to sea. I found an unsuspecting local to take my picture with the backdrop of a grumpy looking North Sea; shortly after while phoning Ali the rain started, rather a fitting end to a wonderful adventure.

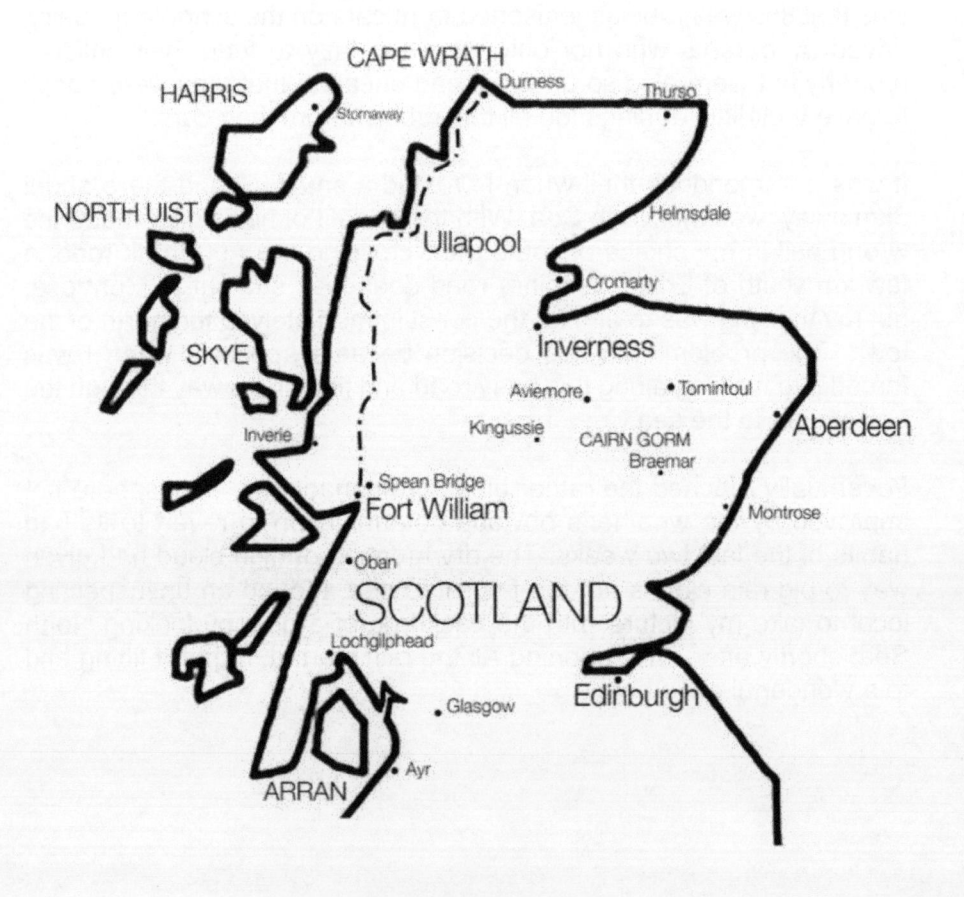

North to Cape Wrath — ‧ — ‧ — ‧ —

5. North to Cape Wrath
THE CAPE WRATH TRAIL May 2004

Part 1 The Idea

During the summer of 2003 one of my regular walking friends lent me a book which he thought would interest me; it was The Cape Wrath Trail by David Paterson. It describes his experience of walking the 300+km from Fort William to Cape Wrath, the far westerly tip of mainland UK. This was published in 1996 and the author can be regarded as the first person to promote the route as another UK long distance walk. By the time I had finished reading the book I was very tempted to plan my own Cape Wrath Trail. At the end of the book David Paterson makes the observation that as there is no definitive route from Fort William to Cape Wrath, that anyone keen to undertake this walk should plan their own route and enjoy the challenge of assessing and overcoming the many difficulties presented by the various sections of wilderness. It is interesting to note that in over two decades since the publication of the book and the inception of the Cape Wrath Trail, it has no official recognition and so remains more of a concept than an actual long distance route. Yet in that time it has become acknowledged as probably the hardest backpacking walk that the UK has to offer and as such every year attracts people from around the world to take up the challenge. Due to the large tracts of mountain and moorland that constitute the North-West Highlands, backpacking is the only viable option. If ever the Cape Wrath Trail did become officially recognised, waymarking would be bound to follow. Then activity holiday companies would move in offering bag carrying facilities and transport to hotels each evening. At present the huge attraction is that to walk your own CWT is to have an adventure you will never forget.

Part 2. Preparation

Once again the sofa became littered with O.S. maps, the S.R.W.S. book and map, sundry other guides and trail books. In trying to keep to a straight line route from Fort William to Cape Wrath there are a few sections where the only logical route is the one David Paterson took, but it was a very interesting exercise working out what I hoped was a realistic route for all the other sections. From the experience the previous year, I knew that I was fairly comfortable with a daily average of 24/25 kms, although I did realise that the Cape Wrath route was over much more difficult and hostile terrain than the 2003 walk. Nevertheless I still reckoned on that sort of daily distance when I tried to gauge where the overnights would be and I reckoned that I could complete the walk in 13 to 14 days; although I did not have enough confidence in this to book a ticket in advance for my return home. Having set my route it became apparent that there were some extensive sections of wilderness. The reality was that the longest section from Glen Shiel to Achnasheen, approximately 58km crossed no public road, only intermittent contact with estate tracks and no house, farm or other human activity. In the three days it took me to walk that section I saw 8 or 9 people on the first day, no-one on the second day and one person on the third day.

Another particular problem with this expedition was the remote location of Cape Wrath. Uninhabited and on the wrong side of an MOD firing range; 15 kms from a not insignificant estuary and river, the other side of which lay civilisation, in the form of Durness. There were no public roads on this NW tip of the UK. I knew that there was a mini-bus service which, in conjunction with a small ferry across the estuary, took sightseers from Durness to Cape Wrath. Thus by implication it could take Cape Wrath Trail walkers from Cape Wrath to Durness. Here such pleasures of the flesh as a shower, a square meal, a couple of beers and a comfortable bed, could be enjoyed.

In order to ensure an orderly end to the expedition there were several crucial factors to be considered
1. When did the MOD firing range operate
2. At what times of year did the mini-bus and ferry operate
3. Contact details for mini-bus and ferry
4. How could I get from Durness to Inverness

In pre-internet days it would have taken a determined effort to find answers to all these questions concerning this relatively short journey. I spent about an hour searching various web sites and found answers to all the questions. The mini-bus and ferry only ran from May to September/October and the MOD firing range was generally not used during that time. The bus operator would know when the range was to be in operation; and there was a daily return coach service from Inverness to Durness. On the Cape Wrath website from which I gleaned a lot of this information there were two words at the end of the detail about the mini-bus and ferry service, *'Weather Permitting'*. Little was I to know then, the relevance of that codicil.

In order that Ali could follow my progress I copied all the relevant sections of OS maps, marking route and anticipated areas where I would overnight. In the event these were remarkably close to the reality. The route involved several major river crossings and I knew that if I was unlucky with the weather all had the potential of scuppering the whole expedition. A slightly less important detail of planning, but one that would make the return journey more comfortable, was to have trainers and clean clothes. This could be achieved by sending myself a parcel to Durness PO.

As with the coast to coast walk, the locations of post offices was not ideal, but perfectly workable. The only options en route were Kinlochewe and Ullapool, which would probably be reached on days 6 and 8 respectively.

So the stage was set, before finalising the dates I needed to check with the mini-bus operator. The daily Inverness bus service departed from Durness about 15.00. I figured that given good luck and a following wind, if I arrived at Cape Wrath by mid morning I would stand a sporting chance of catching the Inverness bus that afternoon. An hour and a half or so for the minibus and ferry, an hour to get up into the village and collect my clothes parcel, and maybe even time to snatch a quick lunch. Mmmm.. the best laid plans of mice and men!

As far as my kit was concerned the only item that had not performed well on the previous trips was my rucksack. After researching the options I finally bought a Karrimor bag with a capacity of about 100 litres, it was a beautifully engineered rucksack but rather heavy, even when empty! Once I had set up the strap adjustments I had none of the shoulder stress that the other bag had caused.

Part 3. The Walk

The journey begins:

My pack seemed to weigh a ton! I cursed my luck that due to the annual motor-cycle trials I had been unable to book a B&B any nearer to Fort William railway station. "After that 12 hour train journey, the walk will do you good" I told myself as I staggered along Auchintore Road at about 22:30 on 5th May. All I could think of was having to walk back to the station the next morning, in order to catch the 08:35 Mallaig train and travel the 6 minute journey to Banavie at the southern end of the Caledonian Canal, the starting point of my walk. It transpired that the B&B was over a mile from the station.

I boarded the train with 2 minutes to spare and settled myself down amidst a happy chattering throng of Shearings holiday makers on their day trip to Mallaig, and possibly a boat trip as well? A few minutes later still perspiring from the dash to the station, I heaved my pack onto the platform at Banavie and watched as the train departed, my mind going back almost a year to when I had made that journey to Mallaig, caught the ferry to Inverie in Knoydart and started my coast to coast walk across to Montrose.

"This is going to be a much tougher challenge" I thought as I crossed the road to where the Caledonian Canal joins Loch Eil. The weather looked unpromising, there was not much to be seen of Ben Nevis or its neighbours and I fancied I felt a drop of rain as I posed my sack for its photo call by the bottom lock of Neptune's Staircase.

Day 1 Thursday 6th May
Walking from 08.45 till 17.00hrs
Distance covered 26K, Height Climbed 650m Camped at NN153694

This 9-10 kms walk along the canal to Gairlochy was a good introduction to the rigours of the next two weeks, an opportunity for the body to get into some sort of rhythm and begin to acclimatise to the unwelcome addition of the pack. In spite of all endeavours to reduce weight the fully loaded pack was about 24kgs. This included 2 litres of water and food for 6 days. This was my first outing with my new rucksack and I quickly began to appreciate its superior design over that of my previous sack.

The views to the east up into the mountains – Ben Nevis and the Grey Corries, are very impressive on a clear day, but on this occasion low cloud meant I had to content myself with looking closer to hand. Nevertheless the hills to the west made a dramatic backdrop to the narrow strip of cultivated land on the other side of the water.

So far, the rain had not been far away and apart from a brighter spell in the early afternoon this pattern carried on all day. Even the rather dull light could do little to diminish the impact of the vast banks of gorse in full flower on the west side of the canal as I neared Gairlochy. I think this year must be a good year for gorse as throughout the whole trip north, I was to come across many wonderful displays.

A young red deer had strayed onto the tow path, presumably from the more open section near to Gairlochy. It had been 'pushed' south by a group of walkers to a section where there was a wire fence close to the path and me walking north, it doubled back past the group, only then to meet up some time later with two ladies who were also walking south. A repeat situation occurred with myself and the two ladies. We stood about 100ms apart and close to the edge of the water, in order to make the deer's escape path as wide as possible. The deer trapped between us repeatedly ran full tilt into the wire fence until in utter panic it ran past me, if only it had gone the other way it would have reached open ground within about 300m.

At Gairlochy I turned left across the canal bridge and right on to the B8005, a quiet little road serving Achnacarry and other isolated dwellings along Loch Arkaig, until it comes to a dead end at Strathan, the portal to Knoydart, some 18kms to the west. For 4kms the road goes through the trees along the bottom end of Loch Lochy, although you cannot see much of the loch. A side road to Achnacarry cuts off a big loop in the B8005 and eventually rejoins it at the eastern tip of Loch Arkaig. My route took me a short way along the loch to Achnasaul, but before I reached there I sat down on the loch shore for a much needed rest and some refreshment.

As I sat looking out over the loch I recalled that I had walked this last section, from Loch Arkaig to Gairlochy at the end of the second day of my coast to coast walk. On that occasion the squalls that had chased me out of Knoydart had consolidated into heavy rain by the time I reached the point where I was now sitting. Then I still had to walk another 10 kms or so to reach the camp site at Torness, on the Spean Bridge side of Gairlochy.

At least this second time around the weather seemed to be improving and by the time I left the loch side road to pick up the path at Achnasaul NN152895 the sun was shining and it was doing its utmost to appear like a proper early summers afternoon. The map shows a nice clear path going north up the east side of the Allt Dubh, as usual reality was not quite so simple. Achnasaul is a small farm and the track passed close by the house and outbuildings. I was seduced into staying on a track that the farmer would have used to get to the higher ground above the farm. I soon noted that I was looking straight ahead, at hills that needed to be on my right hand side! I stopped and a quick reference to the map and looking to my left I saw a little bridge over the stream I was following, about 150ms behind me, I retraced my steps and was soon heading in the right direction.

After that brief diversion the walk became very pleasant, a steady climb with gradually opening views west along Loch Arkaig and in the hazy afternoon sunshine, way in the distance, I could see the faint outlines of the Knoydart mountains. After 2kms the valley narrowed and the only long views were looking south, on either side steep grassy slopes with rocky outcrops. The western flanks of Glas Bheinn, to my right, were particularly dramatic.

By the time I got to the watershed where Glenn Tarsuinn heads east NN165933, the sun had gone and clouds were gathering. This is a beautiful spot, with fairly level ground and superb all round views. East, Meall an Tagraidh, to the north Meall Coire nan Saobhaidh, north-west Geal Charn, south the valley of the Allt Dubh and to the south-east the steep slopes of Glas Bheinn. From here I headed due north for 1.5kms, climbing 250m to Bealach Carn na h-Urchaire NN162946. The weather was deteriorating rapidly, the cloud base dropping and on reaching the bealach, thunder was rumbling around Geal Charn to the south west. Then the rain started in earnest. I walked another 2km north-west over broken ground, made even more difficult by the heavy rain. I decided that with conditions as they were it was best to find a suitable camp site and get some shelter. The confluence of two streams at NN151965 provided a good flat patch of grass with water supply immediately on hand, I soon had the tent pitched and gear stowed inside, together with a fair amount of water!

With the rain still hammering down, there was no immediate prospect of a cup of tea or food because my tent did not have a porch suitable for the sheltered, safe use of a stove. So I contented myself with the recovery formula energy drink, stretched out and was soon lulled to sleep by the watery noises from the two streams outside. I awoke about an hour later just before 19.00, the rain had stopped and the weather was improving again. Interestingly the streams had risen about 100mm since I first made camp. The end of the day routine now got under way and I soon was enjoying my well earned evening meal. This time I had brought cous cous to bolster the powdered soup. I soaked about 40 grams in cold water for 15 minutes, then heated it and added the soup powder. The result was delicious and a great improvement on the powdered potato I used on the previous year's walk. That was followed by the freeze dried 'Real' packet meal, which only required the appropriate amount of boiling water to be added, then left for 5 minutes and was ready to eat.

The weather had now cleared and the signs were promising for a good day tomorrow. I had the opportunity to look round and get the lie of the land. To the NW the rounded outline of Glas Bheinn (the other one!) with the forest further on arcing round to the north. Looking back the way I had come, was the impressive view of the bealach with the craggier Meall Coire nan Saobhaidh, to the left and the rounded lump of Geal Charn to the right.

This is a fairly quiet neighbourhood with few signs of human intrusion. The paths shown on the OS maps are pretty indistinct and intermittent. In places the tell-tale twin tracks of the ATV's can be seen but the terrain here is pretty boggy, with dense heathery grassy carpet which although it may be water-logged and looks treacherous is almost invariably fairly solid and safe to walk on.

Having Dartmoor as my local wilderness, I have developed a healthy respect for bogs. It may not have the crags or exposed rocky ridges of other wilderness areas, but when it comes to impenetrable bogs it wins hands down over any I've come across in Scotland. Walking there at any time demands great vigilance and understanding of the terrain and in very wet spells one is constantly forced into detours to get past bogs. The thing that puzzles me is that in Scotland bogs can look almost identical to those on Dartmoor but will only be boot deep at worst, while their Devonian cousins can be crutch deep or worse.

I now retreated to the tent for the last ritual of the day, that is to write up my log and enjoy a few nips of malt whisky from the hip flask – this year *Knockando*, a good Speyside malt. I was feeling more relaxed, having now got into the walk. I had felt rather apprehensive during all the weeks of planning – many winter evenings spent sitting on the sofa studying maps and books, trying to picture the terrain and decide times and distances.

As I sat there in my tent, thinking through the days walk, I was happy with all aspects. The feet and body reported no problems, all the kit was working well, yet again the Paramo jacket and trousers had withstood the rain, their great feature I think is as long as you keep wearing them they dry out so quickly and remain warm at all times. So I retired to my sleeping bag content that the walk was now on!

Day 2 – Friday 7th May
Allt an Fhithich to An Caorann Mor
Walking from 08.50 to 18.30hrs
Distance covered 24K, Height climbed 650m, Camped at NH088128

Awoke early the next morning about 5.30am and after 15 minutes or so of relishing the comfort of the sleeping bag and thinking of the day's route, I emerged to face the day. It was an absolute gem, the sun low over Meall Tarsuinn, wall to wall blue sky and a slight distant haze that promised a fine, warm day ahead. The streams had retreated again to a friendly babble from their agitated rush the evening before. As I stood outside the tent trying to focus my eyes I could hear what I took to be coughing of deer to the east, but in the bright light I couldn't see them.

I have found on previous walks that the morning routine of strip wash, dressing, brew up and breakfast, then breaking camp and packing up usually took about 2 hours! Sure enough by just gone 8:30 I was ready for the off. The walk across to the Allt nan Glas Bheinn was straightforward and having crossed the river I contoured round the northeast side of the hill and found that the track became clearer and more distinct as I approached the forest. Once within the confines of the trees, the track became wetter and more difficult to negotiate, with one section just before the river forcing me to add a caveat to my statement on Scottish bogs, to the effect that it doesn't apply to bogs in forests!

The track was at least 4 metres wide and completely impassable – tentative prodding with the Leki pole confirmed my suspicions that this was bad. I ended up by forcing my way through the trees, not an easy feat when they are only about a metre apart and all the dead lower branches stick out ready to prod one in unexpected places and catch on any unsuspecting piece of webbing or clothing. I emerged the other side of the bog triumphant, turned round, gave a dismissive gesture to the obstruction, removed a considerable amount of debris from my person, dusted myself down and proceeded on my way, shortly after this I stopped for a few minutes in a sunny clearing by the track and had some refreshment. I was now on the main route into (or out of) the forest and after a kilometre or so I emerged on to the bridge over the River Garry NH133012.

I stood on the bridge to take a photo, blinking in the bright sunshine. Looking east, the view was spectacular, the sun shimmering on the shallows where the river is quite wide as it leads down eventually to Loch Garry. I have a friend who is a great fisherman and he regularly travels north to stay at the Tomdoun Hotel which is only about 2½km downstream from the bridge and talks about the wonderful fly fishing here.

I sat for a while at the side of the road enjoying the sunshine and taking in the view up Loch Poulary towards the power station and contemplating the 330m climb that would take me north to Glen Loyne. Normally when back-packing with a full load I tend to stop for 10-15 minutes every 1½ to 2 hours. This allows the muscles in my neck and shoulders to relax and also is a good opportunity to take on some nourishment – this trip it was chocolate, fruit, nuts, dry roasted pumpkin seeds and a number of energy bars, one of which I now eat - more out of duty than desire – for it had very little to titillate the taste buds.

This particular type, produced by a nutritionist whose face smiled out at me from the wrapper, had the look and consistency of dry putty and not as much flavour. I am a firm believer in natural foods but I am constantly disappointed by the inability of some of the producers of these prepared foods to get any decent flavour into them!

The walk up the Allt a Ghobhainn to Mam na Seilg NH106042 was a bit of a pull, but gaining height quickly has the benefit of constantly widening horizons, so at least there is something different to look at as one gasps for more oxygen. Once through the narrow bealach between Mam na Seilg and Glac Raineach I looked north west over Glen Loyne to the southern flanks of the big mountains that comprise the eastern end of the fantastic South Glen Shiel Ridge. Beyond and to the north, the great expanse of hills, between Glen Affric and Loch Cluanie.

There had been a late fall of snow a few days before I arrived, which had given a good dusting to all the tops over about 800m, and it gave the landscape a majestic definition which was accentuated by the clear sunny atmosphere.

The path from Glen Garry to the Cluanie Inn is SRWS route 248 (the Scottish Rights of Way Society handbook is a wonderful book which describes rights of way all over Scotland. I found it an invaluable aid in the planning of walks in Scotland.) The notes accompanying each route are most useful, neither exaggerating or underplaying difficulties to be confronted. The last sentence of the notes for route 248 is *"This route is not possible if the River Loyne is in spate"*. From my experience of Scottish streams and rivers I know that during and after rain some can rise and fall very quickly while others take a lot longer to react. Consequently the crossing of the River Loyne was an uncertainty in my route planning and mentally flagged by a big red asterisk.

By the time I had climbed from Glen Garry to Mam na Seilg, quite a lot of cloud had built up in the distance, but it was still a good day for being in the hills. As I proceeded north through the gap, the views into Glen Loyne opened up below. Looking back to the south and east was a grand spread of mountains and I fancied I could see the tops of Ben Nevis and Aonach Mor in the distance.

My first sight of the River Loyne was encouraging, looking fairly wide but no appreciable amount of water. Sure enough the by the time I reached the floor of the glen I could see that the river was very docile and I crossed easily without removing boots. The path now led NW up the glen and after about 1½km NH079064 I turned off onto a rocky path that led ENE up the valley side to the bealach between Creag Laithtais and Creag Mhaim at about 480m NH091066. The path then contours round before dropping quite sharply to join the old metalled public road that at one time must have been the direct route from the Cluanie Inn to Invergarry before Loch Loyne was enlarged by the building of a dam at its eastern end.

By now it was late afternoon and I sensed that there was a weather change on the way. The wind was still from the west but it had a sort of urgency about it, as if trying desperately to hold back the forces of weather from the east. Sure enough the whole of the eastern horizon was taken up by a wide bank of cloud.

It was about 18:00 as I took off my pack outside the Cluanie Inn and went in for the much anticipated beer. I phoned Ali from the phone box and got all the news from home. It was good to talk to her and I knew it would be another 3 days before I would get to another public phone and the chance of getting a signal on the mobile in the terrain ahead was pretty slim.

Suitably refreshed, I set off east along the A87 for 2km to pick up the track north up the An Caorann Mor. On the map this glen appears so wild and open that I had wondered how far I would have to go before finding a campsite. As it happened about 1 km up the track I found the perfect spot in a sheltered position, 10 metres below the track next to the stream. I quickly laid claim to it and soon had the tent erected. The weather was still suspect, that big bank of cloud to the east was less prominent but generally I was pretty sure the weather was not going to be so good the next day. But that was another day, I was comfortable here and enjoyed my meal and the post prandial routine of writing up my log, followed by whisky and chocolate, horlicks and then to bed.

Day 3 – Saturday 8th May
An Caorann Mor to Nr Loch Mullardoch
Walking from 09.50 to 20.00hrs
Distance 23K, Height Climbed 1255m, Camped at NH083291

Sure enough the weather changed, there was a bit of rain overnight, a lie-in was encouraged by a steady drizzle and I eventually unwrapped myself from the comforts of the sleeping bag at about 08.00, once the rain had stopped.

An initial assessment of the weather was not good and a further more comprehensive assessment which involved climbing the 10m back up on to the track in order to get a better view north up the glen, merely confirmed the fact that it was a rather claggy day with an unbroken heavy cloud base at I estimated under 1000m. Most of the ridge that was to be my route later that day was covered and the likelihood of more rain was pretty strong.

This was the scenario I had not wanted. In the planning of this expedition I considered two alternative routes from here to Loch Mhoicean (NH077316). The first section up the glen to Alltbeithe Hostel is straightforward. This is the beginning of SRWS Route 253. From the hostel were two options. One was a low level route due west at the head of Glen Affric then north to Iron Lodge and a climb north east up to the Loch. The other and my preferred option, a high level route, onto the ridge from Alltbeithe Hostel up to Sgurr nan Ceathreambhan, then the NE ridge to Mullach na Dheiragain and Mullach Sithidh, due north down to Loch Mullardoch then up and over to Loch Mhoicean. I figured this was more interesting, more direct and also a chance to get on to some tops and bag a couple of Munroes! Then there would always be the option of the Iron Lodge if the weather was bad.

So here I was at 10.00hrs. having had a later start than I would have preferred, due to the weather, plodding north up the glen weighing up the pros and cons of the situation. I decided to go with my preference – the high level route and to hell with the clouds!

The first 3km was a comfortable walk up a good track. The imposing presence of the big hills to the east and west with their crags and rocky buttresses, was enhanced by the clouds swirling around their tops and the dark colouring of the wet rock. The track comes to an abrupt end at the watershed NH079162 – for some reason this must be as far as the stalkers wish to travel in their ATV's and 4 wheel drives. The next 4 km to the River Affric, by the hostel was awful, some of the muckiest and more time consuming terrain of the whole trip. The quote from my daily notes sum it up *"……the latter half of the walk to Alltbeithe was rotten, boggy peaty muck, descent to river over wet tight grassy mossy stuff was like a skating rink, fell over 3 times……."*. It always seems to happen in this sort of boggy difficult terrain, the track appears and disappears like a will o the wisp. It was gone midday before I was standing by the river, feeling thoroughly out of sorts. The falls had only hurt my pride but there is no doubt that when one is out of the first flush of youth (ha! ha!) – 17 going on 57, a fall of any sort especially if accelerated by a 20+kg pack, does have a certain unsettling affect on one!

So temporarily out of sorts was I, that I had removed boots and socks, donned my Teva shoes and forded the river before I noticed that 500metres to the east, just beyond the hostel is a bridge! Feeling a complete prat I dried my feet, put on socks and boots and set off for the hostel and the path up to the ridge. I rested for a time above the hostel and went through the routine of taking on water.

The new Karrimor sack I had bought for this trip has a 2 litre hydration system, I also carried a 2 litre Platypus bladder. The usual method was to fill this from a stream and add the purifier, which has then to be left for 20 minutes. Once it is ready I decant it into the hydration system together with the G push energy food powder. I find this a good system because the built in hydration system allows fluid to be taken regularly and the second bladder gives the ability to carry extra clear water as well as the energy drink.

During the latter part of the morning the cloud base had dropped and I reckoned it was now down to about 850 – 900m. On my way up the path of the ridge I met with two young women coming down and while chatting they said that they had not reached the ridge because the cloud was down and they had decided to return to the hostel!

It was about 14:30 when I reached the bealach between An Socach to the east and the ridge to the west NH080230. The cloud was really thick, so it was very dull, with visibility of only 20-25m. In conditions like this one has no idea of the bigger picture; one can only assess what is in the field of vision and try to judge the features of the mountain from that limited information.
The ridge didn't seem difficult, some terraces with short sections to scramble up or down. I tend to worry on these parts if I lose the main way and I am always relieved when I find footprints or boot smoothed rocks again.

I shortly met up with three guys 'Dave' and his two mates who were on their way down from the summit. Dave was to drive his friends to Inverness later that day and would be returning to the hills the following day, Sunday. They were an affable trio and it was good to stop for 15 minutes or so and talk mountain talk. So far in 3 days walking I had only met a handful of people. The previous day the only words I had spoken to someone other than myself was to order a beer and peanuts at the Cluanie Inn.

Progress seemed slow and it was to get slower once I got to about 1000m. The last 1 km had a snow covering of only a few inches, but as that top section of the ridge consisted of loose rock and moss, which combined with soft snow, meant things could not be rushed. Visibility had been very poor most of the time, just a couple of times the north side of the ridge opened up to reveal glimpses of the corrie, the southern side of the ridge remained completely clagged in for the whole time I was on the ridge.

I eventually reached the East summit of Sgurr nan Ceathreauhnan in no more than 10m visibility and went on the further ½km to the West summit. I have to admit here that for whatever reason I had wrongly fixed in my mind that the track on to the NE ridge went from the West summit. Imagine my consternation when reaching the west summit and in visibility of 15-20m I realised that a NE bearing would take me straight over the edge of what looked, in the poor conditions like a fair sized cornice. On returning to the East summit the visibility had improved a bit and I could see the tracks, through the snow, that lead to the elusive NE ridge. I was soon dropping down on to the narrow ridge above An Gorm Lochan.

It was now past 17:00 and I was beginning to feel tired. I think the strain of coping with the conditions was beginning to have an effect and also I realised I probably had not eaten as much as I should have done that day, although I had been taking on the energy drink. A salutary lesson really, that even with experience it is still possible to overlook certain fundamentals on occasions. I have done many walks, that from the distance and terrain perspective were tougher, but when the stress and anxiety of a day like this, on one's own, is factored in to the equation, I think the effects on ones stamina etc.,. is quite considerable.

There was still a lot to do before I could set up camp, about 7km with three big undulations in the ridge before Mullach Sithidh, from where it would be all down hill. Visibility continued to improve and for the first time, looking back, I saw the ridge that had seemed to take me forever to traverse. Also the view out to the west seemed to encourage thoughts of a pleasant fine evening. It stayed thus till I got to Mullach Sithidh NH082265, by which time I was getting decent views north giving me a view of the start of the following day's route.

I had stopped to chat with two young guys 'Phil and Ian' who were setting up camp in the col above An Gorm Lochan, their mission was not only Munroe bagging but also to bag every top over 3000ft. They had come away for the weekend and were heading south again on Sunday afternoon. Some time after I had left them, I realised they could probably have helped solve a problem that had been nagging me for some time. Although Ali had full details of my route and roughly where I would expect to camp, I felt sure that when I spoke to her last, on Friday afternoon, I had confused the days and had told her that I would be ringing again on Sunday pm, whereas in reality I reckoned it would be Monday afternoon before I reached Craig on the A896 above Achnashellach NH037496 where I might hope to find a public telephone.

As I approached the bealach before Mullach Sithidh, NH078252 I heard 'Phil and Ian' behind me. They had finished setting up camp and were on a light weight attack of the NE ridge to bag the one Munro and three 3000 footers. As they passed by I asked if they would mind phoning Ali the next day. They readily agreed, I gave them details, and we parted for the second time. Sure enough she had a call from them the following afternoon as they were driving south on their way home.

At Mullach Sithidh I carried on down the shoulder that goes off to the NW while they continued NE to bag the 933m unnamed top. The last time I saw them they were half way to their objective, moments later it started to rain and within 2 or 3 minutes the cloud had descended and once again I was in rotten visibility, the difference being that this time it was raining, serious Scottish *"get off these moontins you bloody introoder"* rain. My notes written the following morning put it bluntly *"...just as I had established my route it started to rain. The cloud dropped and it absolutely pissed down. Got down by instinct, occasionally reinforced by compass bearing..."*

In retrospect this was the low point of the whole expedition. A mixture of exhaustion and disappointment that the weather was deteriorating again, brought many thoughts to mind like, *why am I doing this to myself?*. I found it quite a mental challenge to stay completely focussed on the matter in hand – a difficult 500ms descent down the north ridge over Creag a Choir Aird to the glen below.

I came out of the cloud at I reckon about 350-400m and although it was still raining, I could see a wide green strip on the south bank of the river about 1km or so west from the top end of Loch Mullardoch. As I lost height my gaze kept returning to it, becoming more convinced that this was to be my next camp site. Sure enough at about 20:30 hrs I was standing on a beautiful flat grassy sward, "this will do me" I thought and immediately began unpacking my sack. I was completely exhausted. By the time I had pitched the tent and stowed my kit, all I could think of was getting out of my soaking wet kit and getting warm and dry in my sleeping bag, so I just had the recovery drink, half a bar of chocolate and shut my eyes on the day.

Day 4 – Sunday 9th May
Near Loch Mullardoch to Loch an Laoigh
Walking from 10.30 to 17.50hrs
Distance 22K, Height Climbed 380m, Camped at NH023414

I awoke fairly early having slept really well. I lay dozing and contemplating for a little while until about 07.00 hrs when I got out for a much needed pee and to start the morning routine. It was almost eerie looking round, there was not a breath of wind and I was in the middle of a thick white mist, only being able to see about 15-20m. There was a certain brightness about it, which told me there was a clear blue sky not too far above me, not like the dull grey claggy skies of yesterday.

I treated myself to clean dry underwear and put on the Paramo trousers and jacket from the previous night – still absolutely sodden! That's the strange thing about Paramo clothing, it takes forever to dry on its own but put it on and body heat dries it within 20-30 minutes, with the bonus that it is still as warm even when wet. I was starving hungry, having not eaten much the previous evening so this morning I breakfasted like a king – two cups of tea, the usual daily portion of porridge, a cod and potato in sour cream sauce expedition meal, followed by some chocolate! Once I had eaten and sitting in the tent with dry clothes I felt so refreshed, mentally and physically, as I wrote up my log for the previous day, I began to feel a certain sense of satisfaction that I had coped pretty well with what I had always thought would be a tough section of the trip. Although the evening before I was so exhausted that

I had no enthusiasm for continuing, now I felt totally revived and began to look at the map, eager to take in the new day's challenge – today's route promised some interesting and demanding terrain.

The mist was beginning to move and a weak sun was shining. Visibility was variable but seemed to be slowly improving. Looking across the river I could see the bealach above Coire na Breabaig NH077306 which was my immediate objective. I took the packing up routine at a fairly leisurely pace and about 10:30 hrs I was ready for the off, the bealach had been clear for some time, but there was mist on the north side, which occasionally swirled gently towards me.

The river was a boots off job, not particularly fast flowing just lacking in the large rock department. I headed for the Allt na Criche and made my way up it to the watershed, once through the bealach I found myself in really thick mist again. I set the compass on a NNE bearing and made my way down over some pretty lumpy stuff, knowing that I would sooner or later come across Loch Mhoicean. Again there was a complete stillness, not a sound broke the spell and it was a great surprise when I suddenly realised the edge of the loch was about 5 metres away. The surface of the water was like a mirror and just merged totally into the misty greyness. I was only about 100m from the eastern end of the loch, beyond which there is about ½ km of peat hags which is the watershed, and then I began descending into the glen. The mist was literally just over the loch and its immediate environs, for by the time I had got through the peat hags I was looking north down the glen in warm sunshine, with some cloud still around the tops.

This is a huge, wild, majestic glen. The considerable rounded mass of An Cruachan in the distance guarding the entrance to the glen and to the west rising up into the mist, was the massif of An Creachal and Aonach Buidhe with their fearsome crags and buttresses high up shielding the tops of vast steep grassy slopes. To the east the lower reaches of the 2km unbroken slopes that lead up to An Socach 1069m are riven by many streams some of which have over the ages eroded clefts higher up where the slope is steeper.

There was a path of sorts down the glen which then contoured around An Cruachan. I stopped for some refreshment and to review the situation, more or less at the point where the path begins to separate from the river. I had looked at this area many times on the map trying to picture it in my mind and wondering quite how wet it was going to be, the objective being to cross NW for about 4kms to reach the eastern end of Loch Calavie. NH050390 I feared that it had the potential of being quite a difficult section. There is a huge amount of water going through here either east to Loch Monar or west to the River Ling. Now as I sat there looking down on what up till now had been described for me on 25 sq cms of map, I became fairly confident of the route I should take.

I left the path at NH086354 and followed the NE bank of the river for 2km or so till just past Cnoc a Mhoraire by which time I had lost the view to the NW of the dramatic south facing slopes of Bidean a Choire Sheasgaich 945m and Lurg Mhor 986m which overlook Loch Calavie. So after taking a rough compass bearing I set off NNW-ish away from the river. The next 2km or so was to put it mildly 'interesting'. My apprehension during the planning stages that this area would be very wet were not realised, the various streams were comfortably crossed but this is an area of broken moorland interspersed with peat bogs and peat hags, not the Premier League ones I was to see later in the walk but more the Division 2 of the peat bog fraternity, they looked threatening but were quite easy to cross.

It was possible to keep a more less straight line across, without diverging more than 20m or so in either direction,. Looking across, it appeared at a distance like an area of open moorland, the peat bogs with their peaty cliff fringes only become apparent at close range, they could extend for anything up to 100m or more and were quite tiring to negotiate, constantly jumping or climbing down a metre or so into the 'bog' then finding a way up the peat 'cliff' back on to solid ground again. As a result it was about 1½ hours later that I reached the comfort of the track, NH065385, that runs from Pait Lodge on Loch Monar to Bendronaig Lodge. This had been a fascinating bit of terrain, but not one you would want to cross after a wet season. There was an interesting feature just before I reached the track, a wide area of bare peat from which the bleached roots of ancient trees protruded giving it the appearance of a graveyard of huge prehistoric beasts!

Once on the track I had a well earned rest of 15 minutes or so and ate some chocolate, dried fruit and nuts. I made good time walking on the track towards Bendronaig Lodge, about ½ km before the Lodge I turned north on the track that headed towards Loch an Laoigh and Bearness. I chose a campsite at the side of the track about 200m from the loch. In planning I had wondered whether the NE slog up Bearness may be more feasible up the river rather than the part track shown on the map to contour round at high level. I wanted to do a 'reccy' so I retraced my steps from the camp site back to the track and now standing in the early evening sun looking north to the area around the loch and at that part of the river I could see, I more or less decided there and then that a low level route was a 'no no'. It had that distinctive look of boggy terrain, plenty of dark brown ground and countless 'glinty' bits of open water. Looking on up the track I just had a funny feeling that it didn't go anywhere. Still, all that would be revealed the following morning, for now I had an excellent sheltered campsite with my own little stream and I hurried back to set up camp.

This had been a day of no human contact, the only indication of man's existence had been a distant helicopter early in the afternoon and now looking over I could see Bendronaig Lodge and way across the river to the north was the MBA bothy NH021431. More surprisingly the only wildlife I had seen was a raven, rock pipits, two sandpipers and I had heard oystercatchers and golden plover. I still had not seen any deer, although there was plenty of evidence of them in the form of footprints and droppings.

It was now 18:00 hrs and with the tent pitched, I did some washing and also spread out the sleeping bag and thermarest to air. The clouds that had been building up in the east all afternoon, were now over the top of Sail Riabhach and there was the occasional rumble of thunder. Although I was still in sunshine I guessed it would not be long before a storm came. I was wrong and after a brief shower and a few more rumbles, the clouds receded and it was a pleasant evening.

I settled into the usual routine enjoying my meal then sitting in the tent reviewing the day's walk, looking at the next day's route and finally the daily treat of chocolate and whiskey while writing up the daily log. It had been a superb day with good weather. I had walked about 22km through some of the wildest country that our small island has to offer and now I had a good campsite and the prospect of a good walk tomorrow, back into relative civilisation and hopefully the opportunity by the afternoon to find a phone and speak to Ali. I reflected yet again what a fantastic support she is. In the last week or so before I set off Ali could see that I was quite apprehensive and it would have been very easy for her to suggest I call it off but she was always so positive and encouraging.

I made a mental note to thank her for nagging me to take my goretex gaiters, I cannot think why I was tempted to leave them at home – probably the last minute mania for trying to reduce the pack weight. I have worn them continuously so far and they are invaluable for keeping trousers relatively clean and helping to keep feet dry.

I am amazed that with nearly 100km under my belt or even my soles, I have had no problems with my feet, for years I have come to expect blisters at the beginning of a walking holiday as a sort of 'right of passage'. I suspect that the 'Superfeet' boot liners are actually doing what the guys in the Moorland Rambler store in Exeter said they would.

My last inspection of the weather at 21:00 hrs just before I turned in, revealed that the clouds had filled in again following the thunder rumbles earlier on, so I got into my bag wondering what the weather had in store for me tomorrow.

DAY 5: Monday 10th May 2004
Loch an Laoigh to Coulin Pass
Walked from 10.00 to 17.00hrs
Distance covered 20kms Climbed 555m Camped at NH024533

I had a lie-in this morning, although there is no way of seeing out of my tent without unzipping the door, the absolute stillness and amount of condensation on my fly sheet made me pretty certain that the weather had clagged in. Eventually at 07:50 I got out and sure enough, I was in pretty dense fog, or low cloud! I found my way to the stream and filled the washing bowl and had my strip wash. This must always present a funny sight – stark naked hopping on one foot then the other, much splashing, many sharp intakes of breath and exclamations as cold water hit vulnerable places but it is amazingly invigorating and really gets the day into sharp focus straight away.

I breakfasted on one mug of tea, lumpy porridge and a bit of chocolate. As usual the morning routine took about two hours and at just before 10:00 I gave the campsite a last once over checking for any stray item and climbed up on to the track. In the last few minutes I noticed that it was definitely getting a bit brighter, so maybe the weather would be OK. I had been pessimistic though in my choice of dress and was all kitted out in waterproofs.

Having walked along the track for about 100m or so it suddenly came to an end as I had suspected the previous evening. I had already decided on the high level traverse of Bearness having been put off by the boggy appearance of the area near the river. The visibility was still only about 30-40m so I took a bearing and set off across the moor in a roughly NE direction.

The mist cleared very quickly after I had been walking for about 15 minutes and by 10:30 I was getting fabulous views from the SW right round to NE looking up towards Beallach Bhearnais NH064450. By now it was really warm and I soon had to stop to change into shorts and swap the Paramo jacket for the light Pertex jacket.

The walk up to Beallach Bhearnais which lies at I reckon just under 600m was one of those immensely satisfying and challenging walks. I saw no evidence at all of any track or path, but looking way down below to the river, remained convinced that I had made the correct choice. The terrain was very varied, from peat bogs to heathery moorland, from 'clitter' to craggy outcrops. 'Clitter' is a good old Devon word and is used to describe areas of Dartmoor, very often near tors, where there are many scattered lumps of rock of varying sizes sometimes all together, sometimes with heather etc.,. growing around them. The several streams flowing down the NW flanks of Beinn Tharsuinn had all cut clefts to differing degrees into the hillside which added to the excitement and challenges of the terrain. These ravines would suddenly appear out of the heather, the deepest involved about a 30m precipitous descent to cross the torrent then an equally steep climb out.

There were some dramatic views up to the ridge of Beinn Tharsuinn looking up the ravine cut by the outflow stream from Coire Beithe. Nearing the bealach, the views back to the SW were wonderful showing the dramatic beauty of Bearness, a glen which I suspect is more used to being looked down upon than walked in. Climbing the last few metres up to Beallach Bhearnais brought one of those fabulous moments that all those who walk the hills must relish. You know that on reaching the top your whole vista will change, just a few more steps and new mountains are coming into view…………..and all of a sudden, there you are, standing on top taking in that new panorama, a great wide glen to the NE and in the east the wild heights of Sgurr Choinnich with just a few cotton wool clouds around some tops, defying the heat of the mid-day sun.

The bealach NH060450 is a very different place to the glen I had just walked up, here there were clear tracks and because this is the access point to the big mountains all around, it had the feeling of a place that would probably see at least a few visitors every day.

It was now 13:00 hrs and because the walk up Bearness had been rather time consuming (6km in 3 hours), I knew I should press on. I sat for 15 minutes or so just taking in the view and enjoying the complete solitude. I will admit to just a faint sense of satisfaction and achievement having come through over 50km of wilderness since my last human contact 43 hours earlier, about 18:00 hrs on Saturday.

I set off down a good path and soon was able to see the track from Craig to Glennaig Lodge on the far side of the stream. As I rounded a shoulder, below I saw the point where the path crosses the Allt a Chonais to then join the main track and, surprise, surprise, a figure coming up the path towards me. We stopped and chatted for 10 or 15 mins, names always seem irrelevant at these chance meetings of like minded people half way up mountains, so, I shall refer to him as 'Alan'. He was a lean and very fit looking 59 year old, he was climbing not only Munroes but also all the 3000 ft tops, just like 'Phil and Ian' who had been my last contact on Saturday. The previous day he had climbed Ben Avon and Ben Bhuidhe (Cairngorms) no mean walk and was to spend a couple of days here climbing some more of the handful of tops left for him still to bag.

We said our farewells and I hurried on down towards the river which I found was a 'boots off' job. The slip-on Teva shoes are really great for this as they are specially designed for amphibious use. The soles are very grippy and give quite a bit of confidence coping with slippery underwater conditions. I soon joined the good estate road that goes down the valley to the railway track eventually linking with the A890 at Craig. It was a really warm afternoon and the hazy sunshine gave that look of innocence to all the mountains. There was an all pervading scent of warm coconut in the air from so many huge banks of gorse that were on either side of the track all the way down to the road.

It was one of those uplifting occasions when out walking, the weather was glorious, the scenery superb, long views into the hazy distance with dramatic outlines of many hills all around and all was well with the world. Although I had only covered about a third of the walk, I did feel very satisfied that I had negotiated the 50kms (as the raven flies) of wilderness since leaving the Cluanie Inn on Friday, and really enjoyed all the challenges it had posed.

I was nearing Craig and soon I hoped I would be able to phone Ali – even though the OS map did not show a public telephone any nearer than Achnashellach Station 5kms down the A890. Who knows there may be a wonderful tea shop there, selling freshly baked home made cakes and great mugs of freshly brewed tea? Although the OS map shows only about five buildings at Craig it includes the word 'Hostel' which I knew from a conversation with one of the few people I met on Saturday, was the famous 'Gerry's Place'. Anyway it was with a great sense of expectancy that I joined the A890 and turned left towards Craig, the hustling bustling mecca of the Highlands!

Three of the five buildings proved to be large detached dwellings on the north side of the road which in estate agent speak, were in 'elevated' positions with panoramic views of the mountains. Unfortunately there was no sign of a teashop. Gerry's Place was the last building on the left set some 50m off the road adjacent to the railway line. As I approached, a figure emerged and started to walk towards the road and we met halfway along the drive. I greeted him with a "Hi, what a wonderful day…is there a telephone here I could use?". He replied "Yes there's a payphone inside". He turned and headed back to the hostel with me, I guessed he was either Gerry or one of the management – it turned out he was a mate of Gerry who was running the hostel while Gerry was away. He seemed like a very amiable sort so I pushed my luck... "Any chance of a cup of tea?". "Sure thing, I'll put the kettle on while you make your call" he said.

It was now about 15:00 hrs and it is always a bit of a lottery phoning Ali during business hours because ours is a mainly retail business so there is always the chance that we cannot have a decent conversation because of customers needing attention. However, on this occasion we were lucky and I sat in the cool and temporarily empty hostel and had a long talk with Ali catching up on all the news at home. How Devon was basking in early summer sunshine, the latest exploits of the cats, the disinclination of the tourists to spend money and other such news. I could sense the relief in her voice as she realised I was in good heart and not suffering with blisters, bad back, violent stomach disorders or anything else.

I have had to undergo this telephone analysis since an occasion in the autumn of 2001 while walking the West Highland Way, I reached

Rowardennan on the east bank of Loch Lomond and overnight suffered a very bad bilious attack which subsequently turned out to have been caused by a sudden blooming of the giardiasis that I must have contracted whilst trekking in the Atlas mountains in Morocco some months before. The following morning I continued the walk and just about managed to stagger as far as Inversnaid Hotel by lunchtime. Realising I could go no further I had hoped to get a room there, but the Hotel was fully booked. The kindly lady on reception managed to book me in at the small hotel up the hill in the nearby Lodge. I guess her natural desire to help was fuelled by her anxiety to find somewhere else for this pale and gently swaying individual to keel over. Later that day, Saturday, I phoned Ali in a state of some distress feeling very ill and thinking I would have to give up the walk. My dear wife then spent all that evening trying to establish how I could get back to Glasgow and thus home from the wrong side of Loch Lomond on a Sunday. However, the next day I felt so much better that in a call to her on Sunday morning I told her that I was able to cross Loch Lomond, catch a bus north to Tyndrum and thus should be back on schedule to finish the walk and use my pre booked B&Bs.

Since then, understandably, I suppose she has always wanted to convince herself I was fit in body and spirit whenever I have phoned her on one of my treks. On this occasion I had passed with flying colours and signed off promising to call her again the next morning from Kinlochewe.

At the back of the hostel, I found Gerry's mate, sat on a long 'bench' leaning against the wall. This 'bench' is an ancient tree trunk about 4 to 5 metres long propped up on two small chunks of tree, it is in a fabulous position south facing looking across the railway line and valley with its forest to the hills, which are the same hills whose southern flanks I had gazed on from my walk up Bearness earlier that day.

We sat there in the afternoon sun drinking big mugs of tea and talking mountains and walking. Once again the fellowship of the hills – this common love of beauty and solitude provided a short episode of companionship that I will remember for many years.

I left Gerry's Place about 16:00 hrs and carried on along the road, looking for the track which would denote the beginning of The Coulin Pass – SRWS Route 288. This is only about 1km west from the hostel, NH029490 So I was soon sweating my way up the zig zagging path through the trees. The forest higher up had recently been felled so I enjoyed some wonderful views and the relative comfort of a breeze during the last part of the climb. Near the top of the path, it joined a good estate track NH024500 which carries on all the way to Loch Coulin.

About 3km down the track I saw a very good campsite just by the bridge over Essain Dhorca, although I would have liked to have carried on for another 5 or 6km. I realised the track was heading towards the estate houses and farms and finding a suitable spot for a wild camp may well become more difficult and this really was an idyllic spot. My mind was made up – a comfortable campsite was worth the slight drawback of an earlier than usual start the next day.

Camp was very soon established and conveniently placed. Dead trees allowed me to put up a washing line and another large tree nearby provided a suitable hook to hang out my sleeping bag to air. For the next 2 hours or so I busied myself with washing, sorting out kit and food and generally enjoying the warm evening. I looked north towards the Torridon hills, I could see Beinn Eighe in the distance – Liathach was not visible – hidden behind Sgwr Dubh, to the west and south west the dramatic trio of Fuar Tholl, Beinn Laith Mhor and Beinn Liath Bheag.

There was more insect activity than I would have liked, quite a lot of midges and other things had made their presence felt by mid evening – 24 hours on and I would find out quite how active they had been!

All the washing I had done was dry by about 20:30 hours, it's always good to have ones reserve clothing dry and clean for several obvious reasons. The weather had seemed to change a bit, although still clear in the west with sunshine till sunset, clouds had filled in elsewhere and Beinn Eighe had disappeared, so I did not have too much hope for clear weather on Tuesday.

Surprisingly, I found there was a signal on the mobile phone so I was able to report in to mission control and also send a couple of text messages to friends. Being someone who basically dislikes mobile phones I am always self conscious about using one 'in the wild' because I know how it annoys me to come across someone using a phone *"Hi Sally I've just reached the top of this huge mountain on the Isle of Skye!"*. Of course it's different when I use one! My first solo back-packing jaunt to the Cairngorms in May 2000, Ali insisted that I took a mobile phone.

These things cannot be regarded as any sort of safety aid because in my experience the only chance of a signal in most mountain areas is right on the tops, not a lot of good if you get in trouble halfway up! I did keep her informed of my progress, and on the third day climbed up from my camp spot to the top of Cairn Toul to find myself in mist with a clear sky above and a wonderful view over a cloud filled Lairig Ghru with Ben Macdui just protruding on the other side. I decided to report in to Ali and found only a reluctant signal on the phone, but by climbing the extra 1½ metres and balancing on top of the cairn I got a steady signal! While talking, a dog suddenly appeared through the mist closely followed by its master. I felt such a prat and duly was obliged to explain my odd behaviour.

On this occasion by the River Coulin I was undisturbed, the only sounds were the stream and occasional bird call, I had not seen a soul since my friend in Gerry's Place.

As usual I had done all the necessary jobs, sorting out, log writing, map checking by about 21:00 hrs and was now ready for bed. I did a mental body check and was pleased that everything was in good working order. I was so pleased that my feet were standing up very well with no blisters or sore bits. I felt that matter of blisterless feet was mainly due to the new Brasher boots I had bought only a week or so before setting off. The boots I had intended to use suddenly began leaking during a particularly wet walk on Dartmoor. I had suffered so much over the years from sore feet that to have a pair of boots fitting like gloves from Day 1 was sheer luxury. The other pleasing thing was that my new rucksack was so much more comfortable and not causing the shoulder ache that my previous sack was prone to do.

Day 6 Tuesday 11th May.
Coulin Pass to Loch an Nid
Walked from 08.00 to 18.15hrs
Distance covered 30kms Climbed 400m Camped at NH081749

The cloud that had appeared on Monday evening had spread and I emerged from the tent at 05:50 to no visibility and a damp chilliness in the air. There was no wind just that incredible stillness when nature just seems to hold its breath until the fog lifts and the weather decides what it is going to do.

By the time the morning routine was completed and I was ready to start walking, it was about 08:00 hrs and I still could not see very much. Things did improve a bit and by the time I reached Torran Cuillin visibility was reasonable but all the hills were totally hidden so I suppose the cloud base was down to about 250m.

I squelched my way round Loch Coulin along a poor path, which saves one from climbing up through the forest to gain the security of the estate road. The path joins this road at the bottom end of the Loch NH010559 and from here to the main road things are well ordered and neat. To the left there are impressive views across to Coulin Lodge and its gardens, then comes Loch Clair with its classic view west to Liathach, or as was the case on this occasion to thick white cloud!

One of the uncertainties of back packing trips is finding somewhere to attend to normal 'bodily demands'. My hopes of being able to 'hang on' until Kinlochewe where I could enjoy the comfort of proper facilities were not to be! For the last half an hour or so the realisation was dawning that not only may it be quite uncomfortable to walk the 5km of A896 to Kinlochewe, but it could well not afford a suitably private toilet spot should it be necessary. Action had to be taken! So with a muttered apology to the Laird, after checking there was no one in view, climbed up the wall at the side of the drive and carefully wending my way up through the new planting on the wooded hillside gained the seclusion of the open moorland 50m above the lochside road. Suitably relieved I carried on and was soon on the main road heading for Kinlochewe. At this point I should have been admiring the awesome presence of Beinn Eighe with its lofty corries, craggy buttresses and its presence as the majestic guardian of the eastern end of Glen Torridon. Cloud was still down to about 300m so I just imagined it – trying to recall the view from my previous visit with Ali in May……1975!

I reached the village at 11:00 hrs and soon found the post office, which like others in the Highlands was also the general store and in this case a café as well. Here I was to find my parcel of goodies that I had sent off a couple of weeks earlier. It is an odd feeling opening up the parcel I had carefully packed up on my bench at work, while now sitting outside in the midst of all this Highland grandeur (not that I could see much of it).

The parcel consisted of another three Expedition meals, more chocolate, fruit and nuts, tea bags, toilet paper, tissues, individually packed portions of the energy drinks, day portions of porridge mix and also some parcel tape, as there were generally some items that can be returned. On this occasion I sent back some dried fruits and nuts, the maps I no longer needed and a couple of packs of tissues. I would be collecting the rest of my provisions on Thursday at Ullapool so I knew that I could then have a major review of what I needed for the second half of the walk.

As I was busying myself with the re-packing of my rucksack and the rewrapping of the parcel, my gaze kept being attracted to the sign advertising 'All Day Breakfasts'. Business was a bit quiet in Kinlochewe this morning so I sat in solitary state in the café waiting for my breakfast - "something of everything please!" to arrive. The café area is one end of the shop so I could look over the store and post office area. As far as I could see the couple (in their 40's) in charge had no other help so while the lady cooked my breakfast, her partner was dealing with everything else, he moved with effortless ease between dispensing postage stamps to selling groceries and the daily papers while keeping up a cheerful banter with the locals.

I steadfastly worked my way through bacon, fried bread, sausage, eggs, beans and mushrooms with bread and butter, marmalade and a pot of tea on the side. I said to myself "You're going to suffer for this in about an hours time!".

Walking down through the village, I felt more bloated and uncomfortable than I had done since leaving Devon the previous week, I guess that demonstrated how we quickly adapt to a change of diet. I consoled myself with the thought that at least the breakfast had boosted my calorie consumption for the day. I spent a while in the car park where there is a phone box and public loos, both of which I took advantage of before leaving the village. I had a good 6-8 minute call to Ali and again she was lucky not to be interrupted by customers! "Are you sure you've unlocked the shop door?" I chided "You've got to make some money to pay for this holiday of mine!". Again I heard how good the weather was back home. I signed off with "I should be phoning again early afternoon tomorrow from Dundonnell or later on from Ullapool".

This section of the walk is SRWS Route 296, Incheril to Dundonnell.

As I made my way out of the village past Incheril, on to the track up Abhainn Bruachaig to the Heights of Kinlochewe NH070643 , the clouds seemed to have lifted a bit, especially over the lower hills. Beinn Eighe though was still completely obscured. By the time I reached the Heights of Kinlochewe I was feeling a lot more mobile having got over the initial energy sapping digestion of my breakfast. That section of glen from Incheril is pretty rugged with great crags on the steeper NW facing elevation, the farmland at The Heights looked quite lush in comparison .

As I climbed up the track that leads into Gleann na Muice I looked back to the verdant riverside fields around the farm and was pretty sure that I saw a hen harrier, with its distinctive 'floppy' flight, flying low over one of these fields.

The next 4km or so up Gleann na Muice were pretty bleak. It seems to be a particularly desolate place, no long views just the rounded shapes of this typical glaciated valley. Even the vegetation seemed to retain its winter appearance, spring comes late here! The sombre mood of the place was echoed by the estate worker on his ATV who I had watched for some time way up the track, when he eventually came down past me, it was as much as he could do to acknowledge my greeting.

It was about 14:30 hrs when I reached the top of the glen NH063680 and the view to the north west began to open out. By Loch Gleann na Muice the track had become an apology of what it had been lower down. I stopped for a rest and to take in the view towards the big hills at the top end of Lochan Fada.

Although the OS map shows a track going as far as the shore of Lochan Fada, by the time I turned off it, to head NE up towards Loch Mheallan an Phudair, about 300m before the lochside NH055697, it had become pretty indistinct.

It was with a great sense of excitement and anticipation that I turned my back on Lochan Fada and set off uphill, ahead of me was about 5km before I could pick up the track north to Loch an Nid. It is impossible to gauge what sort of terrain one is going to encounter when going 'cross country' I have become pretty good at picturing in my mind how some areas will appear by studying the maps, but as to what will be underfoot remains a mystery until reality takes over.

The first kilometre or so up to the little lochan was pretty straightforward rough terrain with no great surprises. The view all around by Loch Mheallan an Phudair was breathtaking and I think one of the more impressive viewpoints of the entire walk. Even the overall grey skies and clouds hiding some of the higher tops did nothing to reduce the impact of the panorama.

To the northwest the peaks, ridges and corries of Beinn Tarsuin, Meall Garbh, Mullach Coire Mhic Fhearchair and Sgurr Dubh seemed to tower above me. Round to the north the view opened out with a rising foreground partially obscuring the Bealach na Croise, which was my next objective. Framed between the hills on either side of the bealach was Craig Rainich, to the east of Loch an Nid. Carrying on round to the east were the huge rounded hills of Beinn Bheag, Groban, Meallan Chuaich, marching into the distance behind the mirrored stillness of Loch Mheallan an Phudair. Then the high level moorland of the Kinlochewe Forest and finally to the WSW, looking through the bealach I had just come across and still partially hidden in cloud the unmistakable outline of Slioch. Beinn Eighe retained its cloudy shroud and so I continued to be deprived of a view of this classic mountain.

Having finally had my fill of the grand views, I set off again contouring round to the north. Shortly after leaving Loch Meallan an Phudair the view opened to reveal the dramatic, narrow Bealach na Croise. Conditions underfoot were fairly rough, a mixture of peaty boggy sections, rough heather and occasional rocks, not conducive to making good speed. I had not seen any real sign of what I was approaching until all of a sudden I found myself on the edge what appeared at first glance to be a sheer drop into the ravine, that had been eroded by the stream draining the corries of Mullach Coire Mhic Fhearchair. The slight V in the contours on the 1-50,000 map does nothing to suggest the actual nature of the terrain.

"What a sod" I thought "how the hell am I going to get across this?" I looked to the left and right, only to find the chasm extended as far as I could see both upstream and downstream. I guessed it was 25-30 metres deep but as I began to calmly appraise the situation, it was not so much of an obstacle as I first feared. I zig-zagged down the steep side, over good thick grass and heather which provided a sound footing. The stream although substantial was not in spate, so a quick recky of the rocks and boulders over and round which it plunged soon revealed an easy crossing point. The opposite side was steeper but because it was south facing it had good growth of heather among the rocks and I managed to climb up quite easily. Having reached levellish ground again, I gave it a last "it will take more than that to stop me!" look and carried on, only then allowing myself to think, albeit briefly, on what the consequence would have been of slipping down that slope!

The next ¾ km to the bealach were hard going, with a lot of rock, some partially hidden by heather. Once through the bealach I came across a sort of track, stopped for a well earned breather and some sustenance, the mornings mammoth breakfast now only a distant memory!

Bealach na Croise is a strange wild place, it is like a side door out of the valley coming SE from Mullach Coire Mhic Fhearchair and the way I had come, losing height to pass through a bealach seemed odd. The way ahead along the NW bank of the stream was steep and fairly rocky. In the distance I could see clearly the estate road that comes from the A832, all along the glen, past Loch a Bhraoin to Loch an Nid – the lengths some people will go for a bit of fly fishing!

It was now past 17.00 hrs and in the still overcast conditions the narrow confines below the bealach were relatively a lot darker than the surrounding hills, thus adding to the general sense of wilderness. To my surprise I picked up a reasonable path not far below the bealach, which for most of the time kept a pretty good line through all the rock and clutter of the descent. As is so often the case with tracks in remote areas, continuity is not on the agenda. A really clear track can suddenly disappear into a section of apparently virgin terrain and then rounding a large rock there is the track again laughing at you!

By the time I was down in the valley the skies were clearing and all the indications were for a fine evening. With the opening out of the valley came the expansion of views all around. I had my first sight of those incredible boiler plate slabs of quartzite rock to the west, below Meallan an Laoigh. I crossed the stream and gained the track which I had seen from way back up the hill and set off towards Loch an Nid. This is a truly awe inspiring place, the views are just breathtaking, with the track winding up the east side of the loch at the base of the steep flanks of Creag Rainich, a beach at the bottom end of the loch and a narrow defile where the outfall stream forces its way north. As I walked along the side of the loch I looked across to the west, to the even more extensive expanse of shiny slabs reflecting the early evening light. This is a hugely impressive sight – a field of bare smooth rock extending over a kilometre and rising for 300m up the eastern flank of Sgurr Ban, giving such an air of timelessness that it is difficult to think that this sight had changed much in thousands of years.

In the planning of this walk I had anticipated camping somewhere between Loch an Nid and Strath na Sealg, which is another 5 kms further north. I could never have envisaged that such a perfect wild camp site would present itself. At the bottom end of the loch the narrow shingle beach was edged by a low bank and then a level strip of close short grass and heather about 10 metres wide, before the thicker heather took over further away from the water. Without a second thought the rucksack was off and unpacked.

This was one of those magical moments that I just knew I would remember for the rest of my life. I had completed a wonderful days walk through some spectacular and remote country, during which I had been confronted with and overcome some technical challenges. Now I had found a good camp site with all mod cons and would shortly be relaxing and tucking into my evening meal. This was the sort of occasion I would recall at odd times in the future, during the hustle and bustle of daily life and think " Wow! Did I really do that ?"

I quickly pitched the tent stowed most of the gear inside, removed socks and boots, spreading them out on heather bushes to 'air'. I then enjoyed a paddle in the loch, reviving tired feet. Now, as I stood on the edge of the water, was the time to take in the view. The weather was perfect, the thick cloud that had been a feature most of the day, had thinned to a light haze, allowing the golden evening sun to spread over the eastern and southern hills. To the north the ground rose slightly, I guessed that because of the constriction in the glen at this point some glacial material had been dumped here at the end of the Ice Age. Above the near sky line to the north, the unmistakable profile of the upper reaches of An Teallach which glowed gold against the vivid blue evening sky. I had never seen An Teallach from this angle and I realised that the next morning would reveal the mountain in all its magnificence as I climbed north on the path down the glen.

The evening had turned rather chilly so I sat in the tent with feet pointing to the door enjoying the triangular view through the tent flap, of shore, loch and hillside.

After the normal ritual of writing up my log I went outside at about 21.00 hrs. to wash up my horlicky mug and have a last pee, as I stood in the relative darkness of the glen I gazed one last time at An Teallach, still lit by the setting sun but now back lit against streaky clouds and marvelled at the beauty and serenity of this place – talk about loo with a view!

Day 7 Wednesday 12th May
Loch an Nid to B&B at Braes of Ullapool
Walked from 08.30 to 19.00hrs
Distance 32kms Climbed 750m Stayed at NH142932

One of the great features of camping so far north at this time of year is that the nights never really get dark. I slept well for I guess 4-5 hours, and then slipped into a more fitful sleep, in which my dreams seemed to be accompanied by the weird nocturnal sounds of this wild and beautiful place, the eerie calls of red grouse and black throated divers, the odd snuffles and coughs of red deer as they grazed their way across the glen.

I eventually emerged from the tent at 06.10 hrs. and stood swaying gently in the sharp chill of the early morning. The weather was superb, as the evening before I was in deep shadow in the narrow glen, but with a clear blue sky above and the early morning sun brilliantly illuminating the east facing slopes of Beinn Bheag, Sgurr Dubh, Sgurr Ban and Beinn a Chlaidheimh. This really was a morning to remember! A slight breeze was ruffling the surface of the loch, and the two divers that as I first came out of my tent were only about 50 metres off the shore had retreated to the middle by the time my eyes had got into focus, so I never got a clear view.

I completed my strip wash and ran down to the water for an invigorating splash around before gratefully donning some warm clothes. The great expanse of rocky slabs on Sgurr Ban reflecting the morning sun was a spectacular sight, with the lower slopes still in deep shadow. My hopes of a good photo proved later to have been too optimistic, the extreme contrast of light proved to be too much for my 35mm auto focus idiot proof camera.

About 07.20 I heard the unmistakable sound of an ATV and some minutes later at the far end of the loch I saw two figures – I guessed they were fishermen who had made the 10-12 kms journey from the A832 along Loch Bhraoin to fish on Loch an Nid. While I finished my meagre repast and completed packing my bag, they slowly worked their way towards me one on each side, stopping and casting waiting for a few minutes then moving on and repeating the procedure. An hour later just as I was ready to set off, the guy who had come along the eastern shore reached my little beach, we chatted for a few minutes and then I bade him good day and good fishing, turned my face to the north and set off again with high spirits excited at what the day had in store for me.

I made quick progress along the path that clung to the bottom of the steep slope using what small amount of space the river allowed it in this confined section of the glen. I was still in shadow but now had the sunlit majesty of the multi-facetted An Teallach full in view. I had walked for 3kms before I came out into sunshine, where the glen opens out by the Eas Ban waterfall. This is an unusual spot, a wooded gorge at about 350m below the corrie on the north slope of Creag Rainich.

The stream that issues from this corrie is quite considerable and posed a challenge to cross, because the area by the confluence with the main river is flat and boggy, but I was able to gain the security of the track north without resorting to boots off paddling! I know from what I have read and heard in conversations, that crossing these rivers at the top end of Loch na Sealga can be very difficult or impossible at times. I realised then that attempting this route in wet weather may be impossible if these rivers were in spate.

As I climbed the track to Corrie Hallie the view to the NW began to open out and the brilliance of the sky above turned Loch na Sealga and the lower reaches of the river, into a ribbon of cobalt. I took one photo, intending to take another further up. Unfortunately this incredible visual effect was not destined to be captured on celluloid, because my attention was completely diverted when I realised the figure now approaching me down the track was 'Dave' the talkative one from the trio I met the previous Saturday on Sgurr nan Ceathreamhnan.

We stood and chatted for half an hour or so, it appeared that although a Merseysider by birth he had spent a number of years living in Bedfordshire – Ampthill, Flitton and my childhood home , Dunstable – small world!

This was yet another occasion when I experienced the great camaraderie of the hills. I really enjoy talking with people who share this irresistible love of the wild hills and valleys, sometimes described more by expression, tone of voice and body language rather than by words, which often are not enough anyway. We parted with mutual best wishes for the day ahead. He was set on a big ridge walk on the opposite side of the glen – taking in Beinn a Chlaidheimh, Sgurr Dubh, Mullach Coire Mhic Fhearchair, with maybe a high level bivvy, and on to Ruadh Stac Mor etc.,. the following day. That evening as I wallowed in the comfort of my B and B in Ullapool with the wind howling outside I wondered whether he had gone for the bivvy option!

This was due to be a morning of coincidences, for I had only walked on another 3kms or so to the top of the pass, and there ahead of me, sat on a rock was ' Alan' who I had met below Beallach Bhearnais, on the descent to Craig on Monday. I sat down beside him on the rock, and gazed up in awe at the massive bulk of An Teallach rising 700m in front of us. We chatted as we ate our lunch, I nibbling on my healthy dry fruit and nuts and 'Alan' working his way through an appallingly seductive ham and mayo baguette (fresh, purchased that morning in Ullapool) . I consoled myself with the thought that I would be there the following morning, so I too could be enjoying a similar delicacy for lunch tomorrow. Although later, I was to regret not having asked him where he bought it!

We parted about 15 minutes later, I was anxious to get on, pleasant as it was to meet up and chew the fat, I had now rested for the best part of an hour with the two stops and I still had a lot of walking ahead . The path down to Corrie Hallie is a good clear track, as one would expect of the main approach path to one of Scotland's finest mountains. All the views I had seen so far of An Teallach were spectacular and without having set foot on it I was beginning to see why one of my regular walking partners, regarded this as his favourite Scottish hill. The path soon descends into a wooded gorge on the right hand bank of the river, the birch trees in their spring flush of new leaves. To the right, the mean crags of Carn a Bhreabadair. Further down, the river is by now way below the track, and still the natural birch wood extends down the precipitous slope to the water. Looking west across the gorge through the branches of the birch trees were tantalising views of the corries, ridges and the silver screes of Bidein a Ghlas Thuill.

I reached Corrie Hallie just above the road about 12.30 hrs , I stopped for a breather , and as I had a drink I checked my 'phone and surprise, surprise there was a good signal so I took the opportunity to report in, I had a short talk to Ali, she was in good spirits, glad to have yet another confirmation that I was still vertical and breathing! The point where the track joins the road is quite elevated and offers a good view across the valley to the next section of my walk, the path from Dundonnell to Croftown in Strath More at the head of Loch Broom. So as we talked I was idly looking across to try and see where I should be going.

My original plan for the approach to Ullapool was to take the track north, to the Altnaharrie Hotel, from where you can catch, as the O.S. map states, the 'Ferry P [summer only]' to Ullapool. I had been unable to get any detail from the Hotel's website regarding frequency of the ferry across Loch Broom and I eventually discovered from the Post Office that the hotel was closed for business and for the time being the ferry was not running. I would have been more than a little put out if I had walked there to then discover that gem of information. During this process of enlightenment I first telephoned the local Tourist Information Office [as you would] and was puzzled by the young lady's reaction to my enquiry about the ferry service across Loch Broom, because she could only make vague comments about ferries to Stornaway, it transpired, on questioning her, that she was in a call centre somewhere [many miles from Wester Ross] and I suspected she had not a clue where Ullapool was, let alone the Altnaharrie Hotel! Just think, these call centres are set up to make it a better service for us.

The plan was revised, by incorporating SRWS route 303, a much less satisfactory solution, as it meant the approach to Ullapool would be an 11 km plod along the A835 from the top end of Loch Broom. The brief description in their handbook gave no clue to the problems that lay ahead. The SRWS do a terrific job with their work on rights of way all over Scotland, however I suspect that they would readily admit that some of the routes they detail, due to problems with landowners etc.,. are not as well signed or indeed as accessible as they would like. Route 303 proved to be a bit of a frustration in its final stages.
The cloudless skies of early and mid morning were now partially occupied by white clouds and a certain amount of high haze seemed to be filling in from the north and west, but at this stage I had not begun to appreciate the weather change that was on the way. I walked down the road and turned right on to the minor road to Eilean Darach, NH115855 crossed the river to the farm where the path goes steeply up the hillside. There was no distinct indication as to where exactly the path went, and

as it obviously started very close to the farmhouse, I felt it prudent to ask, rather than go wandering around by their back door. The lady of the farm seemed rather surprised when I knocked on her door and asked if she would mind me walking up through her fields [I'm not sure what I would have done if she had said 'No'] The way up was a track used by the farmer on his ATV and the lower section was the scene of a real Scottish rural idyll – sheltered fields running down to the Dundonnell River, young lambs frisking and gambolling in the afternoon warmth, the mother sheep feeding or fussing over their offspring, and all of this overlooked by majestic forests and mountains. I was soon high above on the open hillside, the scene behind me still dominated by the bulk of An Teallach, this time distance allowing a complete view of the massif. The path ahead climbed steadily for about 3 kms all the time going more or less due east, before beginning to swing round to the left towards Loch an Tiompain, NH160847 as the path turned I kept expecting to lose the view behind, but it was not until almost the point where it began to descend that An Teallach finally disappeared.

The spectacular views were now in front of me, across the fertile glen, with its wooded lower slopes, to the open hillside leading up to Beinn Dearg and beyond, with glimpses of Loch Broom to the north. My joy at this change of aspect was short lived, the track I had been following ran out on the top, at the water shed, to be replaced by a good cairned path. Within a kilometre the side of the glen had become incredibly steep and both path and cairns had disappeared. I was about to experience an extremely frustrating hour or so probably best described by the extract from my journal written that night, " .... The descent from below Meall Dubh to the valley was an absolute b*****d started as a well cairned path and then it just disappeared, I was totally stuffed, eventually regained a path of sorts and approached the wood that runs down a ravine to Croftown, where there was nowt but a 2 metre high deer fence. In the end after beating back and forth behind the houses I legged it over a gate and crossed a field of sheep to road. ....."

I guess that one of the causes of my difficulty was that the path is little used and on the steep section down to Croftown what vestiges there were of the path had been masked by the verdant new growth of bracken and heather. I was very pleased to have gained the road, for at one point, before I reached the wood I found myself following a wire fence down what must have been nearly a 1 in 1 slope – not good with a 20kg pack on your back!

It was about 1700hrs by the time I set foot on the A 835, to begin the 11km slog up to Ullapool. This promised to be one of those 'character building' times when you just have to forget physical discomforts, get your head down and walk! How situations change, compared to the euphoria of the previous evening at Loch an Nid and the wonderful start to the day's walking, with its superb views and cloudless skies, now I was tired, having already walked about 19 or 20kms and facing a 2 hour plod on tarmac, with traffic speeding by, before I could hope to gain the evening respite from my travels. To make matters worse there seemed to be a definite change in weather taking place, the wind from west or north-west had increased steadily since early afternoon, bringing in quite dense hazy cloud, that although not covering the sun, filled the western sky, and with my limited knowledge of meteorology filled me with suspicions that the good spell of weather, that had lasted since Sunday, was coming to an end.

In the planning of the walk, after the re-routing of this part, I guessed that there would not be any likelihood of a wild camp along the main road, and I was certainly proved right on that count. The O.S. map shows no campsites on the approach to Ullapool, so the only option seemed to be the campsite on Ullapool Point, which if the map was to be believed had 'extensive sea views' and thus would be fully exposed to the prevailing wind. As the kilometres passed beneath my boots I was fancying less and less a night on the edge of Loch Broom, being battered by increasingly aggressive winds. I had now been walking for 7 days and covered nearly 180kms. I suspected that above Ullapool the walking would become progressively more challenging, so thoughts of a bed for the night were coming to mind with a frequency that was in direct relation to my increasing fatigue.

As I approached The Braes of Ullapool the time was coming up to 1900hrs. I was still 2kms short of the town centre, but a roadside B&B sign proved too much of a temptation. Ten minutes later I was standing in a cheery comfortable bedroom removing my dusty boots and sweaty clothes. Looking in the mirror I saw the sight that, by the admission of the lady of the house the following morning, had prompted her husband to question her wisdom in letting the room to me. As an interesting aside to that she added that whilst not being too impressed by the initial impact of my presence on the doorstep, seeing the quality of the watch on my wrist she judged that I was a safe bet!

I washed clothes, showered, sorted out kit and generally enjoyed the temporary 'good life'. I was really glad to wash my Paramo towel, which had begun to smell quite badly. By the time I did my ablutions the previous day there was a definite incentive to dry naturally.

The last task of the day was to assess my stocks of food, I would be picking up my last supplies parcel in Ullapool so I could return any excess if necessary. Up till now I had not eaten anything like the rationed amounts of dried foods and now had over a kilo of fruit and nuts, two or three bars of chocolate and several packets of pumpkin seeds left from the daily allowances. I decided that the majority of this could be returned to Ali, a decision that I was to bitterly regret four or five days later. Just before I retired to bed I wrote a few postcards which could be posted in the morning.

DAY 8 Thursday 13th May
Braes of Ullapool to Loch a Chroisg
Walked from 10.00 to 18.10hrs
Distance 27kms Climbed 400m Camped at NC230025

Breakfast was at 08.30hrs so I got out of bed about 07.30 only to find the view across Loch Broom virtually obscured by very low cloud, my suspicions regarding the weather had been well founded. All my washing had dried over night so I would start again with all clean clothes. I small talked over breakfast with the other B&B guests, a young couple on a touring and walking holiday reminded me of Ali and I, 28 years ago, when we had a wonderful two weeks hostelling and camping on the Isle of Skye and in Wester Ross.

After an adequate rather than gargantuan breakfast I set off in a thin Scottish drizzle on the 2kms walk to town. The clouds were lifting a bit and by the time I reached Ullapool the hills on the west side of Loch Broom were more or less clear, which indicated a cloud base of about 500m.

I found the little Post Office and queued with the local stamp buyers and pension collectors to retrieve my parcel. For the next 20 minutes or so I received some strange looks as I spread the contents of rucksack and supplies parcel out on a nearby seat. After sorting, I repacked the parcel with the hard rations that I had decided to return as 'surplus to requirements'. Ironically from that day my appetite for the dried foods went up very considerably, to the point where for the last 2 days I was eking out my dwindling rations. When I returned home I received a severe reprimand from mission control for this cavalier dismissal of so much of my rations.

I phoned Ali and with a promise of phoning again later in the day from Strath Kannaird I turned my thoughts to the next most important problem – that of locating a ham and mayo baguette, but I searched in vain, there was no sign of a bakers, and by the time I thought I should ask someone, the streets were deserted. I trudged disconsolate and baguette-less out of town. At least the fine rain had relented and by the time I had crossed the Ullapool River on the edge of town I could almost convince myself that it was getting brighter.

Six days later travelling on the Tim Bearman coach from Durness to Inverness, we stopped for a 40 minute break in Ullapool and going into the Costcutter store (almost opposite the Post Office!) I found they had an excellent bakery section selling all sorts of mouth watering freshly made rolls – including ham and mayo baguettes! I had not bothered to investigate this emporium on my first visit as its name just conjured up visions of own brand washing powder and cheap sliced white bread.

I walked out of town on the A 835 fully expecting to be on the path – SRWS Route 313 - within minutes. The path is shown as leaving the road 500m west of the river, however having crossed the river there is a large waste disposal complex extending some way up the valley, bounded by a high forbidding wire fence. Then just after a stretch of dense gorse bushes, there is what appears to be a track leading to some sort of small holding, but this is about 200 or 300m further on to what is shown on the OS map. I retraced my steps thinking I had missed the path, but eventually decided that the track must be the only option. I left the road and for some time was not at all confident, because there were fences in all directions, the fence to the waste site on my right and deer fences going up the hills in front and to my left.

I kept on contouring around above the waste site, until I really thought I was going into a 'blind alley' when all of a sudden a small gate appeared and in a further 500m another gate lead me on to the open hillside, presumably now back on the original path, which I was pretty sure used to go through what is now the waste site.

The next 3km were over fairly bleak heather covered hillsides, but there were decent views back over Loch Broom. The weather had taken a definite turn for the better since leaving the road, there was very little wind, and the clouds were breaking up to reveal a filtered sun overhead and thick haze all around, similar to the previous afternoon. The light was such that distant views were limited and colours seemed to merge together.

The path climbs steadily to about 200m under Beinn Glubhais, NH135965 before going over the shoulder and leaving the southern views behind, I stopped and sat in the sultry midday warmth, looking back towards Ullapool over the wooded hillsides below. The rather mournful monotonic whistle of the golden plover gave a welcome confirmation that there is animal life in them there these hills, for over the last week I had gone for long periods without seeing or hearing anything of feathery or furry persuasion.

Having dropped down north-east of Beinn Glubhais I soon picked up a good track that comes from the A835 up to Loch Dubh Beag. Another 1.5kms further on, at the water's side there was no sign of track or path continuing around to the other lochs. This small loch is linked to Loch na Maoile and Loch Beinn Deirg to provide the motive power for a little generating station in Strath Kannaird. Someone down below must have left the electric fire on all night, because the water level was quite low, revealing beige coloured slabs of rock between the water and the heathery fringe. I initially thought the going would be fairly easy, but was soon to be disappointed. Sudden changes in the layering of the rock, which I fancy had been caused more by dynamite and JCB, rather than geological faults, meant that I had to resort to stumbling through peat and heather above the 'high water mark'.

At the north end of the loch was a solitary fisherman, but my path through the heather took me about 50m away from him – too far for a nodded greeting and an "I hope you get a big one!" Just beyond, by the little dam and feed channel down into Loch Beinn Deirg, I sat down for some well earned refreshment. It should have been at this time that I sink my teeth into that succulent ham and mayo baguette. Instead it was tasty dried fruit and healthy nuts, plus a big treat – a cashew and macadamia nut bar. I realised that I was still fretting about my inability to have procured that doughy delight, I nearly consigned the nutty confection to the undergrowth after one mouthful so lacking in appeal was it. I cannot understand how the manufacturers of this snacky treat could have taken such wholesome ingredients and turned them into something so totally lacking in taste and sensory appeal.

Within a few minutes of resuming, after my feast break I was on the track around Loch Beinn Deirg and all of a sudden, views opened out to the north. Although I had never been this far north, Little Loch Broom and Dundonnell had been the northerly limit of our trip in 1976. I knew from both looking at maps and also from conversations with friends that the terrain changes as one moves into Assynt and above. This several hundred metres of track illustrated that change so clearly. Gone were the big mountains and ridges separated by great glens, sometimes wide and forbidding, sometimes narrow and secret. Gone were the long deep lochs, gone were the vast tracts of high mountain moorland. Ahead lay the wide open spaces of Assynt, with lonely mountains, standing proudly separate from the low hills and boggy moorland, and WATER everywhere, fractured watery expanses and countless lochans of all shapes and sizes, too numerous for many of them to be granted the honour of a name.

The weather was slowly improving and in spite of the haze there were views of Cul Mor and Cul Beag. By the time I was descending on the track down to the A835 and Strath Canaird I could see Ben Mor Coigach in the N.W. then in the hazy distance the chisel ridge of Stac Pollaidh. Further round the impressive massif that is Cul Mor and Cul Beag, and to their right Canisp about 20km away. Suilven, the near neighbour of Canisp was resolutely hidden behind Cul Mor, but it reminded me of the famous line in the 'Pete and Dud' sketch, about Vernon Ward's duck paintings, when in response to Pete's observation that you could only ever see one eye because the ducks always flew sideways, Dud responded that even so you had the strong feeling that the other eye was straining to look at you round the beak!

The little settlement of Strath Canaird looked so attractive in the soft afternoon sunshine. A cluster of cottages and houses sprinkled along the top edge of an area of green pasture, such a contrast to the wintry brown and beige overcoat the surrounding hills and moors were still wearing. I could see the 'phone box, from which I hoped to call Ali in a short while, by the junction with the track up the River Canaird NC150023. Several cars whooshed by as I trudged up the road to the telephone box, apart from the fisherman I had neither met nor spoken with anyone since leaving Ullapool and the effect of what was now eight days of walking with so little contact with people left me with a rather curious sense of detachment, so that even the occupants of cars did not really register as 'human contact'.

It was good talking to Ali again even though it was only a few hours since the quick call from Ullapool. She was her normal chatty self and told me of the heatwave that Devon together with most of the U.K. was experiencing. She bemoaned the lack of cash rich visitors coming into the shop. While talking I inadvertently knocked a pound coin off the ledge in the 'phone box, it fell down on to the floor and thence into the grass (it is one of the new design box with a gap at the base of the side panels!). We said our goodbyes, knowing it would be a couple of days before we spoke again and I then looked for my misplaced coin. A few minutes later I sat down on the nearby verge to take a drink and chocolate and also to ponder on the ease with which a pound coin can disappear off the face of the Earth.

I contemplated the next phase of the walk which once again led into the wilds, crossing the A837 some time the next morning to then head off into the badlands beyond Loch Ailsh, around the eastern flank of Ben More Assynt to later emerge on to the A894 a few kilometres south of Unapool hopefully in about 48 hours time, which would be my next opportunity to report in to H.Q.

I set off along the track which dropped down away from the main road, past some houses and on up the Strath Canaird towards Langwell Lodge. This was an extremely pleasant walk, with the river down on the right hand side, it was sheltered and very warm in the mid afternoon sunshine. The Landowner must be a keen plantsman; the track passed a very well kept plantation of mature trees. I am pretty hopeless in identifying trees but there were clearly many different species, spaced far enough apart to be able to appreciate their shape and colour. Further up near the Lodge in a sheltered south facing little valley was an enclosed wild garden, full of rhododendrons and azaleas in full flower. A real oasis of colour, in an otherwise brown and grey landscape.

After the Lodge the track runs adjacent to the river for 2 kms or so, then leaves the valley and climbs up the hillside through a beallach between Meall a Chuaille and Ruith Chnoc NC195024 up towards Loch a Chroisg. The view from the high point was spectacular, sunlight reflecting off the river made it appear like an incandescent ribbon below me, further away the lower reaches of the strath, where I had walked two hours earlier, further still, 9 or 10 km away in the sunny haze, sea and sky merged in a silvery uncertainty where the out of focus shape that was Ilse Martin floated ethereally.

Since leaving Fort William I had seen very few deer, those I had come across were extremely timid and quickly moved away with little provocation. In this section of the walk I saw two herds and on both occasions they seemed completely unconcerned by my presence, stopping on higher ground adjacent to the track to scrutinise me before melting into the heathery moorland.

I should have been content, walking in an outstandingly beautiful wild area, warm spring sunshine, wildlife posing in front of me to be seen, I was vaguely troubled though, several things were bothering me. Firstly the weather, I was even more convinced that the change I sensed yesterday was coming. I am no expert, but the build up of thick haze to the west combined with the strong wind, that now I was on higher exposed ground had become much more noticeable, were two indicators I would rather not see. Secondly since Langwell Lodge there were wire fences, stretching up the strath for miles, these were old low fences rather than high deer fences. I was not sure why this unsettled me, except that in an illogical way it tied in with my third worry.

When I was planning the walk I was rather attracted to the option of route 320 of the SRWS. 'Kylesku to Altnacealagh', a 30 km walk which "............ *goes through some very wild and remote country on the east side of the Ben More Assynt range....*". To link this to a route from Ullapool, (the path I had taken so far), left a 10km stretch beyond Loch a Chroisg NC215025 going N.E. across wild moorland with no vestige of a path, before striking the A837 just below the track to Benmore Lodge.

I had felt that this section may cause a problem, because it is obviously a very wet area, many streams draining away in different directions, very reminiscent of Dartmoor. So I had suspected the worse regarding underfoot conditions. Within 24 hours I was to rue the fact that I had been using the 'Crown Copyright 1981' version of O.S. sheet 15, because the 2002 version would have shown the hazard that was to cause me so much grief the following day, and ironically it was a hazard that had not immediately come to mind in the planning of the walk.

When looking for wild camp sites the ends of lakes often provide good spots, level, very often with grassy area adjacent to the water and obviously, ample fresh water! The western end of Loch a Chroisg broke that particular rule on the first two counts and as I continued along the waterside path I began to see the eastern end of the loch and the nearer I got to it the nagging suspicion grew that there was a double disappointment in store. I stopped at the last decent stream that flows into the loch and filled my 2 litre platypus, very fortuitously as it turned out because I did not find a camp spot till I was well clear of the loch and there was no running water nearby. There was a good level area of grass among the heather, I quickly pitched the tent and then went off in search of more water, eventually finding a trickle in the undergrowth, at least it was enough to fill the washing bowl, so I now had water for drinking, cooking and washing!

I had pitched camp at about 1800hrs, and due to my treat of B and B accommodation the night before I had no washing or drying of clothes to fill my time, so I enjoyed a leisurely meal. It was a fine evening, there was a build up of cumulus along the eastern horizon even though the wind was still from the west. However by sunset, 21.30 that seemed to have gone again but there was now a lot of high stratus cloud. The whole pattern of weather over the last 6-9 hours reminded me of that at the end of day 2, and I recalled with apprehension the weather of day 3! The temperature had now dropped and I was glad to have my mug of horlicks and get to bed. I had walked a pleasing 27km. But it had been a less satisfying day than some, I think because of the doubts that were troubling me.

DAY 9 Friday 14th May
Loch a Chroisg to East Side Ben More Assynt
Walked from 08.10 to 21.00hrs
Distance 23kms Climbed 460m Camped at NC346196

I slept well and around 05.00 woke to that rather unsettling sensation of complete still with no sound other than a very gentle whisper of light rain on the flysheet, a few inches above my face. I dozed until 06.15 when I realised that the rain had stopped. I vacated the embryonic warmth of the sleeping bag and unzipped the flysheet flap; the sight that greeted my bleary eyes did little to raise my spirits in expectation of fine walking conditions.

A kaleidoscope of earth colours surrounded me, the near areas of heathery hillside were a riot of muted wet browns, further away these toned into a sludgy khaki/grey. The loch was a sheet of grey; the clouds were a subtle blend of heavy greys, which looked as though they contained too much rain to be good for me. The only actual and metaphoric light on the horizon was way over in the east, where the previous evening there had been a strip of cumulus, now a far away band of thinner cloud back lit by the rising sun.

Since embarking on these solo expeditions I have surprised myself, on occasions when conditions have been less than favourable and there has been little cause to whistle a merry tune, I seem to be able to just get on with things and face the challenges at hand. In my normal everyday life I am far more likely to have a depressive reaction, cuss, bluster, roll my eyes, be grumpy and then get on with it! This I am sure is much to Ali's amusement and irritation.

The (I suspected) temporary lack of rain helped in the packing up process, which together with preparing and eating my meagre breakfast, still took the best part of two hours, as usual. I set off just after 08.00. with the sobering thought that the next 10 to 12 km, which I had always thought likely to be challenging, would be made much more so by the inclement weather.

My immediate route was the 150m climb up the Allt Rapach, to the watershed between Meallan Odhar and Meall a Bhuirich Rapaig NC245035 from where I would hope to see my next objective – Cnoc na Glas Choille. The river is surprisingly wide and fast flowing, considering its relatively small catchment area. Higher up several convergent side streams made progress up the west bank slower than I hoped. Looking from afar the hills give a false impression of rounded regularity, and I was not expecting, as I climbed higher, to have several precipitous ravines to negotiate. These just seem to appear out of nowhere, suddenly offering you the prospect of finding a way down anything from 10 to 20 metres to cross the stream then up the other side.

This gave an exciting and adrenalin fired start to the day, I thought on several occasions that these deep gullies were definitely not the places to fall and break a leg, one could lie undetected for quite a while before being discovered (or not!), I tried to eliminate these thoughts as soon as they wagged their crooked fingers at me.

As I neared the bealach between the two hills I perceived that the sky had darkened, and a few minutes later, standing looking north-east over the vast grey expanse of wilderness, the tops of the hills on either side of the bealach had been swallowed into the clouds, but I was able to identify, way in the murky distance, the rounded outline of Cnoc na Glas Choille NC276081. I quickly fixed a compass bearing, as I suspected that I would not see it for much longer. Sure enough as if on cue the rain started, this was the proper Scottish variety, none of your nancy southern rain here, this was the business! Within the next 2 or 3 minutes visibility reduced dramatically, everything more than about 250 metres away had disappeared into grey nothingness. Studying the map the previous evening I concluded that a straight line route was likely to be as good, or bad, as any other, so off I set compass clutched firmly to my breast, walking to the newly acquired bearing, well protected from the rain which was coming from slightly behind me.

This is a very wild and remote area, not perhaps in terms of proximity to a road, but by virtue of its obvious complete lack of anything that would appeal to the normal wilderness frequenting fraternity. As I plodded, I tried to imagine when was the last time someone walked this route. I could not think many people found their feet pointing in this direction. Other than the track I had taken from Strath Canaird, the O.S. map shows no other paths in the area bounded by the A837 and A835 for some 100 square kilometres or so. Apart from the remains of a very old and rusty wire fence, I saw no evidence of human egress during the next 6 kms.

Conditions underfoot were awful; to say challenging would be understating matters. A constantly changing terrain, ranging from fairly firm clumpy grass interspersed with sparse heather, squelchy bog, peat hags, many streams, to sparse heather interspersed with not so firm clumpy grass, more streams etc.. All good fun when trying to walk a bearing. Occasionally the cloud would lift a bit, sometimes enough to reveal that I was still on course for my destination. The great consolation was that by concentrating so hard on the next step and the compass bearing, I was not thinking too much about the rain lashing down.

As I crossed the river Allt nan Clach Aoil NC265061 I was pleased with my progress, in spite of the difficulties, I had covered the 5 or 6 kms from the watershed in about 2 hours. It was now just after 11.00hrs and my satisfaction was to be short lived, for as I climbed up towards my objective, the clouds had lifted again to reveal the unmistakeable outline of a deer fence across the top of the hill. This was the first of several low points over the next few days. Standing on top of Cnoc na Glas Choille just before 11.30hrs in driving rain, looking north-east, I could barely make out the Glen Oykel forest and Loch Ailsh, which marked the starting features of the route I would follow in due course (SRWS route 320) past Benmore Lodge and skirting Ben More Assynt. Unfortunately I was looking through a 2 metre high deer fence. The other side of the fence was a clear fringe of moorland then I could see the tops of the trees that were now part of a large area of forestry that I presumed covered the slopes running down to the A837. Oh! woe is me, if only I had bought an up to date O.S. sheet 15, I would have seen that the area of forestry to the south west of the A837, between the two rivers, had hugely extended from the very small area shown on my earlier map and now spread north westwards right across the bit of hillside I wanted to cross.

The deer fence was 2 metres high, stoutly constructed of what down in Devon I believe is called pig netting, strong wire mesh about 12cms square, tensioned between posts which must have been 3 to 4 metres apart. I guessed from the look of it that it had been erected within the last year or two, some 100m from the edge of the forest and seemingly stretching forever in each direction. Sometimes ways through the fence are provided, but I was entirely pessimistic that this would be the case here. I walked to my left for 200metres or so until standing on a vantage point I saw that it carried on due west unbroken and disappeared into the mist and rain. I knew that if I continued that way I would be going far off my route, towards Loch Urigill, so I retraced my steps and continued south-east until I realised that I was losing height and heading towards the Allt Eileag and I knew that most likely this could mean big trouble as the river is shown on the map as not exactly a trickle!

Needs must when the Devil rides! Although I had not a clue how I would find my way through the forest once I had got over the fence, I assessed that it was the lesser of several evils. I found a suitable spot for my trespass to commence. There was no way that I could climb the fence wearing my sack so I took it off and contemplated the problems – both physical and psychological – of ridding myself of all means of comfort and support, by throwing it over the fence. Fortunately as I stand at 6 feet 4 inches I reckoned that once I held the bag above my head I would be able to toss it over without the necessity of further height gain. This was no easy matter, lifting a 20+kgs. bag above my head, it took me several attempts before I felt it was balanced and ready for the heave ho! It was as though I was cutting a lifeline, not to mention the sheer value of what I was despatching over this obstacle. What if I could not get over? What if I could not find the bag again if I had to take another route myself? Fortunately confronted with this predicament and the omnipresent heavy rain I did not dwell too long on this philosophical train of thought. The bag thudded into a boggy area of clumpy grass on the other side, I poked my walking pole through the mesh to join it. Luckily the square mesh of the fence was just large enough to safely accommodate the toes of my size 13 walking boots and about twenty seconds later I was reunited with my worldly goods and chattels.

As I stood donning my sack once again I smugly thought 'huh! It will take more than this to stop Big Bob!' Now I had to find a way through the trees on to a forestry road which surely ran across somewhere below me. There was quite a clear area between the fence and the edge of the forest, so I walked back in roughly a N.W. direction looking for any indication of a ride through the trees. When I am out on my own in the mountains or moors, thought processes and powers of deduction always seem to be more highly tuned than when out in a group, I have got lost far more often with my walking pals than I ever have while on my own. It was these powers of deduction that came to the fore now, I think the fact that the fence was so new made me think that sooner or later there must be some evidence of where the fencing crew had driven up through the trees to reach their place of work. Sure enough within 200 to 300 metres I saw faint signs of A.T.V. tracks and these lead me down in a N.E. direction through the trees along a ride that was only a few metres wide, and 5 minutes or so later I was standing on (I assumed) the main forest track. The question now was 'which way will lead to the A837?' Again my clear thinking (ha ha!) suggested going to the right where my map showed a track coming off the road at NC308074 and sure enough that was exactly right.

I was so relieved that the forest had been beaten and as I walked along the track the rain was easing a bit, my spirits rose, ah! life isn't too bad. All of a sudden a crooked finger appeared wagging furiously at me, ' *What if there is another 2 metre fence and a locked gate between the forest and the road at the end of this track?*' Ohhhhhhh S**T!!!!

My fears proved to be ill founded. The rain had virtually stopped by 13.30 as my boots once again hit tarmac on the A837. Often when you hear people talking about taking long trips in the wilderness on their own, they talk about 'finding themselves' in great seminal soul searching experiences. I cannot be doing with any of that, I get involved with thinking about matters of uncertainty, like the question that now bothered me, ' why spend all that money on building a fence at the far side of the forest when the deer can just wander in off the road?' All the way through since crossing the fence there had been ample evidence of deer, in the form of footprints, droppings and bark stripped saplings. Maybe it was to stop deer from going into the wilderness, now there's a thought!

I left the road behind me and set off up the track to Benmore Lodge, I continued for 20 minutes then found a suitable place and with great relief, flopped down for a well earned rest. I had not eaten since 07.00 having been otherwise preoccupied, but times like this I think prove the worth of hydration systems and energy drinks. Throughout the morning I had drunk nearly 2 litres so had taken in plenty of 'emergency rations'. I sat for half an hour enjoying some food and the now complete lack of rain. It was good to mentally unwind after all the trauma of the past 6 hours. The walk up to the Lodge was a gentle relief, the track goes past it and the adjacent cottages and outbuildings but I saw no sign of life, other than hearing some yapping dogs, which were shut up in one of the sheds.

As I left civilisation behind yet again, I mused that apart from a few cars I had neither seen nor spoken to anyone since leaving Ullapool the previous morning. At the confluence of the rivers Oykel and Allt Sail an Ruathair NC330130 two bridges took me on to open moorland above the forest and then north-east along the right bank of the latter. It was now that two facts occurred to me, firstly it was clear that this area had not received the dowsing I had come through that morning and secondly it was with sinking heart that I had to admit to myself that the wind, which had become more noticeable in the last 2 or 3 hours was now what the weather forecasting people would probably describe as 'a strong westerly, gusting to storm force'. I carried on along the path, which was reasonable, but at times needed sharp eyes to pick out and consoled myself with the thought that maybe there would be shelter once I got round on the east side of Ben More.

The weather had been playing quite a significant part in the scheme of things, so it was understandable that my thoughts would dwell more on matters meteorological. The Ben More Assynt range is a formidable massif and at what must be well over 100 square kilometres of high ground, clearly has an influence on weather patterns. I had noticed when down at Loch Ailsh that the two southern sentinels of the range namely Sail an Ruathair and Sgonnan Mor had appeared very differently, the western flank of the former was bathed in watery sun whilst its neighbour cowered under a dense black pall of threatening cloud. This situation continued all the time I walked below them, which was strange because there was no sign of sunlight anywhere else across the whole of the visible extent of sky.

By the time the path headed due north, contouring round the side of Meall an Aonaich NC347157, it was in places what is called on Dartmoor a 'peat pass', that is , a path literally cut through the peaty hillside to the rocky surface below. I had seen no grass or any area which would offer a reasonable camping spot, since leaving the north end of the forest. The first corrie was Loch Sail an Ruathair NC337144 and had offered nothing but bog, rocks and deep heather. The time was now approaching 18.30 and I had been walking for the best part of ten hours. I was beginning to think I had made a mistake not making a camp spot by the confluence of the two rivers, where there had been a welcoming area of flat grassy ground. At the time I felt that I would be sure to find somewhere in either of the two nearby corries which would be more sheltered than the top end of the forest. Now though, after drawing a blank with the first, I approached Loch Carn nan Conbhairean NC347175 with apprehension thinking that being blasted by the wind with the tent securely anchored on solid ground may have been better than the alternatives that were now presenting themselves.

My earlier thoughts of shelter on the east side of Ben More were proving to be wishful thinking on my part, to quote from my log *"……..the wind was gaining strength worryingly and far from giving shelter the wind was crashing down on me from the corries above – way above up in the cloud ……..".* Looking to my left, up the steep mountainside, an ominous dark cloudy ceiling hung 100mts above me, looking to my right the peaty desolation that is Glen Cassley was opening out, giving some understanding to the earlier quoted extract from the S.R.W.S. book *"….through some very wild and remote country on the east side of the Ben More Assynt range..".*

I passed by the loch, very close to the outfall and there was absolutely no chance of camping there, even if a good grassy sward had presented itself, it would have been dreadfully exposed to the ferocious gusts blasting down out of the murky gloom above. Not far beyond I stopped at a point where a high peaty heathery bank gave some protection from the wind, I wearily sat down, my back nestled into the bank and looked down over a vast tract of peat hags. This was a scene that one of those 19th century artists, who delighted in producing pictures with religious significance, could easily have used as a subject for a depiction of Purgatory. I had crossed several areas of peat hags in the last 10 days but what I looked at now put them completely into the shade, these were Premier Division peat hags. These were at the head of the queue when size was being handed out, peaty cliffs up to 2 metres high sometimes stretching for 100 metres, which seemed in most cases to be separated by lagoons of liquid peat.

I was pretty tired and mentally exhausted by now and also feeling extremely hungry, after all this was the time I would normally be camped and preparing the evening banquet. My thoughts wandered southwards and I pictured Ali, back home from work perhaps sitting in the garden, with the cats, enjoying the last of the sunshine before shadows lengthened over our little courtyard garden. I decided that no further decision could be made on an empty stomach and duly began to unpack my rucksack in search of food and stove. While waiting for the water to boil I idly looked out the 'phone and was very surprised when there appeared to be a signal, but it was not strong enough to get all the way to Devon, so hopes were dashed of a comforting conversation with Ali.

An hour and a half later, much refreshed by food and a rest I assessed the options. I could stay put with no chance of getting the tent up and endure a long night in a makeshift bivvy. I could carry on walking for another couple of hours, with the possibility of finding somewhere to camp and at worse stop about 22.00 hours for the bivvy. The great consolation in all this was that there was still no rain. I decided to press on, I hoped at least, to find somewhere eventually to hunker down for the night.

Progress was slow as the path was becoming more difficult to follow, in places a clear path cut through the peat, then moments later no sign at all. For the umpteenth time I pondered the question of why paths disappear and reappear with complete unpredictability. How many times have you looked at a map and decided on an alphabetical walk from A to G, because it shows a nice clear path through B,C,D,E,F and finishing at G. You set off on a splendid path visit B arrive at C and off towards D with no problem, then oops, all of a sudden the path begins to be less defined. Before you reach D you loose it completely, but regain it shortly afterwards. The same thing happens on your way to E except that it takes longer to find it again and when you do it's an apology of a path, not strong enough to leave its mother. On the way to F it disappears without trace, you carry on over what looks like virgin territory – no foot has ever trodden it before - as you approach G you find a path again, that takes you to your goal. So why? Do lots of people set off from A get to between C and D become fed-up turn round and return to A thus making that section even more pronounced? What of those who set off from G to walk to A? Do they go only a short way along the path , fan out across the country, to converge on the intended track somewhere between E and C then all tramp along triumphantly together to A? Such weighty matters concerned me as I carried on my way.

I reached the river Allt a Chnaip Ghiobhais NC348194 about 21.00 hours, the light was fading now, mainly due to the continuing presence of a great pall of dark cloud overhead. This is a pretty big river gathering its load from the corries below the southerly ridge from Ben More. It has cut a considerable watercourse down the side of the mountain and although it did not present any great difficulty to cross, it did have the effect of disguising the path. By the time I had crossed the river and climbed back up to the open moorland I was not at all confident that I was on the path. I walked on for another 300 metres or so trying in vain to pick out signs of a path in the failing light.

I had noted from the map, that a track comes from the east and crosses my path at right angles, but I was not prepared for what I now stumbled on. A wide track appeared from the wilds of Glen Cassley and carried on some way up the mountainside. Since the river I had seen no convincing evidence of the path and I immediately decided that I would be foolish to carry on further. Looking round for somewhere to make a bivvy I saw a large rock standing at the trackside, below it was a sort of ditch with a mound above it, to the side of the standing stone. This little scoop did give quite a bit of shelter from the wind, I felt this was going to be about as good as I could hope for so set about clearing some of the surface stones and tried to make it as homely as I could, the main drawback being that the slope was quite steep.

There had still been no rain since early afternoon and now in the gathering gloom of late evening there was a definite dampness in the air. I fervently hoped that it would remain there and not descend on me, for the experience of contending with rain as well as the wind, was not one I hankered after.

I wrapped myself up in the inner groundsheet section of the tent and lay on the Thermarest and spent a couple of uncomfortable hours trying to relax. This in itself was no easy feat, with wind trying to tear things from my hands and consign them to the wilds of Glen Cassley. It now occurred to me, with a great sense of irony, that this was just the sort of situation that I sometimes jokingly referred to at home. For example as Ali and I snuggle down under the duvet, on a wild winter's night, with the rain lashing the double glazed windows and the wind howling round the roof, I will say something like, "It's not the night to be stood on Exmouth seafront in nothing but your underpants" or "I'm glad I'm not on the top of Yes Tor [Dartmoor] with nothing to cover my confusion".

I must have gone off to sleep because I suddenly became aware that it was much darker and to my great relief the wind had lessened, to the point where it no longer tried to blow anything in its path to oblivion. I looked at my watch, just after 23.00 hours, but there was still just enough light to see to put up the tent. Ten minutes later it was erected, decidedly skewy, but while the wind stayed as it was I reckoned that the few pegs I had managed to partly sink into the stony subsoil should hold it. Two hours earlier when I stopped walking I had put on an extra pair of trousers and my extra coat, now having just removed my boots and feeling like Michelin Man, I crawled into my sleeping bag and was asleep within a very short time.

DAY 10 Saturday 15th May
East Side Ben More Assynt to Unapool
Walked from 05.45 to 16.30 hours
Distance 17 kms. Climbed 100m B & B at Unapool

By 04.30hrs the wind had gained strength once more and I was awoken by the flapping of the tent. This is a problem with my tent, the little cleats on the guys do not hold the cord firmly enough, so in a buffeting wind the guys gradually slacken. I emerged from the tent to salute the happy morn and found that as far as the weather was concerned it was very much business as usual. The flanks of Ben More disappeared into the murk only a matter of several hundred metres from me. The wind was still from the west and huge plumes of lighter coloured low cloud were thrashing eastwards over my head, in stark contrast to the dark pall of higher cloud above. The eastern aspect - looking over Glen Cassley - was incredibly dramatic, gaps of lighter cloud brilliantly back lit by the dawn sun, only served to accentuate the darkness of the thick surrounding clouds. It was a constantly changing cloudscape, but this feature of dark cloud above and sunlit light cloud to the east remained until I escaped from the proximity of Ben More, later in the day.

I tightened the tent guys and took a few photographs, only then realising that the pictures would have looked more dramatic if I had taken them before tightening the guys. I then wandered up the track for a pee, and while I stood there, admiring the view, I saw my path wending its way northwards across the moorland. Much relieved, in more ways than one, I returned to the tent for a morning brew up.

I feasted on Readi-brek, chocolate and a cup of tea, packed up and set off walking at 05.45. My next objective was Loch Bealach a Mhadaidh NC315234 some 5 kms away. The wind still gusted very strongly, as the previous evening, but still no rain! The S.R.W.S. details that this path ends at the loch not to reappear till north west of Gorm Loch Mor, describing the section in between as "… a rough pathless section from the outfall of Loch Bealach a Mhadaidh below the craggy hillside along the S.W. side of Gorm Loch Mor …". In fact well before the loch I again experienced difficulty with following the path, and by the time I was dropping down to the outfall I had given up completely and just tried to pick the best route through what was very demanding terrain – rocks, heather and boggy bits in every combination.

I have always thought corries, especially when accompanied by tarns or lochs, to be quite forbidding places when viewed from below. Maybe because of its remote location, the weather and the potential difficulties I knew lay ahead, but as I looked up into the corrie I had a sense of great vulnerability in a [naturally] hostile area, although at the same time a terrific sort of excitement that I was the only one who could get me through this and back to 'civilization'.

I had been quite concerned by the prospect of crossing this river, as the map shows it to be of significant size, the S.R.W.S. notes on the route make no mention of it and sure enough although it is quite a cataract, I was able to pick my spot and cross it with dry feet. I then dropped down northwards and began contouring around the hillside towards Loch Gorm Mor. Progress had been slow this morning and was about to get slower. The next 3 kms section was very challenging, rather like the walk up to Beallach Bearnais on Day 5, but hugely enjoyable. In places the slope down to the loch was very steep and there were several crags to be got around – either over or under. All my senses were on high alert and I guess adrenaline was in good supply too.

Part way along the loch I stopped by one of the many streams for a rest, food and to replenish my water supply. The time was now nearly

09.00 and as I sat looking out over the dark rippled surface of Gorm Loch Mor, the day did not seem any lighter than it had been 4 hours earlier. 2kms on I had climbed a little and was now in cloud, which did not help matters and for the next 2 kms or so I was definitely Mr. Confused of Assynt. This was partly the fault of cloud but also because of the nature of the terrain, I had the feeling of walking through a canyon like area, which I suspect is the result of the torture that glaciation had imposed on it. It seemed to me, in that fog of ignorance, that the way through frequently changed direction, huge rock buttresses loomed out of the mist and I was literally 'following my nose'. This was the area just to the west of an unnamed lochan at NC297258, depicted on the map by the symbol for 'rock outcrop'. Still in the cloud for most of the time I eventually cleared that section and I slowly climbed up the side of the valley. I had seen no sign whatsoever of the path that is shown on the map coming from the intersection with the main approach path up Ben More Assynt and Gorm Loch Mor. I knew from the S.R.W.S. notes on this route that I needed to aim for the two lochans at NC280270.

At one point the clouds lifted enough to reveal hanging valleys and the strange alignment of Loch nan Caorach NC295277, which is a 2 km long loch nestling in a depression near the top of a long ridge and seeming to drain sideways down the steep valley to Abhainn an Loch Bhig which flows parallel to it. On another occasion I had a fleeting glimpse through a gap in the cloud, of the top end of that finger of sea that is Loch Glencoul. Ahead of me I began to see plumes of spray billowing down into the valley and I guessed, correctly, that I must be nearing the lochan at NC283265. I crossed the stream issuing from the lochan and below me to the right I saw the top of what I imagine is quite a spectacular waterfall, if you could get into a position to see it! I had only gone a few metres beyond the stream when lo and behold there was a very prominent black peaty track, so I guessed that below me somewhere there was a vantage point that warranted the effort for walkers coming from the northern access point to Ben More. Shortly I met three people on just such a mission and we chatted for five minutes or so. They seemed surprised and a bit appalled at my revelation that they were the first people I had seen to speak to since leaving Ullapool, on Thursday morning.

The cloud was still down and the next 750 metres of path to the two lochans, is much more convoluted than the map shows, changing direction and several other paths intersecting. At one point I got out the compass, just to reassure myself that the path which looked as if it were going in the wrong direction was in fact the one I wanted. I had come out of the cloud by the time I reached the two lochans, these mark the departure point of the path westwards to Inchnadamph. I relaxed knowing that I now had a 4 – 5 kms walk down a good path to the A894.

My social life was now a real whirl, because I met up with another 10–12 walkers before I reached the road, in fact so many people that I could not cope with talking to all of them! Ahead of me across the moorland to the north-west was the brooding bulk of Quinag, sheltering sullenly under a thick mantle of cloud. Further on, the hazy expanse of Eddrachillis Bay with its many sunlit islands, which narrows to become the three spectacularly beautiful sea lochs set either side of the constriction at Kylesku, where until recently a ferry would allow travellers on the A894 to continue their journey. Now two dramatic bridges take the road across the narrows, a kilometre west of the old ferry point, enabling north south contact to be maintained without let or hindrance 24 hours a day.

The time was 1500hrs when I set foot on the tarmac of the A894, I walked down a short way and then stopped for a very well earned rest. I sat down in the warm hazy sunshine and feasted on dry fruit and chocolate, washed down with energy boosted water, the occasional car swished by and the last 30 hours or so began to seem a bit surreal, now that I was back in 'civilisation'. I idly turned on the mobile 'phone and to my surprise found a good signal, seconds later I was talking to Ali. I have to admit that after all the challenges of the last day and a half I was a bit choked when I heard her voice. <u>Bad move</u> she immediately became concerned that I was in some sort of distress, and it took a lot of explaining before she accepted I was O.K. I must say that I felt that after having walked 40kms, endured bad weather, overcome very challenging terrain and obstacles and had only about four hours sleep, I was entitled to be a bit emotional when I spoke to my loved one.

The 4 kms walk down to Unapool were a delight, looking down on Loch Glencoul and beyond to the hills north of the lochs. I think sea lochs tend to be more attractive than their freshwater cousins, something to do with the weed covered shorelines and generally more bird life. Now that I was at low level the weather pattern became more apparent, looking around, all the mountains and hills over 500 metres had dense really dark clouds over them, the lower coastal fringe and out to sea were under pale blue skies in warm hazy spring sunshine. The overall effect was a stark contrast of light that robbed the hillsides of any colour and detail, so much so that all the high ground appeared in silhouette only. This weather pattern was to become a feature of the remainder of the journey to Cape Wrath.

Earlier in the day I had decided that because Kylesku is a clear break point in the journey and I would be arriving there probably in late afternoon, it made sense to enjoy the comforts of a B&B if one presented itself! It does not pay to rely on things like that as one can so easily be disappointed. The previous year in my coast to coast walk I arrived in Gairlochy on the Caledonian canal NE of Fort William, 19.30 hrs, soaking wet, having walked the last 2 hours in pouring rain, to find the only B&B full (or unwilling to take in this bedraggled figure!) and having to walk on to the nearby campsite. But as I neared Unapool I did allow myself passing thoughts of a warm shower and soft bed.

Ahead I noticed a sign and was soon looking at a neat little tearoom in a stunning position between the road and the loch. I realised the attraction of sitting down admiring the view, with a pot of tea and homemade cakes and was soon dumping my rucksack and making my order.

Half an hour later having enjoyed copious quantities of tea with shortbread and sponge cake I was preparing to leave and asked if they could recommend a B&B " funny you should ask, but we can help you there as well" replied Deryck. He and his wife Mary had come to Sutherland from Yorkshire after they retired, to run the tearoom while living in a caravan in the garden. After their house was built 'Maryck Bed and Breakfast' was added to their business empire.

Its funny how fortunes can change on a trip like this, 12 hours earlier I was contending with storm force winds and very hostile terrain, now I was ensconced in a comfortable room with the imminent prospect of a shower and then a couple of beers and a 'proper' meal down at the pub by the old ferry slip. Just to put the gilt on the gingerbread Mary had offered to do some washing, so I would be starting on the last leg of my journey with clean socks and underwear!

Later I phoned Ali again on my way to the pub and had quite a long chat, eventually persuading her that I was still of sound mind and fit in wind and limb. The time was about 19.30 as I walked back up the road to Maryck,, there was blue sky above and a warm sun, it seemed a perfect early summer evening, until I looked over to the dark hills with their ominous head-dresses of black cloud. I had no idea what sort of weather to expect on Sunday.

Day 11 Sunday 16th May
Unapool to West side of Arkle
Walked from 09.40 to 17.45 hours
Distance 27km, Climbed 600ms Camped at NC286451

The view over Loch Glendhu was a bit depressing when I first looked out, low cloud down to about 250m so Ben Strome and all the higher hills to the east were obscured; the redeeming feature though was a suggestion of brighter skies to the west.

I set off at 09.40 after a very substantial breakfast and the weather had improved since earlier. Patchy sunshine brightened up the sea now and the clouds overhead were lifting, but all the hills maintained close contact with their cloudy hats. My route followed the road to Kylestrome from where I would pick up a path over the hill and past Ben Strome. The new bridge which sweeps majestically across the mouth of the loch leaves the old ferry points of Kylesku and Kylestrome at least a kilometre to the east and does not rejoin the course of the old road until some way up the hill. For the walker this means at least another 2kms but the view from the bridge is worth it. The wind had lessened since the previous afternoon but other than that there were no indications that any great changes had occurred.

The path I was looking for leaves the old road at NC222345 and as I approached, walking down through the trees towards the old ferry hotel, I could picture things as they were before the bridge; cars accelerating up the hill having just come off the ferry, at busy times maybe a queue of cars going down the hill waiting their turn and just a general quiet bustle. Now it has become a real backwater. I was not at all sure I had located the path but having left the road and worked my way up following a path of sorts, I soon came to a gate which lead out on to the hillside and it clearly was the route I wanted.

The path climbs steadily going eastwards and the views to the right are stunning, Quinag to the south-west with its huge corrie separating Sail Gharbh from Sail Gorm, the upper reaches still in cloud. From this distance the bridge looked like a spindly branch lying across a stream. The two watery fingers of Loch Glendhu and Loch Glencoul stretching away, reflecting only the steely greyness above them. Ben More Assynt still looked in as grumpy a mood as it had for the last two days, its mantle of cloud set stubbornly at about 750mts.

As the path gradually turns north-eastwards the view below opens up to reveal Loch an Leathiad Bhuan NC275358, a large remote loch nestling in the hills 180 mts above Loch Glencoul. It drains into the loch below by means of the Maldie Burn, which must be in line for the 'shortest river in the U.K.' award, but what it lacks in length it more than makes up for in character. The lower reaches of its 2 kms course are a series of spectacular waterfalls, the lochside path from Kylestrome follows the Maldie Burn, to eventually join the path I was taking and would certainly be a good alternative route.

I had seen several herds of deer since leaving Kylestrome, they all seemed unconcerned by my presence, continuing to do their deer things as if I did not exist. Just like the herd above Strath Canaird.

Somewhere close to Ben Strome, on rounding a small bluff my attention was caught by a movement on the hill to my left about 150m away. For probably two seconds I had a positive sighting that really excited me. When one is out in the wild it is such a bonus to see birds and mammals in their own habitat and positive sightings are always to be treasured, remembered and talked about for years to come. We can all recall that golden eagle in the Cuillins of Skye/ Glencoe/ the Galloway hills or wherever, that gannet diving from 50m above the bay at Lamlash on Arran, etc. etc., all our own positive sightings! Well this time I was 100 per cent sure that I had seen a wildcat ---- or was it a fox----- or maybe a really fat hare. Whatever it was it did not have the decency to stay around.

The high point on the walk over to Loch More is the Beallach nam Fiann NC270380, about 7 kms from Kylestrome. The wind here was considerably stronger than down below and I was glad of the ruined shieling to give some shelter while I ate some of Mary's packed lunch. For some time I had been anticipating with delight, succulent sandwiches and crisps as a change to dry roasted pumpkin seeds and dried fruit.

I sat looking north towards Ben Stack and Arkle, both were capped with cloud, but every now and then a shaft of sunshine would break through and bring to life the silvery screes of Arkle but each time I was too slow with the camera to capture the moment. Looking back into Assynt the view was very much the same as it had been, dark hills and heavy cloud.

Suitably refreshed I was soon heading down the track towards Achfary Forest. Loch More and the valley were in sunshine and remained so, certainly for the next hour and a half that I was passing through. This is a very satisfying path to walk on as it angles down the steep side of the hill above the forest, and gradually gets steeper lower down as it nears the trees.

On the O.S. map Ben Screavie NC310396 looks an insignificant hill at only 332mts, but on this occasion in the afternoon sun it appeared like a huge shiny grey whale beached in the loch, being fairly devoid of vegetation the sun was reflecting off the grey rock slabs and screes. The whole effect was accentuated by the shadow and darkness of the higher hills behind.

The path wound down through the southerly edge of the forest, to emerge on the lochside road NC300388 near Lochmore Lodge. The upper part of the forest was memorable for the prolific growth of a moss, which covered everything at ground level except the running water. Rocks, stacks of logs, branches all had a verdant furry green cover. It was like something out of a fairy tale, an enchanted wood where anyone foolish enough to go to sleep would remain there for ever more – just a green mossy shape.

The great banks of gorse around the north end of the loch filled the warm afternoon air with their coconut scent, and I relished the rather parochial feel of this quiet corner of the Highlands. I was soon at the entrance to Achfary Estate NC292396 and my route was along the estate road past the various estate buildings and offices. The track then lead back into the forest again, to emerge after 2kms to the open expanses of Strath Stack.

On the road just by the estate entrance I saw the famous (in a limited way) black and white telephone box. Information gleaned from the internet suggests that the story behind its unique colour scheme was to blend it in with the surrounding estate buildings. I found it worked perfectly and was soon talking to Ali. She told me that there was still wall to wall sunshine over the whole of the U.K. apart from the very north west tip! Devon was sweltering in the extreme temperatures and she was trying to shake herself from a heat induced torpor to go for a bike ride. As I finished the call two guys appeared and we chatted for a few minutes. They said their plan was to drive to Durness and then on Tuesday to go by bikes to Cape Wrath and then on to Sandwood Bay. We parted with the possibility of meeting again two days later. I did not know then, but a bicycle as a means of getting to Sandwood Bay from Cape Wrath is about as much use as a chocolate fireguard!

As I set off up the road a fearful noise assaulted the Sunday afternoon tranquility. I could see about 200m ahead, where the track goes into the forest, a mechanical thing had appeared, which was obviously the source of the hideous racket and the spawn of the Devil Himself. Its progress along the track was so slow that I caught it up within a few minutes. It seemed to be some sort of early prototype motorised wheelbarrow, powered by an exceedingly ancient and environmentally unfriendly 2 stroke engine, which was so finely tuned that it did not need a silencer. It was being driven by an elderly, early prototype tweed clad estate worker, who in sullen resentment, ear defenders clamped to his bowed head, sat slumped upon this Satanic workhorse. As I drew level I did have the passing hopeful thought that maybe being overtaken by a middle aged (plus) backpacker might induce such surprise that he would release the throttle in his shock. I noticed that the load carrying section of this heinous contraption contained no more than 2 bucketfuls of garden rubbish, which shortly afterwards he turned off the track and jettisoned. I reflected that perhaps his life was so dull and boring in this quiet rural idyll that he periodically needed a fix of mind-numbing multi-decibels and carbon monoxide to relieve the tedium.

Having had such excitement the next section of the walk was positively uneventful. This lower section of the track passed through fairly dense forest, sheltered from the wind and cool in spite of the warm spring sunshine above. As the track climbed so the trees thinned and became more scrappy, these trees were the first line of defence against the prevailing westerlies that come funnelling through Strath Stack. The unique shape of Ben Stack, a rocky fin lying on a WNW to ESE axis, cannot be appreciated at such close quarters but its southerly flanks are still very dramatic, rising steeply from the narrow confines of the glen. The track itself slowly became less cared for, to the extent that as it approaches the head of the Strath it is little more than a serpentine peaty scar made by ATV's, as they try to avoid the more boggy ground.

Once I was well clear of the trees I found a sheltered grassy area and stopped for rest, refreshment and for the umpteenth time to go through the water ritual. As I sat leaning against a heathery bank, chewing nuts and chocolate, I pondered on the fact that even though I had found a small piece of grass it was still very wet and boggy. The further up Strath Stack the more is the temptation to turn round, for the views ahead are of boggy tracts of moorland while the view back reveals

Strath Stack in all its remote glory, and to anyone interested in physical geography is a fine example of a glaciated U shaped valley. The NW end of the valley was remarkable for only one thing and that was the ongoing construction of an electrified 2 metre high deer fence crossing the moor in a SW to NE direction. Way over I could see a caravan which must have been used by the construction gang. This was no mean fence, it marched across rock and bog alike and where it passed over solid ground the rock was drilled to accommodate the posts. Not only that but on my side of the fence a second series of posts about a metre high and the same distance from the main fence, carried a single electrified strand to give more protection; but against what?

I was worried, was I on the inside or the outside? What (or who) was being kept in (or out). What was on the other side? What were the cost benefits of erecting such an expensive fence? Was it being paid for by an EEC grant? Should I touch it just to see whether it really was electrified? There being no darkened room for me to lie down in, I wandered off in a NE direction along the path that leads down to the A838 near Loch Stack Lodge. The visibility was reasonable albeit a bit hazy, but Foinaven was there in the distance still with its cloudy headdress, to the east Loch Stack and between them was silvery Arkle.

I turned right on to the road for a short way and then took the road to the Lodge NC268436, crossed the bridge and followed a clear track east then north as it winds its way round a hill then over the moor towards Arkle, this being one of the main access points to that mountain. I was beginning to feel the effects of the days walk and as the time was now 18.00hrs I decided that once I was well clear of the Lodge I would look for a place to camp. Everywhere seemed to be wet, bog plants the only vegetation. Just before the point where the track passes between two lochans I noticed to the left about 100 metres from the track a 'shelf' of higher ground which looked grassier than the surrounding area. I left my bag by the side of the track and went squelching across to investigate, it was by no means ideal but at least firm enough to pitch a tent!

Rising ground to the north of the 'shelf' gave a bit of protection from the wind. I soon realised that it was unwise to stand on one spot for very long unless it was a large tussock because I would quickly get that sinking feeling. I was disconcerted when doing a 'trial lie' to test the comfort of the position and with my ear to the sleeping mat I could hear the occasional drip, drip coming from underneath me! Half an hour later the tent was up and I had foraged for water, having gone at least 400m on to the lower slopes of Arkle before finding running water suitable for filling the water containers.

I had pitched the tent roughly in line with what I judged was the wind direction which meant that from the doorway I looked on to the magnificent silver screes of Arkle's SW face, the weather was still giving me cause for concern, the strong wind brought clouds racing in from the west and meeting the mountains they then delayed to thicken the cloudy ceiling above. Every now and then the evening sun would burst through on to Arkle's slopes immediately transforming the ice cold silver screes into layers of molten lava.

The normal evening routine proceeded and I retired to my sleeping bag by about 21.00hrs happy that at best lying down my weight was spread over the widest possible area, thus reducing the likelihood of my disappearing downwards. As I reflected on progress, with the evening nip of malt, I realised that tomorrow would see me leaving behind the mountains and heading for the sea for the last leg up to Cape Wrath via Sandwood Bay.

Day 12 Monday 17th May
West side of Arkle to Strathchailleach Bothy
Walked from 06.00 to 18.00 hours
Distance 30km, Climbed 435ms Bothy at NC249588

I quote from my daily log "Another awful night, wind changed quarter - thus hitting tent side on and by 22.00 was very fierce, slept only fitfully with tent thrashing around. Amazingly all the pegs held in the flimsy boggy surface. Rain started at 05.00 so everything got wet in packing up."
It must have been about 04.30 that I awoke with a strange sensation, as I drifted into consciousness that turned out to be the clammy tent fabric pressed to my face. The single hoop design tent has an alarming habit in a side on wind to 'collapse' inwards, only to bounce back as the wind speed drops. Because of what happened two nights previously on Ben More I had tied pieces of cord around each of the four guys which stopped them from gradually loosening in the battering wind. I lay there putting off the evil moment but as the rain started I knew that I must get

moving, so I began the routine that I had mentally rehearsed many times.

Question How do you get all your worldly goods – clothes, food, bedding etc.,. into your sack in as dry a condition as possible while it is raining and blowing a gale?
Answer With great difficulty!

The procedure was made more difficult because I did most of the packing while in a sitting position – as soon as I knelt I could feel the ground giving under my knees. The sequence of events was:-
• Roll up sleeping bag and put into compression bag.
• Dress completely including boots.
• Pack everything else into respective bags.
• Deflate sleeping mat and put into its bag.
• Choose a lull in wind to open tent, get out quick, bring everything out and put on to waterproof rucksack cover and hopefully zip up tent before wind peaks again.
• Gather extraneous odds and sods which are outside tent – washing bowl, water bottle, stove, cooking pan, walking pole.
• Take down tent trying to pack outer quickly, to keep inner as dry as possible.
• Pack soaking wet tent plus about half a litre of water into its bag.
• Then it is quick job to put tent, mat and sleeping bag into bottom of sack, then everything else, close sack.

I set off an hour later at 0600hrs in steady rain which slanted across at me. The cloud was well down the watery flanks of Arkle, although at my level the visibility was pretty good. The track is a good one and it winds around the north end of Arkle before heading off to the screey slopes of Foinaven. I was heading for Rhiconich and the logical route seemed to be along the line of the two lochs which lead NNW from NC280470 and hopefully find the path that goes the last 2 kms to the road. Once I had crossed the stream Alltan Riabhach I left the path and headed NW across very broken ground for a kilometre before reaching the shore of Loch a Garbh-bhaid Mor. I had no reason to expect anything but a difficult time for the next 3kms or so but as I pushed my way through the thick heather on the NE bank of the loch I realised that I seemed to be on a path of sorts. It was not clearly defined by any means but I guess sufficiently well walked to be a great help on this heathery hillside sloping down to the water's edge. It was a most strange sensation, for I could see far less of the path than my feet could feel. It was as if I was gliding through the heather on invisible rails.

I had set off walking without my morning cuppa and reaching the far end of the loch I determined to find somewhere to stop as the rain was fading the further I travelled away from the mountains. The river which flows into Loch a Garbh-bhaid Beag proved to be the ideal stopping place. There is a wide shingle delta on either side of the main channel which is so wide and of such considerable force that it was definitely a 'boots off' job. Once I gained the stony beach on the far side of the river NC268499 got the stove going and by the time I was shod again in dry boots my tea was mashing. I sat on the biggest rock I could find and feasted on sesame snacks, chocolate and nuts (Gad! I know how to live)

Near the little boathouse at the top end of the loch the path improves and by 08.45 I was approaching the bustling metropolis of Rhiconich. By 08.46 I had left it far behind me! Although I had intended to make the last camp of the trip near Sandwood Bay, because of my early start to the day and the less than attractive prospect of spending another night in a flapping tent on a bog, I had been pondering on the feasibility of pushing on to Cape Wrath that day. Before I could make any such decision I would have to find out the time of the last minibus from the Cape. Near the junction with the road to Kinlochbervie there is a phone box, I tried phoning the minibus operator but could not get through, so I phoned Ali instead! I think I totally confused her with what was evidently an inadequate explanation of my predicament.

I set off along what is quite a quiet road – compared to most back home! It undulates its way past several lochside communities which I guess for many generations were very dependant on fishing for their livelihood. There is still a lot of fishing in Loch Inchard but I suspect nowadays the boats operate out of Kinlochbervie. The weather was following the same pattern as previous days, much brighter on the coast but still very heavy cloud looking back to the SE over the mountains. There were occasional squalls of rain but mostly it was bright and sunny. I really enjoyed this walk even though tarmac can be unforgiving on the feet, the views more than compensated.

I tried again to 'phone the minibus operator but still to no avail, the question was resolved however when I reached Badcall and went into the London Stores, (a certain irony in the naming of this little wayside Aladdin's Cave, something to do with it being the most westerly shop on mainland U.K. and thus the furthest from London) for during a chat with the proprietor he told me that there is a bothy just NE of Sandwood Bay, so problem solved, a night in Strathchailleach Bothy.

I have to admit here a grave omission on my part, I belong to the Mountain Bothy Association and this is one of their bothies. In the preparation for the walk I went through their handbook and noted the locations of any that were near my route, how I came to miss this one I cannot think, but it certainly was a very welcome piece of information. I succumbed to temptation and bought 2 packets of sandwiches, 2 apples and a packet of eccles cakes, simple fare but so much more appealing than nuts and raisins. I sat outside the shop and consumed the packet of egg and cress sandwiches but they did not really set my taste buds a jingle – then I noticed they were the healthy low fat option – low fat, no this, no that, no taste. The moment was saved though, by 2 eccles cakes and an apple.

There were some magnificent banks of gorse in many places along this road filling the warm morning air with their intoxicating scent; one of the more spectacular was at the side of the road just above Kinlochbervie, the contrast of the yellow gorse and blue of the loch was just stunning. Lunchtime approached and when I came to the little track down to Oldshoremore I decided that lunch sat on the beach looking out to sea would be just the ticket, I also needed to avail myself of the Public Conveniences there. Fifteen minutes later feeling considerably lighter and more relaxed I made my way on to the white sandy beach which was deserted and very windy. I found a sheltered spot behind some huge rocks where I could have my lunch. The trouble was it faced inland and offered a splendid view of where I had just come from.

It was mid afternoon by the time I reached Balchrick, the warm sunshine of earlier in the day had been replaced by thick hazy cloud, I was getting tired, the 06.00 start beginning to tell. Near the start of the track to Sandwood Bay quite a number of cars were parked, this being the nearest access point. During the hour and a half walk to the beach I must have seen more people than at any other similar time since leaving Fort William including those on the beach I guess 30 – 40. The 6 kms walk would be lovely on a fine clear day, but given gale force wind, grey skies and thick mantles of cloud over all the hills to the east I have to say I found it rather a grim plod. However as I got to Druim na Buainn NC215642 I looked down to Sandwood Loch and began to get glimpses of the beach and so my mood changed. The last section of the path drops down towards the beach and is truly dramatic, to the right is Sandwood Loch with the hills behind, in front the bay. This must be about the most inaccessible large beach in the U.K. and all I had read about it had not prepared me for the exhilaration of walking across that wide expanse of sand. It is bounded at both ends by high cliffs, the western end has a rock needle equally as splendid as The Old Man of Storr on Skye, there are also several rocky islets just off the beach.

By the time I reached the beach the sun had disappeared and dark clouds were overhead, which together with the angry sea and spray laden wind only served to accentuate the loneliness of this wonderful seaside gem. I had first seen the gannets while I was still on the path down to the beach, but once on the sand, walking along near the water's edge it was a grand sight, there seemed to be an endless flight of gannets both mature and immature together with other seabirds flying NE to SW along the line of the surf, the gannets were diving from a height of 25 to 30 metres.

On another day I would have relished lingering here to explore the loch and enjoy all the views, but concern about the weather was ever present and I was anxious to find the bothy. As I walked along the beach I looked north, a view which on a clear day would have revealed the last headland about 1 km south of Cape Wrath, but on this occasion I reckoned I could only see to just beyond the Bay of Keisgaig.

Towards the NE end of the bay I splashed across the outfall river of Sandwood Loch and climbed up the rocky cliffs, which are at quite a comfortably climbable angle, trying to keep traversing the cliff and hillside above in roughly a ENE direction. The terrain here is very wet and spongy, but firm enough to not cause too much worry. I soon reached Lochan nan Sac NC240657 and turned almost due east from the top end, shortly after that I saw in the distance the bothy, nestling on the left bank of the river.

I arrived at the, unoccupied, bothy about 17.30hrs and explored the facilities,
• Sleeping room 4 metres square most of the floor area taken up with a raised platform.
• Small kitchen no sink, no running water, just two work tops.
• Sitting room possibly 4m x 5m with a few assorted chairs and a rickety table.
• Passage way by door housing spades – for cutting peat and toilet purposes.

The unpacking of my rucksack revealed an extremely wet sleeping bag and Thermarest. In the excitement of breaking camp that morning in the wind and rain, I had put the tent inside the waterproof liner, so all the water that was on the fabric of the tent, having been squeezed out into the bottom of the liner was then soaked up by its absorbent neighbours. I rang out as much water as I could but the sleeping bag did not dry out to any significant degree. Fortunately the bags filling did not loose any of its thermal qualities by being wet.

One of the 'Rules of the house' was to maintain the stock of cut peat, so there would always be a supply of dry peat for the fire. Once I had sorted myself out I prepared for my first experience of this ancient art. Armed with spade and plastic sack I teetered across the river, a substantial flow some 5 metres wide and found the peat cutting face some 50 metres away. This is a very satisfying pastime, slicing down through the deep deposit, trying to cut brick size lumps. Fresh cut 'bricks' are left on the surface to begin the draining process, partially protected from the elements by strips of plastic sack. I then filled the bag with 10 kilos or so of partly dry 'bricks'. I found it even more hazardous recrossing the river, tired legs, wet rocks, a spade and an unwieldy bag of peat was not a recipe for surefootedness.

The lumps were then stacked in the dry lean-to store of the bothy. Having done my duty I set about trying to light a peat fire, no easy task, but a reluctant form of combustion did eventually occur. Had the weather been 10 degrees colder though, I would have spent a very cold evening in front of it. The smell of burning peat is unique and I thought quite pleasant. I tried to ignore the vague recollection that peat smoke is highly carcinogenic.

I was destined to spend the night on my own, which although I am normally quite a sociable person I felt it was rather fitting, having been on such a solitary venture for 12 days, that I should not break the pattern for the last evening. There were a couple of squalls after the peat cutting episode and the wind was as fierce as ever. All of a sudden around 20.30 the gloomy interior of the bothy was lit by golden evening light, reflected from the surrounding moor. I quickly found my camera and rushed outside. What an incredible sight! The low sun appeared like molten iron ore – reminding me of a visit years ago to the steel works at Corby and seeing the Bessemer Converters discharging the liquid ore. The contrast of light, sunset red clear sky to the west, the rest of the sky a mixture of heavy rain clouds, blue patches and lighter, higher cloud. All this combined with the burning colours of the moor, deep shadows both on the stone walls of the building and also among the thick clumps of grass. I just stood out there and marvelled at its beauty, until another sudden squall sent me scuttling in once again.

This is an extremely remote location, amidst lonely bleak moors; I could only begin to imagine how conditions were in the middle of winter when any combination of snow, ice, Atlantic gales and very short hours of daylight would make this seem to be a very hostile environment. With only 2 kilometres of flattish moor between the bothy and the ocean, gale force winds of any description from the west would present a severe hazard to both body and building alike.

The bothy was occupied for a number of years by a colourful character, who having forsaken life working in the heavy industry of Glasgow came north, found the deserted building and moved in, thereafter living the life of a hermit. He would walk to the London Stores to collect any supplies he needed. With an inexhaustible supply of peat and water within 100 metres he had all that was required for a frugal lifestyle. Many of the interior walls of the building are decorated with murals that he painted, which depict a whole range of subjects. It is probably true to say that most bothies are buildings with an interesting history, but Strathchaillach must rank as being pretty unique.

I really enjoyed my evening meal; it was eat up night, thus a larger than usual portion of soup with couscous and best of all my favourite 'Real' meal – cod and potato in sour cream sauce, saved for the occasion. The feast was rounded off with the last two Eccles cakes. The light was fading while I wrote up my daily log and a suitably erudite entry in the bothy 'visitor book'. My literary endeavours aided by the post-prandial delight of malt whisky and chocolate, being careful to leave just enough whisky to drink a toast on reaching Cape Wrath the next morning.

By 21.00 I was beginning to flag, it had been a long day, 30 kms and 16 hours since being forced into action early that morning. I spent another 20 minutes enjoying a cup of Horlicks while straining my eyes reading some of the visitor book entries. A last check in the kitchen area that what meagre supplies of food I had left were stored in a plastic bag hanging from a hook – to prevent mice from taking nocturnal nibbles, a last pee (outside in the designated 'toilet' area) and then to bed.

Oh what luxury, lying in a warm and snug (and damp) sleeping bag, drifting off to sleep with the sounds of the wind tearing at the nearby window and whining in the eaves.

Day 13 Tuesday 18th May
Strathchailleach Bothy to Durness via Cape Wrath
Walked from 08.40 to 16.00 hours
Distance 28km, Climbed 400ms

The wind increased again during the night, several times I was awoken by either the wind crashing against the building or torrential squalls thundering on the corrugated iron roof, how I relished the warmth and security of the bothy! I gave more than a passing thought to the group I had seen camping near Sandwood Loch, as I snuggled even deeper into my now dry sleeping bag. They must have had a truly horrendous time.

To say that at 06.50 I sprang out of bed would be to stretch reality a bit too far, but I had a great sense of excitement that within a few hours I would be standing at Cape Wrath. At home with the luxury of hot showers and dry towels, the morning ablutions can be savoured and enjoyed. One of the drawbacks of wild camping is that they generally consist of standing stark naked, at the mercy of the elements, washing using a bowl of water about 300mms square and then a splash rinse in a nearby stream or lake, then attempting to dry oneself on a damp towel about the size of a dish cloth.

I spent nearly two hours breakfasting, sweeping and tidying the bothy and packing my sack. At 08.40 I shut the door and set off on the last leg of my journey. My first task was to get across the river. I stood on the bank and looked with dismay at the place where the previous evening I had crossed on the peat cutting foray, rocks which then had been well above the water level were now completely submerged. The overnight rain had caused the river to rise by 150 - 200mms and there was now no possibility of a dry crossing, so off came the pack, off with boots and socks, on with the Teva shoes. I was soon across and a few minutes later had dried my feet and was dry shod again.

The weather was dry, lots of cloud and no sign of the sun or blue skies, the wind had eased a bit and I fancied it had backed a little to a south-westerly, which if anything would help me on my way.

I had read somewhere a piece of advice concerning this last 10kms section to Cape Wrath recommending a route well back from the coast, because of the steeper nature of the terrain near the coast and also greater difficulty in crossing some of the streams close to the cliffs.

Given the position of the bothy I had decided to keep to more or less the same contour to the east of Loch a Gheodhe Ruaidh,

then under Cnoc an Daimh to contour round NW and then through the bealach to the west of Cnoc a Ghiubhais NC260705. From there a due north course would take me on to the track about 1.5kms from the Cape.

In spite of some pretty wet ground this route did not present me with any problems or delays. The excitement of seeing and then reaching Cape Wrath together with a favourable wind on my back meant quick progress. This is a large area of wild lonely moor and one does not get much impression at all of being so close to the sea, the only really memorable view was from the bealach looking SW to the Bay of Keisgaig. The sea was still angry looking and a thick sea mist meant that sky and water combined in shades of grey. Just after 10.00 I stopped for about 10 minutes on the north side of the bealach which gave me a good view of Dinan Mor, the large hill 500metres south of my goal. I ate some chocolate, nuts and dried fruit. Since leaving Ullapool I had eked out supplies, I bitterly regretted sending so much back to mission control. At the start of the day I had only half a bar of chocolate and under 100 grams of fruit and nuts left. I guessed (correctly) that I would get it in the neck from Ali when I got home.

Cape Wrath is a fairly inaccessible place. A large chunk of this northerly extremity of Sutherland comes under M.O.D. jurisdiction, being a firing range. There is no resident military presence but it can be closed several times a year for exercises. Outside the summer months of May to September anyone arriving at the Cape from Sandwood Bay and intending to get back to civilization via the A838 and Durness, will have to do so under their own steam. Every spring two minibuses are tied onto a large rowing boat and taken across the Kyle of Durness, after this they spend the summer conveying sightseers the 16kms from the little passenger ferry to the lighthouse at Cape Wrath. The ferry across the Kyle and the minibus service are run by different people but are mutually dependant on each other.

When I was planning the walk I garnered all this information from the internet in a matter of 5 minutes, together with the names and phone numbers of the ferry and minibus operators. A few more clicks of the mouse found details of a daily return coach service between Inverness and Durness, run by Tim Bearman Coaches. I rang the minibus number and spoke to a very helpful lady who assured me that by mid May they would be running a regular hourly (ish) bus service every day starting about mid morning. On enquiring she also told me there was no public telephone at the Cape but if I needed to phone there should be no difficulty in getting a signal for a mobile. The return coach to Inverness left Durness at 15.15, so I figured that as long as I reached Cape Wrath by midday I could comfortably make Durness, collect a post restante parcel of clean clothes at the post office and be on my way south that afternoon. I needed to find a B&B near Inverness railway station to make it handy for catching the train home the next morning. I also ascertained that there were no military exercises in May, so everything was falling nicely into place, nothing could go wrong!

About 10.45 I set foot on tarmac turned left and followed the road as it gently climbs 50metres or so clockwise around Dinan Mor. I expected at any moment to have to step off the track to make way for a minibus – with the happy faces of holiday makers pressed expectantly against its steamy windows. It is only in the last 300-400metres that the lighthouse and other buildings come into view, but still no glimpse of dramatic cliffs or sea. There is a large, bleak deserted building up a little track to the right, which I imagine at one time had some military significance. The array of buildings around the lighthouse, which I would guess once housed a substantial team of people are now all empty and boarded up.

This must be the place where the minibus stops, yet there was not the slightest indication of human activity, no bus, no group of cagoule clad visitors, crouched behind the walls to escape the bullying buffets of the gale.

It was now, as I sheltered by an outbuilding next to the lighthouse, that I felt a huge clash of emotions. I was immensely proud of myself, that I had completed the 320kms walk from Fort William, achieved all that I had spent so much time planning, yet for some reason, by the part of my mental filing system flagged 'Cape Wrath minibus' a large red warning light was flashing.

I toasted my success with the last mouthful of 'Knockando' malt whiskey, then found the mobile phone, surprise, surprise, no signal! I left my rucksack by the wall and just with camera and phone walked the last 200metres past the lighthouse and on to the almost northerly tip of mainline U.K.. This is an impressive bit of coastline, the wind incredibly strong – no gusts – just a continual blast. The visibility out to sea was rather hazy to the west and north, not quite so bad looking east. Going due north from here there is nothing other than sea until you reach the ice floes of the Arctic. The little rocky lump of Dustic, with its white surf collar, looked rather forlorn a kilometre or so to the NE.

I took a couple of shots on the camera, then turned the phone on again. To my dismay the signal was too weak to leave its mother. I returned to the shelter of the wall, no minibus. In spite of the gale I had still not worked out the reason for its non-appearance. The time was now 11.30 and I decided there was no point in waiting for the possible non-arrival of any vehicular passenger transport. If I really legged it I figured I could do the 16kms to the ferry in 2.5 to 3 hours, leaving just enough time to get up into the village to collect my parcel. At worst I could flag the bus down on its way south from Durness and forego picking up my goodies.

An hour earlier I had assumed my walking to be almost done; now I was retracing my steps, this time into the wind. I had already revised my earlier opinion that the wind had eased, I was now in the strongest wind of the whole trip. Near the point where I had joined the track it turns SE and heads in that direction for the next 12 kms, the SW wind was hitting me broadside, continually pushing me across the road. Several times I found myself having been pushed onto the heathery verge. Occasions like these and my anxieties, lead me to express opinions of the wind, with some vigour, in less than flattering terms, but nobody heard!

I developed a technique to counteract the effect of the wind, using the walking pole at an angle to brace against the sideways force, trouble was after a time my left arm ached like hell – you cannot win. From the bridge over the Kearvaig River the road steadily climbs about 120metres over the next 3kms to the bealach between the impressive rounded lumps that are Maovally and Sgribhis-bheinn. As I approached the bealach I was soaked by a violent squall. Having had thousands of miles of unimpeded passage across the Atlantic the clouds clearly resented having to lift themselves over these hills and accordingly dumped some of their load to express their displeasure. The wind was unrelenting in its constancy and ferocity.

Dropping down on the east side of the bealach the view east opened out and I expect in better visibility one could see Durness, the time was 13.00 and I was still just about on the pace. I tried the phone again and to my great relief there was a good strong signal, I took off my sack, the noise of the wind was so loud I had to find some shelter before I could make a call. Lying in the heather at the side of the track in the lee of my rucksack the wind noise was reduced to a bearable degree, I punched in the minibus number. I still had difficulty hearing what Donny, the minibus man, said, but I did hear him say that the ferry could not operate because conditions in the Kyle were too rough. I felt completely pole axed as I realised that there was now no way of keeping to my travel plans. While we talked, all kinds of thoughts and options were rushing through my mind.

Donny was really very helpful and sympathetic in the circumstances. He answered several questions and the salient points that came out were; there was no guarantee that the ferry would be running the next day, as far as he knew it was possible to walk around the Kyle from the ferry point, there was a bothy at Kearvaig I could use if I wanted to 'sit it out', and a throw away remark that he thought it may be possible to walk across the Kyle at low tide, this last gem of information received no second thought, until about two hours later! His parting comment was that if I did manage to get on to the A838, I had only to phone him and he would come out and pick me up.

I ended the call and for a few minutes just sat looking east into the hazy distance, at Faraid Head, Balnakiel Bay and just a glimpse of the mouth of the Kyle. I decided that I really had no choice, staying on this side of the water was out of the question, food stocks were down to two squares of chocolate, four hazelnuts, one raisin and half a litre of energy drink. Looking on the map at the west bank of the Kyle below the ferry point it was difficult to guess how easy a walk round would be, but it could not be any worse than other terrain I had overcome in the last fortnight.

I then phoned Ali and once I heard her voice, the heady mixture of elation, doubt, disappointment, fatigue and frustration boiled over in a fairly emotional conversation. As always she was so concerned and determined to do all she could to sort out the predicament. We ended the call with a promise that she would investigate the chances of my flying back from Inverness that evening, or the next morning. The travel plan I had allowed for meant I would not be back home for another two days.

As the road dropped down to the bridge over Daill River I noted that the outer end of the estuary showed signs of exposed sand bars. Having found shelter amongst a bank of windswept gorse I sat down for a much deserved rest and consumed the remainder of my rations. Refreshed and rested I set off and half an hour later I passed a little lay-by, just before the ferry landing, where the two minibuses sheltered smugly, from the wind. At the ferry point I climbed up a very steep rocky cliff through heather, gorse and rock on to a small headland. I then started an exciting 1kilometre traverse SE, above the estuary. The 1-50,000 map gives no indication of the craggy nature of the terrain here and it turned out to be quite an enjoyable scramble.

The further round the headland I went, the more I could see of the middle and upper part of the Kyle of Durness, and it was clear that the tide was very low, revealing acres of golden sand, I now recalled Donny's remark about walking across. The stream that flows down from Beinn an Amair has cut a sharp cleft in the last few hundred metres of its descent to sea level and as I approached I assessed that my best option was down. Some minutes later I was standing on the foreshore which was encouragingly solid. I continued along the edge of the sand for another 300 - 400metres till I was round the point and there is a channel close in to the rocky foreshore. Looking across the sandy wet expanse, the A838 beckoned me seductively; this was the narrowest point and the road no more than 500metres away. I thought 'To hell with it, I'll give it a go!'

Off came the boots, Paramo trousers unzipped and their flapping legs tucked into my waistband. The first channel was only about 20cms deep, then a long stretch of firm sand again until the main channel which was close to the eastern side of the estuary, this was knee deep and once clear of it I was back on dry ground within 25m or so. All the way across I had been using my fully extended walking pole to test for quicksand, but the crossing was without incident and only took about 10 minutes.

As soon as I reached the side of the road I 'phoned Donny. True to his word Donny arrived a minute or two after I had finished drying my feet and putting boots back on. He drove me up into Durness, where we drove round until he had found me a B&B, stopping on the way at the post office to collect my parcel.

Ali had been unable to book a flight because of my not having any photographic identification, so I spent a leisurely time the next day, caught the Tim Bearman coach to Inverness, getting there about 20.00 in time to book a ticket for the London sleeper train.

I stepped on to the platform at St. David's station in Exeter at 11.00 on Thursday morning to be met by Ali. By 12.00 we were back at our business in Budleigh Salterton. The end of a fantastic adventure.

6. THE INTERVENING YEARS

In the months following the previous two solo trips I had been enthusiastically planning the next challenge, but in the summer and autumn of 2004 I felt curiously deflated. I spent a great deal of spare time writing up the log of the trip and preparing it for publishing on the internet but I had no inspiration concerning another venture. In respect of long distance walks the Cape Wrath Trail ticks all the boxes, it is a straight line route starting at Fort William which in my mind is synonymous with mountains and adventure. It finishes at Cape Wrath, probably the most wild and remote point on the British coastline, which for centuries has had huge significance for the seafarers of Northern Europe. I somehow felt that it would be a very difficult act to follow. Nevertheless I was back in Scotland during May of the next three years, twice on solo backpacking trips and once with my friend Tom for a two week Munro bagging trip, mixing wild camping with the easy life on campsites. Both solo trips were cut short, the first by a combination of bad blisters, a dodgy knee and appalling weather, the second time in 2007 bad weather again in the form of very heavy rain that turned every stream and river into un-crossable cataracts. It was on this last trip that I began struggling with my eyesight, finding difficulty, especially in poor light, in 'reading the landscape' and also map reading when viewing through a film of water on the map case. I realised then that it was no longer prudent to take myself off alone into the wilderness.

With solo walking off the agenda and my old walking companions less inclined to undertake the types of walks of our glory years, my interest in cycling was revived during many discussions with my friends Adrian and Mark. In 2007 I purchased a new Dawes Galaxy bicycle. For the first time in my life I was riding a quality cycle that was the correct size for me. Over the next eight years I rode thousands of miles, mainly in Devon, acquainting myself with its byways and villages, much of which were completely new territory for me.

Other factors were also at play, retail trade had become more challenging during the previous few years and became even more so as we headed into the recession of 2008/9. Our business of picture framing was heavily reliant upon my good eyesight, so my declining acuity was beginning to impact on our long established procedures. Then there was gig rowing. In 2006 I was introduced to the mainly West Country sport of pilot gig rowing and a whole new world opened up.

Cornish Pilot Gigs are traditional clinker built rowing boats, manned by 6 rowers and a coxswain. They were used in the Isles of Scilly and Cornwall during the 18th and 19th centuries as general purpose rowing boats. Perfectly designed for coping with the prevailing sea conditions they were used as supply boats, passenger boats, lifeboats and most importantly to facilitate the very lucrative business in the Isles of Scilly that of piloting. A pilot would be put on board an incoming merchant vessel where he could then be commissioned to pilot that ship through the treacherous coastal waters to London, Liverpool or wherever. They continued to be used in a very limited way through the 20th century, especially on a local basis for competitive rowing. In the 1980's this sport began to gain popularity and by the turn of the century there were a good number of established clubs in Devon, Cornwall and the IOS.

I joined the River Teign Rowing Club based at Teignmouth, in 2006 and have been rowing ever since. I rowed competitively for about twelve years and took part in eleven World Championships, run annually in the IOS, from 2007 to 2017. Rowing has been a wonderful substitute for hill walking, although I do still get misty eyed when I think of the mountains. Between about 2010 and 2016 I did have three backpacking trips with two friends; one to the Cairngorms and two to Knoydart, but now my sight is so bad that even a walk on Dartmoor poses me some real problems. The last time I set foot on a mountain was in the autumn of 2016, when together with a group of rowing friends we took on the Three Peaks of Yorkshire Challenge, Pen-y-ghent, Whernside and Ingleborough in under 12 hours. I completed the walk in about eleven hours but had great difficulty on several of the steep descents.

Five men on a bike

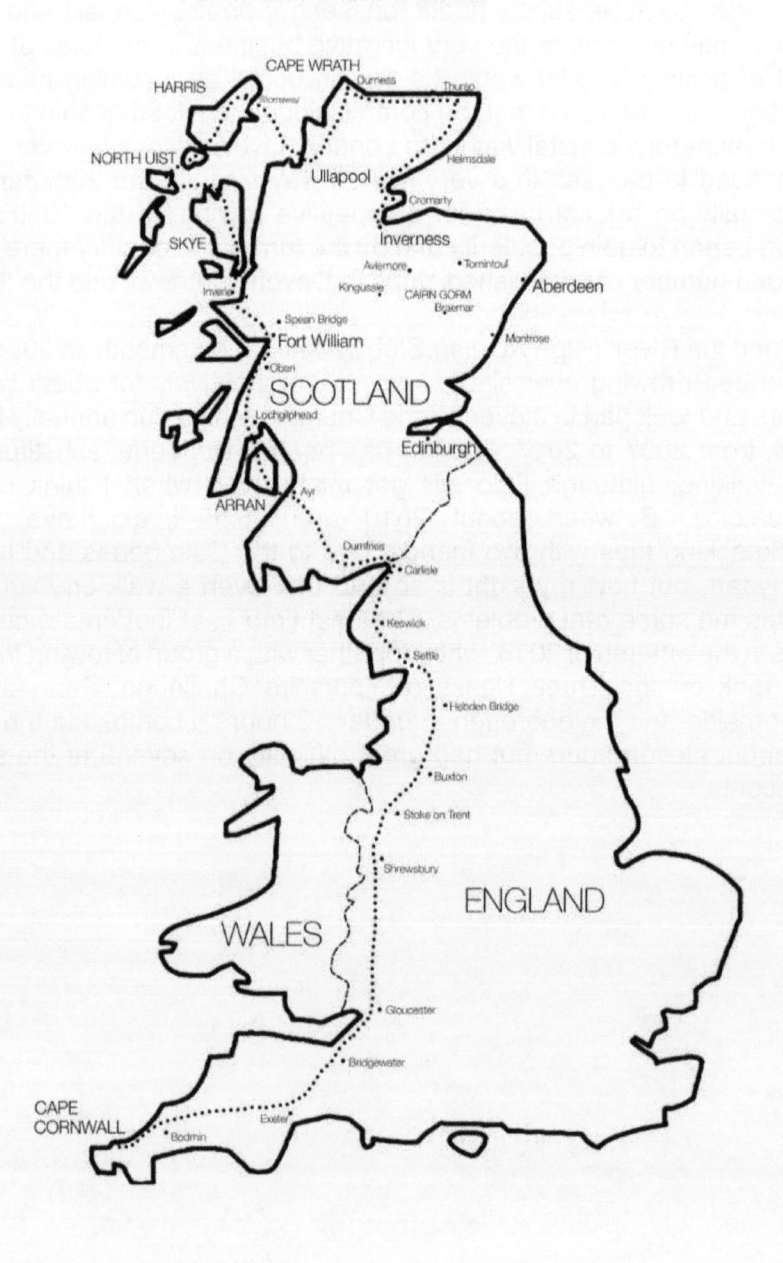

7. FIVE MEN ON A BIKE - A TANDEM TALE May/June 2017

Part 1 - The Back Story

It was late afternoon on what had been a glorious, shimmering late September day in 2015. The East Devon countryside displayed all the magnificent colours that autumn could muster. I had returned home after a 40+ mile cycle ride with 3 of my cycling friends; yet as I sat in the kitchen with a big mug of tea I felt a heavy sense of gloom; for I knew that 'the decision' had to be made. Since my retirement in 2012 I had enjoyed many miles of cycling, both on my own and with a small group, but for 6 months or so I had been finding cycling more and more challenging. Convincing myself that I was still safe on two wheels had become more and more difficult.

In 2006 I had been diagnosed with a degenerative eye condition; that caused me to give up driving in early 2009. Since then my trusty Dawes Galaxy cycle had become my lifeline to independence.

On that late September morning we had set off from the edge of Exeter and headed up to the right of the M5, then swung east on a circular route that eventually took us to the coast at Budleigh Salterton, then back home via Exmouth and the Exe estuary. Unfortunately for me the clockwise direction this route took meant we were cycling into the sun for most of the day. In spite of the help of my friends the ride had been a nightmare for me, much of the time squinting, desperately trying to see in the glare of the sun, crashing into potholes I had no hope of seeing. 'The decision' had to be made, that was the end of my solo cycling, I could no longer feel safe to ride. My beloved Dawes was now put into early retirement.

It was later that year, enjoying a beer with two very good friends, that the seed of an idea was sown. Adrian and Mark were the same friends who ten years earlier had persuaded me 'back into the saddle'. They were both keen cyclists and tandem owners and they suggested that I should consider buying a tandem. They would both be happy to pilot me and felt that it was quite reasonable to suppose that I would be able to find others in the retired cycle fraternity who would be prepared to share piloting duties.

So it was that after much thought and talking things through with my wife Ali, that in June 2016 she and I went up to Thorn Cycles in Bridgwater and ordered my tandem. A month later Adrian and I rode the magnificent bright yellow tandem - The Beast - over The Blackdown Hills to its new Devon home.

The autumn and early winter of 2016 saw the familiarisation process of getting acquainted with the Beast. It acquired the nickname early on, because at 2.5m long it can be very skittish to manoeuvre by hand rather than by foot, especially along our narrow hallway, through the chicane, up into the kitchen, through a 90 degree turn into the conservatory, its resting place. On the road though, a pure thoroughbred, stable and predictable.

As I became more and more drawn into cycling the idea of a Land's End to John O' Groats journey began to hover in my mind. I cannot say this had always been a burning ambition, but the idea of travelling the length of our country had long held a certain allure. In 2010 I was planning to do this as a solo ride but called it off because I realised that navigating on my own would present too many challenges.

Part 2 - The Beast

A 'Raven Twin' steel frame tandem from Thorn Cycles, size 'large/large' and painted bright yellow.
Wide 66cms handlebars give very good control and manoeuvrability

Rohloff 14 speed hub gears, front dynamo both with bright red hubs.

V brakes front and rear plus Hope disc brakes on the rear.

Brooks saddles, rear carrier for panniers plus Carradice rear carrier top bag.

26inch wheels with 50mm tyres give very good cushioning and road adhesion.

Part 3 - The Plan

As summer merged into autumn and I became more familiar with riding the tandem I realised what a splendid machine it was. Most of those who came on board as pilot loved it, great fun to ride, quite hard work on hills but on the level or downhill it was superb, very responsive and quick. Needless to say it was not too long before thoughts of the 'big end to end ride' surfaced once more in my mind.

Yet again Ali's agreement was pivotal to the trip going ahead. In the last 20 years or so she has become quite resigned to me wanting to go off on solo backpacking trips, that she agreed quite readily, possibly with the thought that with 2 of us there would be a 'safety in numbers' factor. By the early winter 2016 I had mentioned the idea to Adrian and Mark, and also Ian from Churchill in Somerset, with whom I had cycled many a mile. From that time the whole project developed a momentum of its own. I wanted a route that my pilots and I wanted to ride rather than a straight line type of Land's End to John O' Groats route. I was attracted to the idea of a 'Cape to Cape' route. Cape Cornwall to Cape Wrath. So it was that we decided a 4 week trip at 50 or so miles a day and 4 pilots each taking a 6 or 7 day stint. The fourth pilot became Peter, Adrian's brother and by mid December dates were set, the route was roughed out and those who needed to had booked leave from work. As Ian my last pilot had been able to book a longer break we decided to stretch the last section to include the Outer Hebrides, two days in Durness, then along the north coast to Thurso from where we could go to Dunnet Head the most northerly part of mainland UK then back through the Flow Country to finish at Inverness.

Two days in Durness would allow a visit to Cape Wrath. I was a bit sceptical as to whether we would be able to cycle there as the road across the MOD range is very rough so the minibus alternative would probably be the sensible option.

I have to say that as we moved into the New Year the trip was becoming more ambitious as witnessed by the planned itinerary:

May 15th Peter and I set off from Cape Cornwall
May 20th arrive Cheltenham
May 21st Adrian takes over

May 25th arrive at friends in Settle
May 27th Mark takes over
June 2nd arrive Fort William
Ali joins me for 3 days
June 6th Ian takes over
June 17th arrive at Inverness our final destination
June 18th fly to Bristol

As map reading is almost impossible for me now the pilots would be responsible for plotting routes for their sections. We all agreed that minor roads and Sustrans NCRs (national cycle routes) would be the order of the day. The question of mapping needed a lot of thought, we did not think that paper maps were the option for two reasons, even using OS 1:50,000 around 50 sheets would be required, this then creates a logistical problem, adding to the amount of baggage carried. So it was decided that to 'go digital' was the answer, I purchased a downloadable version of OS 1:50,000 which could be comfortably held on an iPhone. Purchasing the download gave access to the app which had so many bells and whistles that I think we should all have attended a course of evening classes to familiarise ourselves fully with the system. It is a very clever app allowing the plotting of routes then the ability to set up a sat nav feature which shows the exact position and the selected route. There was a slight problem, it was very demanding of power and we quickly realised that full use had to be made of power packs and recharging via the USB port from The Beast's hub dynamo. My iPhone would be used and I bought a special holder which fixed on to the handlebars. Inside the zipped lid of the holder was a compartment exactly the right size for the 'phone, this held it against the acetate screen which allowed full touch screen operation. There was room inside for cables and a couple of power packs. Advertised as waterproof the first two days use revealed it was anything but, resulting in a screen fogged with condensation.

Neither Ali nor I could picture Cape Cornwall although we felt we must have walked there years ago on one of our coast path treks. So in late April having a few days in Cornwall we took the bus to St. Just and walked to the Cape and then along to Botallack. I was a bit alarmed to discover that the car park at Cape Cornwall is at the bottom of a steep hill which rises about 80m, the prospect of tackling this hill immediately after setting off did bother me!

Part 4 The Ride

Day 1 Monday May 15th
Cape Cornwall to St. Newlyn East
47.3 miles
3077 ft ascent

It all seemed like a familiar dream because in my mind I had played it through so many times; the early morning start, the drive down the A30, the car park at Cape Cornwall. As it happened on the morning of May 15th 2017 it wasn't quite as I had envisaged, or would have wished.

Weeks before a very good friend and neighbour, Ian J., had readily agreed to transport us and the tandem to W. Cornwall for the start of my big ride. Just before 6.00am Peter, my first pilot and Ali carried the panniers and I wheeled the Beast up the path and round the corner, to Ian's house. Ian was already there sorting out the van and we managed to repeat the success of a few days earlier when on a dry run we fitted the 2.5m tandem into his VW camper van. The projected weather forecast for the next few days was not good, but we were trying to look on the bright side. After all it was not actually raining as we drove through Exeter. However the rain started almost as soon as we left the city behind, heading down the A30. The drive west was not encouraging, accompanied the whole way by the swish swish of windscreen wipers, I had no faith in the old adage 'rain before 7 dry by 11' because I had seen the forecast. We stopped at an ASDA on the outskirts of Bodmin for breakfast, that did nothing to lift the spirits either. We arrived at Cape Cornwall at 9.45. The car park was exposed to the full force of the westerly winds, low cloud/sea mist was eddying around the headland about a quarter of a mile away. The rain had eased to a spiteful drizzle and we could hardly open the doors as the wind was so strong. We gazed with utter disbelief at the two 'lucky' ravens above us. The only luck we could imagine was on their part - that they were not being torn apart by the wind. The whole process of unloading, then getting the tandem ready to roll, pedals fitted, saddle adjusted, handlebar set, was so difficult and cold that by the time everything was sorted I think we all felt utterly numbed. Now all of a sudden goodbyes had been said and it was just Peter the Pilot and I. Apart from a brief run the previous January, this was the first time Peter and I had ridden the Beast. We rode out of the car park and powered up the steep hill past the golf club, before I had time to worry about it. The road levelled on the approach to St. Just, and as we entered the village Ian and Ali passed us with a cheery toot and arms waving. We were soon wheeling along the coast road from St. Just, the cold and very damp sea mist was swirling up the cliffs, across the fields and over the road. This wasn't a dream, at last it was the start of my Great Adventure!

Very wisely Peter had decided on the N. Cornwall coast road as this is a relatively less hilly route than other more southerly routes. We left the car park at 10.20 and having breasted the hill we turned north at St. Just and followed the coast road through a string of little villages and hamlets, Tregeseol, Botallack, Pendeen, Morvah and on. To say that we were seeing a riot of colour would be doing the forces of subversion a disservice, more like a symphony of grey, where all the colours of the few flowers brave enough to show themselves were as nothing but the tinkling of a triangle against the grey's orchestral might. We headed for Hayle avoiding the fleshpots of St. Ives. We had decided to find a cafe in Hayle but that was not to be. We cycled under the railway and past the row of shops that constitutes the shopping centre of town, no cafe could be found. We carried on along the east side of the estuary, confident that there would be one at the sea end of the road, conveniently placed to satisfy the endless demands of holiday makers and dog walkers, for cups of tea and coffee. Our expectations were boosted by the unmistakeable, enticing smell of frying bacon but alas a comprehensive search failed to locate a cafe, a vendor of pork products, or even the source of the smell. Afterwards I did wonder whether this was a new twist on the olde folk lore, phantom smells of frying bacon set to lure bacon bap crazed cyclists to an untimely demise. On reflection I dare say that if we had ventured into the huge monolithic superstore near the railway station we would have found sustenance, but that would have been more than a step too far.

Peter and I had known each other for about ten years, initially he was living in Essex but after moving to W. Hampshire he and his family were more frequent in visiting the West Country outpost of the family. We had met up on many occasions through Adrian his brother but this will be the first opportunity we would have had to spend much time together.

Having failed in our search we stopped in a car park for ten minutes, long enough to consume an energy bar and a drink. We left Hayle behind and followed the road past the vast area of sand dunes that form the eastern section of coast. At Hell's Mouth we were delighted to find a welcoming and warm cafe and enjoyed a real 'cyclist' size bowl of homemade soup with buttered roll and tea. Not long after resuming our journey the rain started in earnest, the enduring dampness of morning was replaced by a steady cold and penetrating rain.

Our coast road left Camborne and Redruth to the south, cycling on we skirted round the edge of Perranporth where we negotiated several steep hills but at last there were many really splendid gardens. Even the weather could not hide their beauty. Cornwall is a county of so many contrasts due to its geographic location. The higher parts which are exposed to the full force of the Atlantic gales that are blown in by the prevailing westerly and south-westerly winds, are often bleak, treeless and windswept. Any trees that are audacious enough to survive and grow are eventually stunted and contorted by the onslaught. However the climate is very temperate, with many sheltered gardens boasting sub-tropical plants. So any journey through Cornwall will display sharp contrasts, sometimes within quite short distances. As one descends into a sheltered valley majestic trees, verdant hedges and colourful gardens will replace the stone walls, open fields and threadbare hedges of the higher ground.

It wasn't long before we arrived at our first overnight stop, St. Newlyn East. This was a really comfortable B & B, where we received a warm welcome, plenty of tea and biscuits and a drying room!

Day 2 Tuesday May 16th
St. Newlyn East to Launceston
52 miles
2929 ft ascent

The new day started very much as the previous day finished. We endured rain or heavy drizzle all day and again there was heavy mist over higher ground. Once again the clock stood at 10.20 when we finally put foot to pedal. Looking at our route we doubted whether we would find a coffee and food stop before Bodmin and that proved to be the case.

Riding a tandem is such a different experience to a solo bicycle, one of the main prerequisites is that both pilot and stoker must have complete trust in each other, this applies particularly to the stoker who must accept that the guy on the front has sole control over steering and braking. The stoker must also have a keen sense of balance because manoeuvring especially at low speed will be unpredictable and potentially dangerous if the stoker's weight suddenly shifts or is anything but positioned 'dead centre'. The first day's ride had gone well and I think we both relaxed a bit thereafter and really enjoyed cycling together.

Conversing with one another was generally quite satisfactory even with my rather challenged hearing. I had noticed though since becoming a card holding stoker, that during a conversation a pilot would slightly turn their head, whereas when a remark or observation, "look at that …. over there," was spoken, there would often be no turn of the head; the words were thus propelled forward and very often escaped on the wind before I had been able to listen to them, of course traffic noise and wind often impaired things somewhat.

The ride to Bodmin was rather a curate's egg, there were sections of beautiful countryside, even in the rain, and other parts that were bleak and cheerless. We witnessed a rather strange and amusing incident during the morning; Peter was looking for a right turn so we had stopped opposite a T junction and while he checked the mapping I could see a horse box type of lorry approaching us along the side road. As it slowed down at the junction a cat emerged on to the offside of the roof just above the cab and when the lorry had almost stopped it launched itself down to the verge, a good 3 metre jump and then ran off at high speed in front of the lorry as it turned right in front of us. Peter had seen that we needed the next right turn so we pedalled off after the cat and the lorry. I was rather concerned for the long term prospect for the cat. Happily cat and owner were quickly reunited. A few minutes later as we approached our right turn we saw ahead the lorry parked at the junction, the driver, and we presumed, the cat's owner stood in the road clutching the wayward flying feline. We rode off happy that the cat had successfully negotiated another of its 9 lives

We arrived in Bodmin around midday and through a slight navigational misunderstanding between Peter and I, found ourselves down by Bodmin Jail near the access point to The Camel Trail cycleway. We were anxious to assuage our need for a drink and food and with my limited knowledge of Bodmin thought the best chance to find a suitable establishment would be in the town centre. However I had not been clear enough in my directions resulting in us being some way from the centre and standing in front of the old prison. Having posed for a selfie or two we carried on to pick up the northerly section of the Trail and were encouraged to see a signboard advertising a cafe on the cycle way. We headed north in search of it, then finding nothing turned and headed south till we got back to where we had started. There followed a farcical fifteen minutes during which time we performed, rather neatly I must add, two 180 turns, cycling down the drive of a private house and going round in a circle - again. In the end we gave up on trying to find the elusive cafe, which subsequently we discovered to be about 6 miles away at the northerly end of the Trail, and cycled back towards town to find a good pub for an early lunch.

The 'upper' section of the Camel Trail is superb and I think more picturesque than the section down to Wadebridge. It runs for about 6 miles along the east bank of the R. Camel through a beautiful wooded valley: the old railway line contouring along high enough above the river to provide grand views in all directions. Even in the rain it was wonderful, on a warm sunny early summer or spring day it would be breathtaking.

This section of old railway line was part of the Wenford Bridge to Fowey line which in turn connected with the Bodmin to Wadebridge line at Wenford. It then continued through Bodmin General, Bodmin Road (now Bodmin Parkway) and then down to Fowey. This long forgotten line was part of a very extensive network of mineral and passenger lines throughout central and east Cornwall in the 19th century. China clay and slate were the principle materials to be transported on these lines. Now in the 21st century Sustrans the new pioneer of pastoral bicycle byways have extended the trail from Wenford Bridge on through the lanes to the outskirts of Camelford as part of National Cycle Route 3.

We left NCR 3 east of Camelford and headed for higher ground, this of course being Bodmin Moor, not particularly pretty at the best of times let alone on a day of rain and heavy mist over high ground. Unfortunately this was the only viable option we had to reach Launceston, the alternative was the A395, not a road to be cycled out of choice as it takes a great deal of heavy traffic and cars from the A30 to the north coast. . The day had been cold and wet and as we gained height the visibility deteriorated and the temperature dropped. On several occasions we passed the ghostly outlines of wind turbines eerily chomping at the mist. There was an unnerving and then amusing incident as we wound through the lanes on the climb up to the moor. We were cycling up a steepish lane and we heard behind us the sound of a heavy vehicle following us up the hill. I kept looking over my shoulder but saw nothing. The lane was narrow and winding and we did not really want to lose momentum so we kept going. The sound got louder but still I could see nothing through the mist. 'Very odd' we thought as we judged from the the noise that it was very close. We reached the top of the hill and the noise was fading; then it dawned on us that the vehicle must have been in the field the other side of the high Cornish bank.

I had known for many years that there was an airfield at Davidstow but I had no idea of its history. We pedalled along in the mist and drizzle. It was cold, the elevation here being just 1000ft. The road was straight, running between stands of conifers. After a time I realised that the road must be part of an old runway as there was evidence on both sides, of the old concrete showing through some way beyond the edge of the tarmac road. We left the conifer plantation behind and came to a cross roads where we turned right and for the first time were cycling into a strong headwind. Clearly we were now in the main part of what would have been a large airfield, we guessed that the road was built on one of the main runways. The road seemed interminable and we were getting colder! Along the whole way we could see there was an intricate network of runways and taxiways going in all directions. Eventually we turned left and were now beyond the confines of the airfield. As we lost height and the headwind, the world seemed a slightly better place.

The airfield was part of the WW2 Coastal Command system, it was built in early 1942 and came into operation by mid-1942, a truly remarkable feat, to construct many miles of runway, the hangers, offices and ancillary buildings in such a short time. It was known as RAF Davidstow Moor and remained operational till December 1945, having many different squadrons based there for varying periods, employed in a wide variety of duties: giving cover during the Normandy landings; air-sea rescue; anti submarine patrols; reconnaissance and other defensive and offensive operations. In the early 1950s it became a motor racing circuit for a short time, even running several Formula1 races, in fact the then newly formed Lotus Team had their first success here.

In view of the acute shortage of comfortable cafes we pulled up opposite a farm where some buildings and trees gave a bit of shelter from the wind and rain. An energy bar and swig of cold water is no substitute for a good cuppa and a big sticky bun, but there again beggars can't be choosers. Suitably refreshed we carried on to Pipers Pool where our route crossed the A395 and the next 6 miles or so to

Launceston were on a very pleasant minor road contouring along following the river.

On arriving in Launceston we quickly found our digs, an old town centre pub, not the best accommodation of the trip, 'adequate' probably about describes things. We were comfortable though and had a reasonable evening meal with a decent pint. The main problem was the shared bathroom and toilet as the WC cistern stubbornly refused to operate and the only way to flush was to fill the toilet brush holder with water and whoosh it down the pan.

Day 3 Wednesday May 17th
Launceston to Topsham
48.1 mile
2647ft ascent

The next morning was as wet and dreary as the previous two days so we were in no great hurry to set off. Peter had been looking at the supposedly waterproof 'phone holder and saw that the moisture seemed to be getting through the stitch holes around the acetate screen cover and seams. Peter is one of the most practical people I have encountered, always seeming able to find a solution to a problem. When I was fully sighted I used to pride myself on my ability to solve practical challenges, but I belonged to the 'Jack of all trades, master of none' brigade, whereas Peter is one of those gifted people who can, without the aid of precision equipment, make precision objects, whether it be a wooden flageolet or a complex shaped piece of wood to repair a rotten area on a wooden spar on a boat. He announced at breakfast that before we set off he would go out and buy a tube of super glue, which he thought if applied strategically to the offending holes in the 'phone holder, would improve its moisture resistance. Subsequent careful application to all the stitch holes he could find did indeed improve the situation. Although he had to admit that the whole exercise was governed by the 'silk purse, pig's ear' factor.

Once again it was well after 10.00am when we left Launceston, in heavier rain than we had been subjected to at the beginning of the previous two days. We dutifully posed for pictures on the town bridge over the R. Tamar which is the boundary between Devon and Cornwall and soon we were climbing. The route Peter had planned was basically following the old A30 which for most of the way to Exeter is fairly quiet and clear of too much heavy traffic. The river bridge is at an altitude of about 260ft so in the 18 miles or so to the high point above Okehampton the gain in altitude is about 900ft, nothing like the climbing we would encounter further up country but nevertheless it did mean two hours of steady climbing.

The weather seemed colder than ever and by the time we reached Bridestowe on the northwest edge of Dartmoor we were both pretty cold. We stopped at a bus shelter and we both donned an extra layer, then headed for Sourton to pick up The Granite Way cycle path which would take us to the cafe at Okehampton station. We pinned our hopes on the cafe being open, if not the only option would be to go down to the town, thus losing about 400ft of altitude most of which would have to be reclaimed on the climb out of town. The approach to the station from the west is pretty impressive even in the rain. Having left the open moor the track passes through quite a sheltered section of deciduous woodland then all of a sudden on to the Meldon viaduct adjacent to the now disused quarry which affords views in all directions, especially down. To our great delight the cafe was open and the heating was on!

The Granite Way is part of the Sustrans network, NCR 27, and has received many plaudits for being such a picturesque and spectacular cycle path. It runs for about 11 miles from Okehampton station to Lydford, mostly along a disused railway line. Its elevated route around the north-west edge of Dartmoor affords grand views of the nearby moor and distant views to the north and west. It crosses two viaducts at Meldon and Lake which further adds to its dramatic credentials. The railway line was part of the alternative route from Exeter to Plymouth. In the railway boom of the mid 19th century a group of small independent railway companies were consolidated into the London and South-Western Railways in an attempt to compete with the Great Western Railways south coast route. The first trains of the LSWR reached Plymouth in 1876. The central section of the line was closed in 1968.

Several pots of tea and pieces of cake later, not to mention the increase in our core temperatures, we left the comfort of the cafe and were delighted to find that the rain had almost stopped and the world looked a brighter and more pleasant place than it had for the last three days.

By the time we had made our way through to the old A30 about 2 miles east of Okehampton the rain had stopped and views south to Dartmoor were opening up.

The old A30 really is a cyclist's delight especially travelling from Okehampton to Exeter as there is a net loss of about 500ft. of altitude. The road is wide, well surfaced and relatively clear of heavy traffic. There are several high sections affording magnificent views in all directions, notably south to the hills of Dartmoor and north when on a good day Exmoor can be seen. The road passes through a string of villages most of which are situated on the tops of hills. Nearing Exeter there are three superb descents on leaving the villages of Crockernwell, Cheriton Bishop and Tedburn St Mary. There are climbs before each village but it always seems to me that heading east the ups are less than the downs. After the descent from Tedburn St. Mary there is another short uphill but then a long downhill followed by a fast level run that covers the 6 miles or so to the edge of Exeter in 15 to 20 minutes.

Our third night was to be spent at home in Topsham. Just after 5.00pm Peter and I cycled up the path to be met by Ali and Ian, who an hour earlier had arrived having cycled down from SW of Bristol in even worse conditions than Peter and I had endured. His work shift pattern meant with three days off he could get in some cycle miles before his turn as pilot in about three weeks. He planned to cycle back with us the next day and then on the Friday lead us round the north end of Bristol and over the Avon bridge. Ian volunteered to wash The Beast while Peter and I got ourselves sorted, three days of rain and muddy roads had left the tandem in a filthy state. It was during the wash and brush up that he found a broken spoke in the rear wheel. This came as a real shock, although we knew that two adults and about 20kgs of baggage put a lot of strain on the rear wheel, but we had understood from Thorn that suitably strong wheels had been specified. Fortunately the next day on our way to Ian's home where we were to spend the next night, we could easily divert to Bridgwater in order to get a new spoke fitted at Thorn's workshop. This would add 5 or 6 miles on to an already long day but at least it would resolve the problem of the wheel. There was nothing more to be done now other than enjoy a splendid meal and relax for a few hours. I did find things a bit disconcerting - to have left Ali at Cape Cornwall three days ago now back with her for a short time then another goodbye this time for over two weeks.

Day 4 Thursday May 18th
Topsham to Churchill
78.1 miles
2496ft ascent

The day dawned fair, the forecast was good so we really felt the bad weather was behind us for the moment. We were on the road before 9.00am, Peter and I with Ian accompanying us. We stopped about 20 minutes later to call Thorn, as we hoped they readily agreed to sort out the broken spoke while we waited. In spite of the sunshine and knowledge that the wheel would be repaired I felt really out of sorts on the ride up to Bridgwater, a combination of the second goodbye, disappointment over the wheel failure and the long day ahead all conspired to cast a shadow over the first part of the ride.

The one thing that I believe contributes most to an enjoyable cycle ride is being able to plot a good route, one that avoids as much as is possible busy roads and offers the rewards of splendid views. Of course the other factor is a cafe renowned for its selection of cakes, about two hours in, which really gives a ride gold star status. Heading into Somerset from East Devon the only realistic option to achieve this is over The Blackdown Hills, that big range of hills that lie to the east of the M5 and extend from near Honiton in the south to a few miles S.E. of Taunton in the north. They stand at about 800 - 900feet so any route across will involve a steep climb and working on the basis of what goes up must come down, a steep descent as well. The route we took failed dismally on the cafe front but scores very highly with regard to the other parameters. Our route took us through the wonderful lanes and back roads of East Devon towards Payhembury where the real climb starts up to Hembury Fort, an Iron Age hill fort standing at about 900 feet. Just in the last stage of the climb before crossing the A373 there is a steeper section, marked on O.S. with a black arrow (denotes gradient between 14% and 20%) and I do admit here that for the only time in the entire trip we ran out of steam, however a brief stop of about 2 minutes gave us enough puff to complete the climb. The top of the Blackdowns is an undulating plateau fairly devoid of trees and exposed to the elements. On this occasion there was very little wind so we had a comfortable ride, enjoying the knowledge that although we were barely halfway, there were only a few short climbs left to do that day and looking forward the following 3 days would be the least hilly of the trip.

It was while Peter and I were rolling along, Ian was some way ahead, that we were hailed by a lady cyclist coming from the opposite direction. It was Liz, a cyclist friend from Wellington, a week or so earlier while talking to Bob, her husband, I mentioned that we would be cycling that way on Thursday 18th. Being at a loose end and needing to go to Cullompton anyway, she decided to go the pretty way on the off chance of meeting us. It was good to see her and after a few minutes chat we went our respective ways, she resuming her rather convoluted route to Cullompton. The descent down on to the Somerset Levels has two sections where we could really give The Beast her head, top speed recorded that day was 42 mph. On one of the descents Ian watched us go by and said later it was quite an awe inspiring sight and even slightly frightening, although I would add that later in the trip when he was 'at the helm' he tried in vain to beat Adrian and my 49mph achieved somewhere in N Yorkshire.

Having descended to the lowlands we picked up the cycle way along the Taunton - Bridgwater canal. This should be a fairly uneventful part of the ride apart from the excitement of negotiating several gateways on the edge of the bank. Peter misjudged things somewhat on one occasion catching my handlebars badly on the upright. We came to a shuddering wobbly halt lurching uncontrollably towards the water, I lunged for the upright, it creaked alarmingly and surprisingly it held us; it was in pretty poor shape and was unlikely to withstand too much more abuse from wanton cyclists. Then there were the 6 occasions where the towpath passes under a road bridge. The towpath is quite narrow and kinks alarmingly as it passes underneath bridges. So any slight misjudgement by the pilot could result in the stoker - me - catching a shoulder on the arch and pitching us into the water. We did cycle the first two but then discretion became the better part of valour and we dismounted for the subsequent challenges. We arrived without mishap at Thorn Cycles just after 2.00pm. The repair was made within about 40 minutes, enough time for Ian and Peter to find a cafe just up the road, they returned with tea and doughnuts which were most welcome.

Fortunately when the mechanic appeared with the wheel, we had the presence of mind to ask if he could let us have some spares. He gave us 8 and little did we know then how necessary they would be.

We set off in good heart, much relieved that the repair was straightforward. We had been worried that riding 50 miles with a broken spoke could have caused the wheel to go seriously out of true, which would have then needed a lot more work to rectify.

We were now on Ian's home territory, although the Somerset Levels are a joy to cycle there are so many rivers , waterways and channels that any route is governed by crossing points and a close inspection of the next 20 miles does convey that fact very well. Near Cossington we had a lovely encounter with 200 Friesian cows and a farmer's wife. Cycling along a very pretty quiet lane we found our way blocked by a smiley lady and a line of cows coming towards us on their way to the milking parlour. They were persuaded into the farmyard then up an inclined path, which ran parallel to the road, into the milking shed. We chatted to the farmer's wife and generally enjoyed the antics of the cows as they dillied and dallied on their way. The weather had been perfect all day, not too hot, good visibility and only a breeze to cool us, such a joy after the trials of the previous days.

We arrived at Ian's house to be greeted by his wife, Ruth, copious quantities of tea and cake were consumed before washing down the bikes, owing to the previous day's rain the canal towpath had deposited a considerable amount of itself over the bikes and panniers. For the second time we enjoyed the home cooking and relaxed evening before a well-earned comfortable night's sleep.

Day 5 Friday May 19th
Churchill to Olveston
34 miles
799ft ascent

Another beautiful day, warm and sunny, it certainly felt that the weather had forgotten the grudge it bore us at the start of the week. After breakfast we pottered around doing a few little jobs on the tandem. The plan was that Ian would cycle the first 25 miles or so with us, which would take us round the north end of Bristol then over the Avon bridge, he would then peel off and return home, ready for the reality of early shift at work the following day.

We left about 11.00am and soon picked up the cycle path to Yatton Station. This is part of the Strawberry Line Cycleway that runs from Yatton to Cheddar, and is mainly along the route of the former railway line. In 1869 a branch line was opened, running from Cheddar to join the GWR mainline at Yatton. For nearly 100 years this enabled the many strawberry growers situated in the villages on the southern edge of the Mendip Hills to transport their fruit quickly to markets in London and the North. In recent years Sustrans have incorporated this cycle path into NCR 25.

Leaving the Strawberry Line at Yatton we headed north towards Clevedon and our first crossing of the M5 that day. The cycling was easy, so good just enjoying the warm weather and pleasant views. Our route took us north and east through the narrow belt of rural countryside that lies between the Severn estuary the M5 and the north side of Bristol. We were never far away from the motorway. By the elevated section we were down below cycling along really quiet roads past secluded houses with beautiful gardens. It was odd to realise that the centre of Bristol was only 6 or 7 miles away to the S.E.. We crossed the M5 again and passed round Easton in Gordano before turning back towards the motorway. All of a sudden we popped out on to the cycle way that took us over the R. Avon on the side of the M5 bridge. Having driven over the bridge so many times it felt very odd cycling across just a yard or two from 8 lanes of rushing traffic.

In a short while we arrived at Blaise Hamlet, Ian's planned lunch stop, the cafe in a local park. We enjoyed a leisurely lunch sitting out in the sunshine, Ian then bade us farewell, and set off on his return journey to Churchill. Peter and I stayed on for another hour or more, whiling away the time with smalltalk, tea and ice cream. After four days of cycling it was such a luxury just sitting in peaceful surroundings soaking up the warmth. Some time after 3.00pm we set off on the 8 or 9 mile ride to find our next B & B. This was in a farmhouse near Olveston and very comfortable it was too, situated about a mile from the village pub where we rounded off a grand day with a couple of beers and a good meal.

Day 6 Saturday May 20th
Olveston to Cheltenham
43 miles
693ft ascent

The warm sunshine of day 5 was replaced by high cloud cover and a decidedly chilly temperature. The cycling was easy, we wound our way along quiet roads, through a succession of charming villages, taking a route that roughly followed the Severn estuary north-eastwards, reaching Purton by mid morning. The village is situated at the lower end of the Gloucester canal near the point where the canal runs along the S.E. bank of the R. Severn before joining it at Sharpness. This lower section became more vulnerable to erosion at the beginning of the 20th century as a new channel was naturally forming closer in to the shore. In order to reinforce the bank between the estuary and the canal, old barges and similar vessels were towed by tugs from the canal on high spring tides and beached on this narrow strip of land. Holes were then knocked in the bottoms of the hulks, this allowed the deposition of silt inside which further stabilised them. The first barges were beached in 1909 and the practice continued until the early 1970's, indeed so successful was it that the level of this section of bank was raised to such an extent that in places hulks are lying two deep. This practice was not confined to wooden boats, there are a number of both concrete and steel vessels to be seen in this strange graveyard. We did not explore the full extent of the site, as it continues for some distance. It must be a pretty unique place in the respect of unintentionally becoming a museum of 19th and 20th century barges. The whole area is strewn with relics, some have plaques adjacent which give details of the vessels, in other places just a few ribs or sections of hulls protrude from the ground.

Peter and I parked up the tandem and wandered along the river bank, it really is a most unusual place. The wind was very chilling and had a damp feel about it. We spent about half an hour exploring the river bank and would have happily spent longer but the weather dictated otherwise. Looking downstream we could see a big squall heading our way, the whole width of the estuary obliterated by a curtain of rain. We decided that retreat was the prudent option and managed to reach the warmth and shelter of a cafe before we had got too wet.

Suitably refreshed we set off again and followed the cycle path along the canal towpath all the way into Gloucester Dock. The rain had cleared through but the weather remained cheerless and chilly. This section of cycle path is poorly surfaced and there were quite a number of badly designed cycle unfriendly gates to negotiate. These gates are situated at points where roads cross the canal. Most of these gates or barriers were locked in order to restrict access to the canal side. Clearly this needs to be the case, but it seemed to us that a little more consideration for cycle users would not have come amiss. Most of the cycle gates were in the form of a 'holding' area at the canal end of the main barrier, with entry and exit gates. To negotiate this barrier the cycle is pushed through the first gate into a small fenced compartment, turned 180 degrees to then exit via the second gate. We managed several with there being just enough room to turn the tandem, we then came to one which was slightly smaller, our only recourse was to remove all the bags then lift it over. We were so cross that we positioned the tandem to demonstrate the predicament and were about to take photos which we could then send to Sustrans together with our thoughts on the gate design, when a man appeared brandishing a set of keys. He unlocked the main road gate saying he didn't want anybody complaining. We were glad of his intervention but did feel justified in our irritation because we saw no sign indicating there was a key holder nearby and what would happen when he was off duty?

Subsequently during the rest of the trip we encountered several impossible obstructions on cycleways and a great deal of poor signing while following Sustrans National Cycle Network routes. Sustrans have carried out wonderful work in setting up the local and National networks and do admit that more needs to be done with regard to the matters of gates and signage. However they do have to work with other agencies and it is unfortunate that they sometimes get the blame for issues over which they have no control.

Gloucester Dock is a fascinating place and we really enjoyed an hour or so wandering around. Peter was absolutely in his element being a sailor and very familiar with traditional sailing vessels. One of the first sights is the lightship SULA moored alongside the towpath. Until her de-commissioning in 1985 she was stationed at Spurn Head in the mouth of the River Humber. As we moved around past piles of spars, rusting winches and all sorts of marine paraphernalia, every now and then Peter excitedly exclaimed, having identified some unusual item and then proceeded to explain its function. On the quayside near the workshops of a marine engineering company were two piles of assorted spars and masts, some of truly majestic proportions. One in particular caught our attention and on enquiring were told that it was the topmast of HMS Victory.

We expected that the run through to Cheltenham would be straightforward as a cycle path goes into the town centre. Reality was different, in places difficult to follow its rather convoluted course. To make matters worse we were running very low on power for the iPhone. We didn't manage that as well as we should and the phone died on the outskirts of Cheltenham, this made life very difficult for Peter, trying to find the hotel, hidden within the one-way system.

Peter waited while I found the bike a resting place in the underground car park and checked into my room. That was the end of Peter's piloting responsibilities and I walked with him to the railway station. It had been a grand 6 days and I am so grateful to him for getting the adventure off to an excellent start.

....

The train pulled out of Cheltenham station and I was alone, in a sort of limbo until Adrian arrived the next day.
I had noticed a small fish and chip restaurant quite near to the station and a further inspection proved to be encouraging so I ventured in. I enjoyed a really good meal of cod, chips, mushy peas and a pot of tea. It was odd being on my own but I spent the evening washing some kit then tackling the Facebook blog and my other records that I was keeping of the trip.

Day 7 Sunday May 21st
Cheltenham to Worcester
29 miles
433ft ascent

Breakfast was quite a challenge! As in a lot of the chain hotels it is a do-it-yourself meal. Everything is there - cereal, milk, all the constituents of an English breakfast, bread, a toaster, jam and marmalade, all types of tea and coffee, cutlery, hot water plus of course a pressing throng of people who can all see exactly where things are and if not can read signs in an instant, they take no prisoners in the quest for early morning sustenance. There is also an ad hoc seating system which just involves staking a claim on any vacant seat. To aid the process and help it to run smoothly there are a couple of staff constantly refilling empty dishes, tidying up used cups and plates and facilitating the removal of crumbs and sticky finger marks. Eventually with some help I equipped myself with tea, toast, knife, fork, food, and somewhere to sit. Having drunk my first cup of tea and eaten my scrambled egg with trimmings I left my defenceless plate of toast in order to replenish my teacup. When I returned to my table I found that my plate of toast plus marmalade had been removed by an over zealous tidy upper. To further complicate the situation my table had been taken over by a family of three. I re-toasted and re-seated myself. A few minutes later, on a quest for more toast I kept the tidy uppers under close scrutiny lest the same fate should befall my unprotected teacup.

Adrian was not due to arrive until gone 1.00pm so having vacated my room and left my bags with Reception I ventured forth to see what delights Cheltenham town had to offer. It was a lovely warm sunny spring morning and having wandered around for half an hour or so I found a pleasant little park. I found a shady seat and spent a couple of hours people watching and dozing in the somnolent warmth.

I walked down to the station to meet Adrian. The train pulled in on time, I waited at the barrier scanning the people, size, shapes, emerging from the gloom of the station foyer. To my great relief a tall yellow shape approached, morphing into the reassuringly authoritative figure of Adrian.

This was the start of the second part of my big adventure. We walked up into town and lunched in a Wetherspoons pub. We sorted out The Beast, fitted Adrian's cleat pedals and set the saddle height. It was just after 3.00pm when we pedalled off in the warm afternoon sunshine. Adrian mastered the mysteries of the View Ranger navigation system and we easily found our way out of Cheltenham. We were soon riding through the gentle countryside on quiet roads. Although not really The Cotswolds it still had the feel of being 'the garden of England'. We knew that this section to Worcester was the last part of the respite from hills that I had enjoyed since crossing the Somerset Levels.

An hour later we entered Tewkesbury to the sound of the Abbey bells. We rode into the Abbey grounds thinking there may be a reception committee waiting for us but alas no! The ringing, to my inexpert ears, seemed extremely precise and impressive. I expect that campanologists would be prepared to pull lots of strings to get the opportunity to ring in an Abbey of that standing.

We continued our leisurely way to Worcester passing very close to Upton upon Severn. This place has particular significance to many morris dancers, it being the home of a stick dance, imaginatively named The Upton upon Severn Stick Dance. Both Adrian and I list morris dancing among our hobbies but we resisted the temptation to divert into the town in order to cut a caper and carried on our way.

We arrived at our Worcester accommodation around 6.00pm. Ye Olde Talbot Hotel proved to be very comfortable and the management were gracious enough to grant The Beast a room of its own. Before our evening meal we walked along the river and found the old canal basin, now a very up market housing development. On our way along the riverside Severn Way we passed the Michael Baker Boathouse of Kings School, an impressive award winning design building overlooking the river.

Day 8 Monday May 22nd
Worcester to Shrewsbury
56 miles
3338ft ascent

Another fine sunny warm day. We breakfasted well and were all set for a prompt start when we were brought down to earth by the discovery of another broken spoke as Adrian wheeled The Beast out from its private room. Our tool kit did not include a spoke key but fortune smiled on us, there was a cycle shop next door to our accommodation. Adrian was able to replace it without having to remove the wheel. However he realised a few hours later as we found broken spoke number 3, that we should have spent more time checking the wheel. We set off in ideal cycling conditions. Our route took us along quite minor roads through England's rural idyll. For the first couple of hours we rode on gently undulating roads but as the morning progressed undulations became hills.

Today's ride clearly demonstrated the success of the decision we took at a very early stage of planning, that each pilot would plan his own route. We were all of one mind that main roads would be avoided at all cost and while maybe not to plan for gratuitous climbing we would not shy from using hilly routes if that fulfilled the main criteria. Having left Worcester we took to minor B roads and did not touch an A road until we were at the outskirts of Shrewsbury. A wonderful journey through or past villages that could have graced any of John Betjeman's poems Lower Broadheath, Kenswick, Great Witley, Stottesdon, Neenton, Middleton Prior and so on.

Of course the reality of this rural ramble was that none of these villages boasted a cafe so by lunchtime we were hoping to find a pub. At Stottesdon we found one but it was closed Monday lunchtimes, however there was a community shop at the rear where we were able to buy filled rolls, crisps and sausage rolls. We encamped in the pub garden and enjoyed lunch in the sunshine. Before we set off again Adrian checked the rear wheel and to his dismay found another spoke had given up the ghost. This time we turned The Beast upside down and he spent about half an hour rotating the wheel back and forth, tensioning spokes here and there in an endeavour to true the wayward wheel.

In due course we continued with our yellow road ride, much like the morning quiet roads winding through rural Shropshire. We passed to the west of Bridgnorth and likewise resisting the lure of Telford we left it alone a few miles to the east. At Monkhopton we had to endure a few hundred yards of main road in the form of the B4378 before turning left on to another yellow road that would take us over Wenlock Edge and then on for a few miles to Shrewsbury.

Adrian was keen to find a cycle shop as his lunchtime spoke tinkering had revealed the deficiencies, quality wise, of the spoke key we had purchased in Worcester. The wonders of the internet and smart phones! Just a couple of minutes was all that was needed to provide the necessary information backed up by Mr. Google telling us how we could find them. By 5.00pm Adrian had acquired a top of the range spoke key and we were sorting ourselves out at The Bull Inn

Day 9 Tuesday May 23rd
Shrewsbury to Buxton
72 miles
3941ft ascent

A big day and thankfully free of wheel traumas. We made a relatively early start, getting on the road by 8.40am. Under grey skies but with the prospect of sunny weather later we made good progress in the cool of the morning. We knew we were in for a hard day and a lot of climbing, with the hills being unevenly distributed to the second half of the day. Rural Shropshire shows many similar features to the more southerly counties of Worcestershire and Gloucestershire. Mixed farming with fields bounded by hedgerows, colourful gardens, beautiful displays of laburnum and horse chestnut both in full flower and many majestic weeping willow trees. All this was about to change as we cycled further east and north. By mid-afternoon it would be quite different.

The problem of the breaking spokes had undoubtedly cast a bit of a shadow over the last few days. The question remained of how we could resolve the issue. In some ways we were lucky that it was happening on Adrian's 'watch' because he is a very able wheel builder. If the problem persisted there would be two major issues. Firstly both Mark and Ian, my pilots 3 and 4 were good basic cycle mechanics but neither would be confident enough to replace spokes and true the wheel, secondly the further north we went the more remote our situation, making the possibility of outside help much more difficult. Somehow we had to try and get the matter sorted before we left Settle in four days' time. To this end we had decided to 'phone Thorn to put the ball in their court as it seemed very likely that the problem stemmed from either poor wheel construction or the quality of the spokes.

Around mid-morning we arrived in Newport and found a suitable place to park up and have a breather. We took this opportunity to call Thorn and after a lengthy discussion they agreed to send a complete set of new spokes to the address of Adrian's friends in Settle, where we were due to stay Thursday and Friday nights. This would allow Adrian and Clive to rebuild the wheel using the new set of spokes. Thorn did admit that they suspected a quality issue with a batch of spokes they were using in 2016 at the time I purchased The Beast.

We continued on our way, by now the sun was shining and we were heading for The Potteries. I had wrongly visualised that this section of the ride would entail a good deal of urban riding as we found our way through quite an industrialised area. I was wrong, we passed through the small town of Eccleshall and on to Stone where we had an early lunch at a pub by a lock on the Trent-Mersey canal. We sat in the sunshine eating a good lunch while watching the barges as they rose and fell. Because our table was lower than the lock side it appeared as though the barges were ascending from or descending to the bowels of the earth.

Just a couple of miles before Stone we passed over, on a series of bridges, a complicated railway junction which is where a main line from the south splits with lines going on to Crewe and Stoke-on-Trent. Not only that but also within this area of no more than 800yds by 800yds two fairly significant roads cross by means of two roundabouts and amidst all this is the confluence of two rivers. Within such a small area is a cats' cradle of road, rail and water all tidily sorted by a triumph of civil engineering.

Suitably refreshed by a good lunch we carried on heading N.E. and after about 4 or 5 miles passed through Blythe Bridge which is a satellite town now all part of Stoke-on-Trent. We were now on course for Leek and The Peak District. We had passed through the Potteries without so much as a sniff of fired clay, so much for my pre-conception that the Potteries are a vast wasteland of fumes, dust and degradation. Undulations were now just a distant memory as our route lead us literally up hill and down dale. It was round about here that we began to notice that stone walls were replacing hedges and by the time we reached Leek there was no doubting that we were now in the north country. At Cheddleton, to the south of Leek, we dropped steeply down to cross the R. Churnet then more ups and downs through Cheddleton Heath and up into Leek, where we found a grand little teashop right in the centre. Even though it was well after 4.00pm and the staff were clearly winding down prior to closing, they very willingly plied us with copious quantities of tea and cake.

The Peak District boundary is only 3 miles or so from Leek and the transition is startling, giving a clear indication of what is to come. Even before entering the national park there is a climb from Leek of over 700ft through Thorncliffe. There is a view point more or less on the boundary affording magnificent views to the north and west at what will prove to be one of the highest points in the whole ride of over 1500ft. We stopped at the view point to enjoy the moment, not only powering The Beast up a pretty challenging hill but with a grand view in the late afternoon sunshine. We still had another 15 miles or so to Buxton and a lot of climbing, the road crossed a large expanse of high moorland varying in height from about 1200ft to the high point just north of Dove Head which weighs in at about 1600ft. Although this was an hour and a quarter of really hard cycling, coming as it did after we had already covered about 60 miles, it was hugely enjoyable with terrific views, exhilarating high speed descents and leg straining climbs. We had the last glorious descent into Buxton and easily found our digs, a very comfortable little guest house on the edge of the Pavilion Gardens which looked absolutely superb in the evening sunshine.

After showering and another cup of tea we stretched our legs with a walk through the town. Then back via the opera house and gardens, stopping en route for a pub dinner and a well earned beer.

Day 10 Wednesday May 24th
Buxton to Holmfirth
39 miles
3460 ft ascent

Although this was an easier day in respect of miles covered it was a considerably harder day when considering feet climbed per mile, after all we were cycling across the heart of the Peak District.

It was with relief that a post breakfast check of the rear wheel revealed no more problems. Once again the forecast was good but early morning mist and cloud were slow to lift. We made a fairly prompt start and pedalled up out of Buxton by 9.00am. Our route took us north-east over the high moorland passing to the south-east of Chapel-en-le-Frith. We made good progress and by 10.15 were approaching Castleton from the west. The final descent past the Blue John Cavern certainly cleared any remaining cobwebs showing a speed of 45 mph on the hill which registers a double black arrow (steeper than 1 in 5). Moments later we free wheeled into the village to join the tourists, parked up and went in search of a cup of coffee.

There were two pressing matters to be addressed before we resumed our journey. Firstly and most importantly Adrian needed to buy a postcard for Sam his young son who looked forward to a daily update from Dad. Secondly as we were unsure whether we would be able to find somewhere for lunch we had decided to play safe and buy suitable comestibles while we had the opportunity. While we enjoyed the delights of Castleton the clouds dispersed and having successfully made our purchases we set off in warm sunshine under a cloudless sky. The next 5 miles or so were easy going, gently down to Hope and Brough along the valley of the River Noe. Just beyond Brough we turned left and headed north up the Derwent valley. All of a sudden we rounded a corner and what a spectacular view presented itself! We found ourselves on the approach to the dam of the Ladybower Reservoir. This was built between 1935 and 1943. Finally being opened by King George V1 on 25th September 1945. It is a Y shaped lake and the lowest in a line of three reservoirs situated within the narrow confines of the Upper Derwent Valley. The River Ashop flows into the western arm of the reservoir while the River Derwent feeds into the northern arm, after having first flowed through the Howden Reservoir then the Derwent Reservoir. The views from the footpath-cycleway across the dam are wonderful, to the south long views over rural Derbyshire, while looking east, west and north the lake and high moors above the Upper Derwent Valley. This lake is a clear reminder of the contrasting pressures that confront this area. Located in the moors it provides water to quench the thirst of East Midlands industry and residents. The moors, which are the remnants of a remote and wild region, are now preserved and protected and will hopefully withstand the strains put upon them by 21st century life. Within relatively short distances in any direction, lie many towns and cities forming the industrial heartland of England.

We continued on our way with a stiff climb away from the reservoir up on to the moors again. We had no option but to follow the A57 for a few miles until we could take a left turn on to a minor road that took us over Strines Moor then past two small reservoirs, Strines and Dale Dike. We found a suitably shaded verge with grand views to the south and decided to stop for lunch. Just to prove that there will always be downs to accompany the ups, both cycling wise and fortune wise, it was now that Adrian discovered broken spoke no. 4. My immediate reaction was "Oh no, not again!" Adrian was not at all phased, I suspect his thoughts were along the line of "well it's a sunny afternoon, we are in no great rush, there's a good view and somewhere comfortable to sit and tinker with the wheel, so let's just enjoy it."

Adrian spent over an hour sat turning the wheel back and forth, tensioning here slackening there as he worked to true the wheel. He finally announced that he thought it was as true as he could hope to get it under the circumstances. The issue that had concerned him all along was that a permanent kink in the rim could have occurred early in the ride. As Peter and I had no cause to check, the first spoke could have broken at anytime during the first three days. So it was possible that we had ridden for some distance before its replacement at Bridgwater on the fourth day.

Back on the road again we rode along quiet roads that skirted round the area of high moor to the east of the Upper Derwent Valley that rises to over 1600 ft. There were several steep climbs and descents as the road went from high exposed moor plunging down into sheltered wooded valleys. Altogether a great ride and as Day 9 all the effort of the climbs was continually rewarded by stunning views and speedy descents. One of the features that had been so prevalent over the last few days was the incidence of beautiful buttercup meadows. Most of the small fields seemed to be down to pasture and were a mass of yellow. The conjunction of the grey stone walls and the buttercup yellow fields was indeed memorable.

We came across three more little reservoirs and just beyond the last, Langsett Reservoir we had no choice but to join the A616 for about three miles. This was not a pleasant experience, with the volume of heavy vehicles, which while not being outright hostile to us were clearly reluctant to give us anything but the minimum of room. There was a certain black humour knowing that this was the point where we left the Peak District. After crossing the River Don we had a short climb and then escaped the vehicular maelstrom, turning left on to the friendly little B6106. A last leg straining climb - infinitely preferable to the traffic - and then a final high speed descent into Holmfirth. Then a slightly anti-climactic realisation that our digs were half a mile up a steep hill from the town centre. As this was to be the road out the following morning we did not really mind, after all what is another climb between friends?

I had booked all the accommodation in January and February. All the pubs, guest houses, hotels, hostels and B & B's had been found through the internet, but of course the internet does not always tell the whole story! When I booked by 'phone the Holmfirth stopover, the lady told me she just had two single rooms. I replied that was fine and she quoted me £60 a night one room being £35 and as the other was smaller it was £25. I suspected nothing. The house was a fairly new semi-detached house in an 'elevated position' overlooking the edge of town and the moor beyond. The lady of the house was kindly but a little eccentric. Having stabled The Beast Adrian joined me in the kitchen where tea, cake and biscuits were being laid out on the table. Some time later having indebted ourselves to her by consuming all the refreshments she led us upstairs to our rooms. She opened the first door announcing this was the larger room, I said to Adrian he should have that one. The second door was then opened revealing what even in many estate agents parlance would have been referred to as 'a walk in cupboard'. Furnished with a 2ft 6ins divan bed with a miniscule bedside cupboard. Circulation space was 18 inches along the side and 12 inches or so at the foot. We had to see the funny side of it! Everything was very clean and tidy and she did prepare a grand breakfast for us the next morning.

Our hostess had recommended an Indian restaurant, we took her advice and enjoyed a superb meal. As far as I was concerned, not being a great connoisseur the best Indian meal I had eaten. Both of us felt a bit stiff legged as we walked back up the steep hill to our hobbit rooms.

Day 11 Thursday May 25th
Holmfirth to Settle
55 miles
4998 ft ascent

We had thought Day 9 was a big day! This was our first real encounter with urban riding and there is a certain irony in the fact that in spite of our encounters with the Scottish Highlands later in the trip, in terms of hill climbing Day 11 would take all the prizes. Many of the challenging ascents and descents were within urban areas. We collected a veritable quiver full of black arrows, modesty forbids stating how many. There is no doubt that if the O.S. were as keen to mark urban hills as they are to mark rural hills we would have acquired even more in our virtual quiver.

Not only was this the hardest day but it also turned out to be the hottest! Later Mark and Ian would snort with disbelief as I talked of the joys of cycling with Adrian feeling the hot sun on our backs. No morning mist this morning. We left Holmfirth just after 9.00am and straightaway into a steep long climb out of town and across the moor to Meltham Mills. From there our road took us to Slaithwaite with several ups and downs before a long descent to cross the River Colne in the town centre. What goes down must go back up again and so we did. The hard climb out of town to the north of the river brought us back up to the moorland. Much of the higher moorland is now enclosed, there are some areas of bleak exposed land but the extensive pattern of stone walls does afford some protection for the more fertile land.

More undulations before a steep off road descent on a sort of cycle path towards the M62 and Scammonden Water, a small reservoir that lies immediately to the south of the motorway. In fact the bridge carrying the road is adjacent to and on the same level as the wall of the dam along which our cycleway ran. We stopped to take photos and enjoy the view down the lake, rather odd with the never ending stream of traffic rushing by only yards away.

At the far end of the dam cycleway the path rose at an impossible gradient then a gateway cum barrier, presumably designed to discourage motorbikes. To that end though it became a major obstacle for tandems. We had to remove the panniers and bar bags then between us lift the bike over the steel defences. Our humour was not improved by the discovery that I had evidence on my shoe that this was an area favoured by dog walkers. Having crossed over the M62 we headed north through Krumlin and Barkisland, up and down more hills before reaching Sowerby Bridge. This area very clearly demonstrates the part that water played in the industrial growth during the 18th and 19th centuries. There are many towns and villages along the rivers on either side of the Pennines that grew and flourished because of the ready availability of water power. Our route turned north-west at Sowerby Bridge down the valley through Mytholmroyd to Hebden Bridge. The river valley is quite narrow and steep sided but nevertheless contains not only the river but also the Rochdale Canal, a main road and a railway line, such was the ingenuity of the 19th century civil engineers. We rolled into Sowerby Bridge about 11.30, hot and gasping for a drink. We found a pub serving coffee and were glad to sit down in the cool of the bar, alongside the early morning drinkers. On resuming our ride the first priority was to find the canal. We had anticipated that a mixture of towpath and Sustrans cycle route would soon take us the 6 miles or so to Hebden Bridge. Our overall experience of the National Cycle Routes we used during the whole trip was pretty positive. We did use them for many miles throughout England and Scotland. However this short section demonstrated many of the problems that face the maintenance of these NCRs especially in urban areas where a higher proportion of routes will be off road. This short stretch to Hebden Bridge should have only taken us about 30 minutes. Adrian had a torrid time trying to follow the cycle route which ranged from canal towpath to roads through housing estates to wooded riverside paths. Problems that all conspired to delay and frustrate us were, bad surfaces, cycle unfriendly barriers and gates, poor or non existent signage and misleading badly positioned signs.

Well over an hour later we arrived at Hebden Bridge, hot, harassed and hungry. We parked up near the main shopping centre and found a little bakery then retired to a nearby park and enjoyed a very tasty picnic lunch sitting in the cool shade under a tree. We may not have been so contented had we realised quite what was in store for us. We left the town on a busy main road for only a few hundred yards and then turned off and immediately started climbing out of the valley on a quiet road that took us through Heptonstall, a village clinging to the hillside from where it gazes down with superiority on to the town below. The narrow cobbled road through the village was lined with very attractive cottages and houses, clearly this was the desirable up market residential quarter.

We continued climbing for a while after leaving Heptonstall behind, by now we were back up to an elevation of about 900 feet. For several miles the road wound across the moors at heights of between 900 and 1200 feet, until a steep descent to cross Hebden Water then surprise, surprise another steep climb to take us past the Widdop Reservoir. As with much of the last few days we led an up and down sort of existence for the next 10 or 12 miles passing through open moorland, sheltered verdant little valleys, past working farms and smart smug looking houses with colourful gardens.

The large conurbation encompassing Burnley was not too far away to the west and in the late afternoon we descended into Colne which together with its well decorated friend Nelson, form the north-eastern arm of this large urban area. We were hot, thirsty and tired after a couple of hours hard riding. We sat in the cool bar of a town centre pub and consumed copious quantities of tea and cola. Suitably refreshed and with our water bottles refilled we set off for our next port of call - Barnoldswick. Adrian assured me that once the leafy haven of Barnoldswick was reached there would be not the merest sniff of a hill before our final destination of Settle. The 6 miles to Barnoldswick took us past two more small reservoirs up and down a few hills but already it felt that for the time being the leg straining hills were behind us. A brief pause to take on some more fluid and we were off for the last few miles of the day's ride through Bracewell, Horton, Paythorne and Wigglesworth to Settle and our next National Park - The Yorkshire Dales.

True (more or less) to Adrian's prediction this last run in down Ribble Dale was a real joy, coming after a huge day of hard climbs, breathless downhills and more black arrows than you could shake a stick at. This was the final section of Adrian's stint as pilot and what a wonderful job he had done. Five days had brought us from The Garden of England to the edge of the North Yorkshire Moors via the hills of Shropshire and The Peak District, 251 miles and 16,170 feet of ascent. Mark who was to be my next pilot had arrived at Clive and Sarah's house in Settle earlier that day. He had borrowed one of Clive's bikes and gone off for a spin. Just as Adrian and I were about half a mile from the house Mark appeared so the last stretch was accompanied by a babble of conversation with each trying to catch up with the other's news.

When we first planned the changeover details we were not quite sure of exactly when Mark would be able to get to Yorkshire or how many days would be needed for Peter's and Adrian's stints. So we played safe and allowed for a possible day off in Yorkshire. As route planning developed it became clear that we would have that day off with friends Clive and Sarah in Settle. Due to the breaking spoke saga this did give us the opportunity to sort out the wheel before continuing northwards. Adrian was confident that he could rebuild the wheel with the new spokes, these had arrived from Thorn that morning.

The next morning dawned bright and sunny, Mark set off fairly early on Clive's bike, only too keen to blow away more work cobwebs from his head. Adrian set to, dismantling the wheel in the garage which looked more like a cycle workshop with bikes and bikey bits all over the place. I found the day interminable, there was very little I could do to help Adrian yet I knew that to a certain extent the rest of the trip could be greatly affected by the outcome of his work that day.

I need not have worried, by teatime he had spent several hours spinning the wheel this way and that, checking it with, mostly, improvised tools. I could tell from his demeanour that he was confident with his handiwork. At this stage I will say that not only did the wheel behave itself for the next 900 or so miles of the trip but also for several hundred more miles until I could get the wheel back to Thorn for them to check.

Day 12 Saturday May 27th
Settle to Hawkshead
55 miles
4435 ft ascent

Another big day and as it turned out a day full of contrasts. Mark was very glad that he had managed to arrange an extra day in Yorkshire, this had enabled him to get some Yorkshire miles under his wheels before we set off on the third stage of the ride. Any route from the Yorkshire Dales National Park to the Lake District National Park does not have to work too hard to come up with some beautiful and challenging countryside. Most features that a road cyclist would ask for were supplied in abundance by the route Mark had planned.

The house was strangely quiet that morning, after the hustle and bustle of the previous evening. Adrian had left by about 6.30am in order to catch an early train back to Devon. Clive was still asleep, he works in a computer support role which demands he is on call through most of the night. The weather was bright with high cloud and the promise of sun later. Although the forecast had predicted that there could be thunder storms over the Lake District later.

The Beast had been passed fit by Adrian and Clive so Mark and I checked things over before loading up the bags. We finally bid farewell to Sarah about 9.20. We cycled past Giggleswick and Settle on the west side of the river and then headed up Ribblesdale on a beautiful quiet road. Settle lies at an altitude of about 450ft and we climbed steadily to Helwith Bridge. This gave us the first contrast of the day, here the landscape is very open with few trees, whereas only a mile or two back towards Settle the dale is still quite sheltered, with plenty of trees and snug looking farms. At Helwith Bridge the road crosses the Ribble and continues up on the east side to Horton in Ribblesdale. This is the start and finish point of the Yorkshire 3 Peaks walk, a gentle stroll of some

25 miles distance taking in Pen-Y-Ghent, Whernside and Ingleborough. The heights of these monarchs of the moors is between 2300 and 2400 ft. In the autumn of 2016 I had completed this walk with some friends, in just about 11 hours. It was rather strange being back under very different circumstances and seeing the familiar features, the car park, the cafe and footpath off to the first peak.

After about 12 miles we reached the Ribblehead viaduct and joined the many sight seers for a photocall. The viaduct is quite dramatic, set as it is against the backdrop of some pretty bleak moorland. The altitude of over 1000ft means that even on a good day the weather can be chilly and windy. From here we turned sharp right and continued climbing, into a really strong headwind. We were in effect going round the lower slopes of Whernside. After about three miles our road turned left and we escaped the grip of the headwind, although we kept climbing for another mile or so, to a height of about 1400 ft. Then within a very short distance we were beginning a ten mile descent down Dentdale. Another huge contrast, from pedalling up a long and exhausting hill into a headwind, ten minutes later we were coasting down the most beautiful dale. Following the River Dent the valley is quite narrow and quickly becomes wooded. A really wonderful descent, at times a high speed headlong rush, then less steep sections enabling a more sedate freewheeling that allowed us to enjoy the views of the river and trees still in the full flush of early summer beauty.

We passed through the very attractive village of Dent and we both thought that would be the end of the descent, but no, we kept on losing height for another four or five miles until we rolled into Sedburgh. By now the sun was shining, the sky was blue and all was well with the world. We found a good bakery selling filled rolls and a nearby seat ensured we could enjoy our lunch and the early afternoon warmth.

While we relaxed over lunch we had no real views to the west so it was not until we left the comforting embrace of Sedburgh's lovely old buildings and narrow streets that we saw a build up of cloud to the west. A short stretch of main road took us past the bottom end of the Howgill fells, we then turned right and headed north on a minor road. There followed a long climb of nearly 700ft. The first half mile had two single black arrow sections then the gradient eased into a steady climb. After two miles we reached the high point and the road curved round to the west. The views opened out, behind us superb views of the Howgills and ahead of us a wonderful panorama of Lakeland's southern fells.

Unfortunately we could also see the bank of extremely hostile cloud that hung over what appeared to be our intended destination.

We were approaching Kendal and the area where the north south communication routes are squeezed into the ever narrowing pass between the Howgills to the east and the Lake District to the west, until at Shap summit they can burst through exhausted and descend with relief over the wide plain to Carlisle and Scotland. We crossed the M6 and continued westwards above Kendal to pick up the B5284 to Bowness-on-Windermere. This is a great way to enter the Lake District, through a succession of little villages, Lambrigg, Docker and the wonderfully named Scalthwaiterigg - imagine trying to explain that to someone in an offshore call centre. We had left Sedburgh in the sunshine but by the time we turned off the A684 on to the minor road the sun was being dissolved by the clouds. Any hopes that we had entertained of missing the forecasted bad weather were dashed by the time we crossed the M6 as it was obvious we were heading directly for the darkest section of sky. Yet another contrast, within about 30 minutes going from sunshine and distant views to torrential rain. There was no messing about with introductory drizzle, the light deteriorated very quickly, we stopped to don waterproof jackets and these had hardly been zipped up when the rain started. There seemed to be no point in trying to shelter as this was the sort of downpour that has no hiding place. By the time we reached Burneside, north of Kendal the rain was easing but the roads were awash, in place about 6 inches deep. Climbing a steepish hill out of the village, for a way we had to take a course on the extreme right to avoid the torrent flowing down the left hand side.

From Burneside we had a few miles of quiet roads but then turned on to the B5284 which although only a B road was busy with bank holiday traffic. The rain had for the time being reduced to a grudging drizzle, but looking heavenwards one could be forgiven for thinking that the weather was looking for even the flimsiest excuse to discharge yet more rain upon us. On another day with better weather and less traffic this run down to Bowness would have been a pleasure for the road undulates comfortably over the low fells to the east of Windermere.

We headed straight for the ferry slip, now devoid of cars and saw the ferry retreating into a misty shroud. Second on our list of priorities was tea, we cycled back to the car park where a number of picnic tables with umbrellas lead us to a kiosk dispensing liquid goodness. We barely had time to dismount and park the tandem when lightning and a huge thunderclap announced impending doom. This was followed immediately by strong wind and more torrential rain. The irony of these tables with a large umbrella emerging from a central hole is that the main area of protection from the elements is the table itself. There only has to be the merest breeze and anyone sitting or standing under the umbrella gets wet. Our first cup of tea was consumed with the minimum of dilution from the rain but as more people sought shelter from the storm, the second cup fared less well. The whole interlude was extremely uncomfortable and left us both with less than favourable impressions of Bowness-on-Windermere.

Our second visit to the ferry slip was more encouraging and we joined the dozen or so cars already waiting. This was to be the first of many ferry crossings, we must have looked a bit sorry for ourselves because the ferryman let us travel for free. Both Mark and I although refreshed by the tea were now cold and stiff and for once I looked forward to the few miles on the opposite side of the lake which would take us up and down several steep hills before gaining the sanctuary of Hawkshead Youth Hostel.

Mark found the hostel easily. It occupies a grand house - Esthwaite Lodge , that commands views over Esthwaite Water. We checked in and were soon in our comfortable en suite room. Some time later having showered and changed we went back to the main house to locate the refectory and were rather taken aback by the presence of a dozen or so young ladies waiting to check in, together with what seemed an unduly large number of huge pink suitcases. We concluded they were probably here for a girlie weekend but could not imagine how they could amuse themselves for two or three days in such a remote location.

Later we went out for a walk to shake the creases out of our legs. The weather was still grumpy but with only the faintest suggestion of wet in the air. One of the pubs in the nearby village had a reasonably strong wi-fi service so we were able to post our daily facebook log while enjoying a beer.

Day 13 Sunday May 29th
Hawkshead to Carlisle
49 miles
4068ft ascent

The day started cool and misty with low cloud hanging over the fells. We breakfasted in the hostel refectory and were on the road without much delay. I have to say that Mark's route planning skills were more than matched by his subsequent ability to then follow said route. Our mission for the day was to travel north through the Lake District and on to Carlisle. It was Sunday of the late May bank holiday weekend, so there would be plenty of traffic around.

One of the features, especially of the early and middle part of the ride, was that I did not always remember to get briefed on the day's route. This was not due to pilots withholding information or lack of interest on my part, more due to the fact that evenings and early mornings were so taken up with the multitude of daily tasks to be sorted. Very often by the time showers had been taken, kit unpacked / packed, logs written etc. I would not think about the next route until I was just dropping off to sleep or as we were already on the road. So it was this morning, I knew where Ambleside and Grasmere were in relation to Hawkshead but had no idea what Mark had planned. I had visited the Lakes many times over the previous 50 years but invariably when travelling around would have just used the more major roads. Close inspection of the OS map reveals an absolute cat's cradle of little roads in this part of the southern fells.

As I looked forward to the ride I thought this day's cycling could be challenging, the mix of heavy bank holiday traffic, big hills and main roads was not conducive to relaxed cycling. "Worry ye not" Mark is in control. We rode down the drive turned left to Hawkshead, through the village, deserted and enjoying the Sunday morning lie-in. Then what ensued was more like a magical mystery tour. Our route twisted and turned as we pedalled along narrow leafy lanes, mostly through a wooded landscape, up and down sharp little hills, across bridges, past tiny lakes, pools and streams. T junctions and cross roads came and went, the misty cloudy conditions meant I could gain no clues on direction from the position of the sun. Several times I asked Mark as we turned at a junction "what did that signpost say" the variety of answers ranged from "Ambleside, The Langdales, Grasmere, Skelwith Bridge", all of which I knew were in different directions.

In spite of this uncertainty it was a most wonderful ride and we encountered only the very occasional car. All of a sudden we rounded a bend and there on our right was Grasmere lake. We stopped leant the bike against the inevitable stone wall and drank in the view. The breeze was just ruffling the surface of the water, the wooded fellside beyond, which hid the main road, was a mixture of those vibrant greens which only show for a few weeks in late spring and early summer. Just the merest hint of brighter light was reflecting on the open fell above the trees. From our vantage point we had no real sighting of the sky as our little road ran through a lakeside wood and we looked out from underneath its canopy. A short time later though we could see that the dense cloud and mist of early morning was thinning and there was a promise of brighter things to come. While we were taking our photos a cyclist appeared from Grasmere direction and stopped for a chat. He was on a west to east route across the Pennines, he kindly took a photo of us, then after a few minutes of cycling chat we went our separate ways. It was only a short run down into the village and I soon recognised the road as one I had walked in the past. We skirted round the edge of Grasmere village, dinging warnings of our approach to the unwary tourists. I expected at this point we would join the main road, but no! We were off again into the little lanes for another couple of miles. We came eventually to the A591 halfway between Grasmere village and the brow of the hill above Thirlmere. Almost at the top a cycle track goes off to the left, so after only 2 miles of main road we were back into a cycle friendly environment. The track led down and within three quarters of a mile we were on the little 'scenic route' road which loops off the main road, follows the lakeside around Thirlmere for about 4 miles, crosses the dam and rejoins the main road. It was a delightful ride we saw only a few cars which surprised us as we knew that many sightseers use this route. The explanation became clear when we reached the northern end of the lake, the road across the dam was closed for maintenance.

Our plan was to call on Ali's aunt and uncle in Keswick for lunch. Fortunately they live at almost the highest point of the town, coming in from the south theirs is the first turning off the main road. This was good news for us because it meant we avoided losing several hundred feet descending into town only to have a long climb eastwards out of town on the A66. Having left Thirlmere's lakeside road we had a couple of miles cycling along the stone wall lined roads past sheltered farms and eventually turned left on to the main road. Within a few hundred yards a sign confirmed it was 2.5 miles to Keswick. So in the morning's ride we had travelled through the most busy part of the Lake District with no more than 20 minutes on the main road.

Having enjoyed the company of Ali's relations and the splendid lunch they provided we retraced our route for half a mile then turned left on to an extremely narrow little lane that took us in another half a mile to Castlerigg Stone Circle. This is one of about 1300 stone circles in the British Isles that were constructed as part of the megalithic tradition that endured from about 3300BC to 900BC. Although it stands on a plateau above Keswick at a height approaching 700ft, in the wider context it is almost as if it is at the centre of a vast amphitheatre, because all around in the distance are the highest mountains in the Northern Lakes, Helvelyn, Grasmoor, Dale Head Causey Pike Grisedale Pike, Skiddaw and Blencathra. All of which together with the lower fells, on a clear day, create a breathtaking, majestic panorama. The morning mist had now cleared leaving only a hint of hazy mist in the warm afternoon sunshine. Mark and I happily wandered around taking photos and just enjoying the peace and drinking in the stunning views.

We set off again, having another 25 miles or so to cover before we reached Carlisle. The next 10 miles up to leaving the National Park north-east of Mungrisdale were in many ways one of the more memorable sections of the whole ride. We immediately launched ourselves on a fabulous descent to Threlkeld along a network of little lanes. Just to our left across the valley were the guardians of the Northern Fells, that awesome duo Skiddaw and Blencathra, below us spread out like a scene taken from a Heaton Cooper painting, pastures, trees, stone walls and farms. We soon arrived at the A66, crossed over and entered Threlkeld on what I would guess was the old main road. Now the traffic sweeps past in a seemingly endless stream, most people being unaware of the charms this grand old Lakeland village has to offer anyone willing to travel through in a less frenetic manner. In a couple of miles we were back alongside the A66 for a short while until at Scales we bade the trunk road a fond farewell. The little lane from Scales to Mungrisdale on this sunny early summer afternoon was about as perfect a cycle ride as could be imagined. For about 4 miles it contours round the lower flanks of Blencathra, looking to our left we saw the grassy slopes already shewing the new fresh green growth of this season's bracken. While looking to our right, very often through trees that lined the road for a lot of the way we saw fields, farms and the occasional secluded house. This road belongs to what must now be a very small and select group. It is a gated road, the O.S. 1:50000 map shews 5 gates but I feel sure I dismounted and re-mounted considerably more times than that. This of course meant that it was almost traffic free which added greatly to its charm.

We rolled into Mungrisdale in the late afternoon ready for a pot or two of tea, we were not disappointed and sat in the garden of the local pub, replenishing our fluid reserves and enjoying a generous slice of home-made flapjack. The little village lies about a mile inside the national park and soon after we resumed our ride we were heading north-east into what was a very flat area. The contrast was quite acute, within such a short distance we had left the mountains behind and entered the large plain that is the borderland between England and Scotland to the north and south of the Solway Firth. We made very quick progress through quiet lanes, the Lakeland hills were soon absorbed into the retreating panoramic vista. We knew that the next 30 to 40 miles were just a brief respite from the daily menu of hills that had formed the primary constituent of our diet since leaving Cape Cornwall. Mark found our hotel easily after successfully following what seemed to me to be a labyrinthine route through a large housing estate on the southern edge of Carlisle. The hotel was a characterless concrete and glass building owing its existence to 60's (or 70's) architecture. The sort of place favoured by travelling salesmen, unfaithful husbands (and wives) and cut price conference organisers. It was comfortable though and the staff pleasant. The Beast was given a large meeting room in which to relax.

Later Mark and I walked into the town centre and found an Italian restaurant for a most enjoyable meal to round off a fabulous day.

Day 14 Monday May 29th
Carlisle to Castle Douglas
57 miles
2354ft ascent

What a difference a day makes, in fact not even 24 little hours later we awoke to lowering skies and the prospect of imminent rain. We eased The Beast from the warmth of the overnight accommodation and parked it under the canopy over the entrance. By the time we had fitted panniers and other bags, sorted out the iPhone with View Ranger running the rain had started yet again, a heavy drizzle. We launched into the morning traffic, which seemed unusually heavy considering it was a wet bank holiday Monday. We crossed the River Eden on the main bridge out of the city centre but then turned left immediately on to a smaller road that followed the north bank of the river through a most attractive residential area. As only about 20% of the city lies north of the river, within less than a mile we were out of the urban environment and heading for Scotland!

The rain had stopped for the moment and 40 minutes after leaving the hotel we were posing by the 'Scotland Welcomes You' sign. It had been 13 days cycling, about 700 miles and approaching 40,000 feet of climbing to get here and we were not even halfway through the ride. We diverted into Gretna to buy a few things including a toothbrush for me, to replace the one I had left in Settle. By the time we pedalled out of Gretna the rain had begun again, this time in earnest. Good progress was made through the flatlands of Dumfries but conditions were wretched. Annan was our next port of call, we were still on a cycle route so we had little traffic to contend with, just rain. Mark had planned our route to use part of the National Cycle Network from Carlisle to Dumfries and on to Castle Douglas. The purpose of the NCRs must be to keep cycles away from busy roads thus providing a safer and more pleasurable cycling experience. They achieve that aim admirably but in doing so they do on occasions follow quite a convoluted course. From Annan we headed to Powfoot which is on the coast of the Irish Sea/Solway Firth just a few miles further on. Heavy rain was still falling as Powfoot came and went, our road now ran along the coast. To our left a strip of dull characterless beach beyond which were mudbanks, water, mist, grey sky and rain; to our right, scrappy grass, a large caravan site, mist, grey sky and rain. It came as no surprise that very few of the caravans seemed to be occupied. Compared to our West Country holiday resorts the Solway Firth and Powfoot seemed to be rather lacking in the essential elements required for a varied and fulfilling holiday.

It was probably due to the drop in temperature of a few degrees as we came into the salty embrace of the seaside breeze that both Mark and I began to realise how cold we had become. For some time we had hoped to find a cafe but Eastriggs, Annan and Powfoot do not go in for such frivolous enterprises. The wind coming off the sea sucked any last remnants of warmth from our bodies and we needed to find shelter so we could put on more layers. Shelter presented itself in the form of a less than salubrious flat roofed, windowless concrete toilet block, that looked more like a WW2 emplacement than a public convenience, but any port in a storm! With teeth chattering energy bars and other goodies were consumed and we soon resumed our journey in slightly better spirits. We made fast progress and at Bankend we decided to take the direct road to Dumfries rather than the NCR which made a big loop south and west following the east side of the River Nith. Conditions were improving, the rain eased and it was slightly warmer away from the sea. The sky was brighter and the rain had stopped as we entered Dumfries. Mark's ability to locate good eateries soon found us at the Stove Cafe in the main shopping area. The whole world seemed a better place after a good lunch and we set off again in good heart.

We left Dumfries on the A711 and after a couple of miles turned right on to a minor road that ran roughly parallel to the main A715 all the way to Castle Douglas. We were now well clear of the flat flood plain that bordered the Solway Firth and the landscape had become more varied with some rolling hills. These were not the fully qualified variety that we had conquered earlier in the ride, but more the trainee type of hills that we had dismissed with hardly a sideways glance on our journey through Worcestershire. Progress was steady and we were well on course to arrive in Castle Douglas with plenty of time to relax, shower and think about the evening meal. However on reaching Haugh of Urr signs at a cross road tried to persuade us that our road was closed. When put in this situation I suspect that the response of most cyclists would be as ours, a rather contemptuous 'roads are never closed to cycles'. So we carried on and in due course met up with a bevvy of workmen complete with tar sprayers, chipping dispensers and heavy rollers. It was too late for second thoughts and we pressed on, passing them with cheery disobedient waves. There followed what seemed to be a long stretch of freshly top dressed road that extended all the way to Castle Douglas where our minor road met with the main road into town. At the junction we must have run over some glass, for we had only ventured a few yards along the main road when we experienced that deflating sensation that cyclists dread.

There was a conveniently wide entrance to a country house hotel immediately on our left. The Beast was soon relieved of its burden and inverted, of course it had to be the rear wheel!. Repairing the puncture did not pose any particular problem, however Mark was concerned that there were several nicks in the tyre as a result of either the glass or possibly the fresh road chippings. The repair delayed us by about 45 minutes and it was just a short run into town to find The Imperial Hotel, rather a grand name for a comfortable but ordinary town pub with rooms. After we had checked in Mark had a text conversation with

Adrian, the result of which was to switch the damaged tyre to the front and in the process reinforcing it with a patch on the inside. The landlord showed us where we could carry out the work, fortunately under cover as a steady drizzle had developed. Maybe because we were tired but the job took longer than we hoped. Mark was very diligent inspecting the offending tyre, which paid off as he extracted three more pieces of glass. Eventually The Beast was restored to road worthiness and we retired back into the pub, only to be told by the cheery landlord that the kitchen was now closed! No worries though because there was the choice of four eating establishments just along the road.

We just washed our hands and set off in our quest for sustenance. It has to be said that Castle Douglas on a wet Monday evening is not exactly the mecca of fine food that the landlord had suggested. The Chinese, the Indian and the two other places were all closed, so we retraced our steps to the Greek restaurant nearly opposite the Imperial, that our landlord had not mentioned. By now the time was about 9.00pm and The Nikos Greek Restaurant was about to close, but we were welcomed in and joined a dozen or so diners and were treated to a superb meal.

So, all things considered, day 14 had been a day of very mixed fortunes and thanks to some very kind Greek chefs and waiters it finished on a high. We retired to our room for belated showers then the landlord was kind enough to sort us out with a late evening pot of tea.

....

The shoes were becoming a bit of an issue! Earlier in the year I had thought it prudent to replace my old cycling shoes which I bought in 2007 and had worn for thousands of miles cycling. They had been soaked through and covered with mud on countless occasions with no undue consequences, all I had ever done was to wash off mud when necessary and leave them by the radiator in the hall to dry out, they had never smelt or been offensive in any other way! However I am sorry to say that in horse racing terms in The Cycle Shoe Chase, my new shoes had fallen at the first hurdle. During the ride to Hawkshead on day 12 our shoes were completely soaked through by the time we reached the hostel. No worries though, there was an excellent drying room. The following morning although our shoes were still a bit damp Mark's were just a tad musty but mine were registering towards the 'extremely toxic' end on the scale of olfactory sensations. Not only that but much as a dog shares its fleas it was now becoming clear that the noxious odours had been generously passed on to my socks. The only explanation I could come up with was that the fabric of the shoes was encouraging some sort of ghastly bacterial reaction resulting in the quite powerful unpleasant mouldy smell.

What to do about it, was a pressing issue. I bought some baby powder in Gretna. This was not effective in any remote way. On reflection I should have realised that if a baby smelt as bad as that it would take more than scented powder to restore it to the centre of parental affection. All that happened was that the scented powder completely failed to hide the mouldy smell and the resulting combination of odours was even more anti-social.

At the hotel in Carlisle the shoes were banished to a wardrobe on their own, but we did have a twinge of guilt the next morning wondering how the next occupant would react when going to hang up their smart business suit. From then on they were either double wrapped in carrier bags or left with The Beast in its resting place. Socks had to be washed daily which was a bit of a nuisance. In Fort William de-odourising spray was purchased, this had only a limited and temporary benefit, the can being exhausted well before the end of the ride. For the time being Mark was quite understanding about the problem.

Day 15 Tuesday May 30th
Castle Douglas to Brodick, Isle of Arran
78 miles
2562ft ascent

This was one of the days that I had mentally flagged up with a red exclamation mark. A longer day with a ferry crossing at the end. Fortunately the Calmac ferry service between Ardrossan and Brodick is quite a popular one with the last crossing at 19.20. Nevertheless it did give the day a certain urgency. Another factor that the previous day had added to the mix was that we really wanted to try and acquire a spare tyre which meant diverting into either Ayr or Ardrossan. We had decided to make an earlier start and to aim for catching the 16.40 ferry. It was with a certain relief that on checking the Beast as we prepared for the day that both tyres were still fully inflated.

Galloway cannot compete with the Scottish Highlands when it comes down to matters of size, its highest peaks weighing in at a miserly 2800 feet or so and it lacks the dramatic mountain scenery of the more northerly regions. It is though a relatively sparsely populated area and as such offers a substantial amount of moorland with lochs and rivers, ranging from the lower fringes of 5-700 feet to the high peaks of the central area. A considerable portion has suffered from the attention of The Forestry Commission and is covered in a coniferous overcoat which does few favours to anybody or anything. Like other similar parts of Britain, the lack of too much good farming land together with the more difficult moorland has resulted in there being fewer roads. Travelling as we were from south-east to north-west, unless we took the much longer coastal route we only had three options, the A76, A713 and the A714. The A713 more or less chose itself and I was encouraged when looking on Google Street View that it seemed to be quite a quiet rural road. How does Google remove all that traffic from its film?

We set off at 08.20, grey skies overpowered all the countryside's attempts to look colourful and the weather forecast promised rain by the early afternoon. There was a westerly wind but it did not really bother us too much as it was a crosswind but slightly behind us. In spite of the grey the scenery was very attractive, for miles the road follows a wide shallow valley on the east side of a river then continues along Loch Ken which extends all the way to New Galloway, some 16 miles. So, looking to our left we had a grand view of the distant hills and the loch in the near foreground. To our right more distant hills. It had been noticeable that since leaving the Lake District the roadside bushes of choice were may and gorse, however as we headed further west towards Castle Douglas broom began to replace gorse. Now the gorse had disappeared and the more yellow broom was performing a spectacular duet with the may. Another observation was that initially the may was almost all white but as the day progressed more of the bushes became suffused with that beautiful pale pink. I felt that this wonderful display more than compensated for the, at times, very stressful riding conditions. In places the bushes of broom and may jostled each other in their desire for attention, the may forming banks of blossom up to 12 feet high, the broom smaller but on occasions appearing to be a solid mass of yellow. Even on this grey cheerless day the display was very uplifting.

It became apparent shortly after leaving Castle Douglas that we were not going to have a quiet ride, the traffic was not constant or particularly heavy, but it gave us no quarter, during the run to Ayr we had worryingly close encounters with a bus, an articulated logging lorry and a large articulated container lorry. By lunchtime I had seen more bad, thoughtless driving than in the previous 750 miles. One of the reasons why traffic seemed so intent on making such manic progress could be that there is so little development along the road. After the little village of Crossmichael a couple of miles from Castle Douglas there is nothing apart from the occasional house or farm until St. John's Town of Dalry about 20 miles on. Even the grandly named New Galloway which lies to the west of the A713 is little more than a small village. We blinked and nearly missed St. John's Town of Dalry but it mattered not because we still had more miles to pedal before we had earned a lunch stop . Once Loch Ken had become a memory the road began to climb, gaining about 400feet of elevation as we approached a clearly defined pass through the hills where the road reaches nearly 1000 feet but the hills on either side attain the lofty heights of up to about 2000 feet. Once through the pass there was a thrilling descent of about a mile and a half then we took a right fork which lead us into the village of Dalmellington where we found a bustling cafe and a well-earned lunch.

The forecasted rain arrived on cue just as we set off after lunch and it quickly became apparent as we hit the open road that the wind had changed quarter and was now a north-westerly headwind. Also as is often the case when rain starts wind increases. The next 15 miles or so to Ayr were pretty uncomfortable and hard work, the traffic still giving us a hard time. The rain stopped as we reached Ayr and on the outskirts we pulled over and Mark checked the situation with Mr. Google regarding cycle shops. We did manage to locate a tyre of the folding variety, it was a 1.75 inch rather than a 2 inch as fitted but it would certainly do the job if we had a tyre failure.

We still had about 15 miles to cycle but we felt we were on course to reach Ardrossan in time for the 16.40 ferry. We set off along the coast, at last free of the threatening occupants of the A713. Ayr and Prestwick merge into one sprawling seaside development, after Prestwick along a wide open promenade to Troon. Two elements were now slowing us down, firstly the really strong headwind from which there was no escape so close to the sea and secondly the twists and turns of the cycle path. Several times it seemed like one pedal forward and three pedals sideways. At Troon we went past the famous golf course, then on to Irvine, Stevenston, Saltcoats and finally Ardrossan. Time was running out, still 20 minutes on the clock but there was the 'going home' traffic to contend with. By now we were weaving in and out of stationary queues, somehow Mark still able to see the route. We finally roared into the ferry terminus about 16.30, I rushed breathless into the booking office ......we were too late! This was to be the first of seven ferry crossings on Calmac ferries and it became obvious that they run a very efficient service which relies on rules regarding times of boarding etc.,. to be strictly adhered to, this way very quick turn round times can be achieved.

There was a little cafe bar next to the ticket office and we enjoyed cups of tea and chocolate biscuits while we waited. We duly boarded the 18.00 ferry, by now the weather had taken a definite turn for the better with blue skies and dramatic clouds. The first time I went to the Isle of Arran was over 40 years ago but I well remember that crossing and someone on the boat pointing out the famous 'sleeping warrior' profile of the island. Mark and I spent the whole trip on the top deck. The views were stunning, behind us the low hills of coastal Galloway, in front the lowering sun casting a silvery pathway across the sea towards us. The island initially masked by the bank of cloud in the western sky but as we sailed nearer the lighting subtly changed and we could see the outline of Arran. Brodick is not a large town, in fact it is not even a large village. It basically consists of one road that runs along the seafront. Needless to say, mainly due to my misunderstanding we turned right off the ferry slip instead of left. However in the process of cycling unnecessarily through the village/town we did note where the options for an evening meal lay. We soon found our very comfortable B and B. After sorting out and showering we rounded off a very mixed day with an excellent meal in the local hotel.

Day 16 Wednesday May 31st
Brodick to Kilmichael Glassary
58 miles
3833ft ascent

Our guest house had been very comfortable and the lady proprietor was attentive and anxious to please, but did give rise to the strange episode of 'the porridge'. Now you would think that being in Scotland hotels etc. were no strangers to requests for porridge. Mark is not too demanding but there are two things that help to ease his day along, one is Earl Grey tea and the other is, yes, porridge. I am not at all averse to this oaty delight appearing on my breakfast menu, but if it does not come with the prospect of lashings of muscovado sugar then I probably would not bother. However Mark is happy to pile into his porridge dish handfuls of nuts, dried fruit and fresh fruit in whatever combination is available. During the trip with Mark I did on several occasions agree to having porridge in the, probably, misguided thought that it would ease the burden of the kitchen staff to have a worthwhile quantity of porridge to make. I must say that the lady in Brodick was not the only proprietor to react, when asking 'what would you like for breakfast?' As if Mark had requested fresh guava with yak's milk yoghurt, or something equally exotic. The contents of the two bowls that were presented to us this morning, bore more resemblance to bowls of polyfilla than the oaty breakfast dish so loved by all self-respecting, kilt wearing shot putters. I had asked for brown sugar and was presented with a handful of the sugar bearing paper tubes that will sometimes accompany servings of coffee. It took a good deal of fortitude to work my way through to poached eggs, toast and marmalade.

So, with stomachs suitably lined with energy giving porridge we sallied forth into a beautiful spring day. There was a rather chilly breeze but skies were blue and all was right with the world. We had another ferry crossing, this one a short trip from the north of the island to Claonaig on the Kintyre Peninsular, but the service was frequent so we had no pressure to catch a particular ferry. We stopped briefly in the local store to replenish stocks of energy foods and then before hardly having time to draw breath we were climbing. Just towards the end of the village the 'main' road turns sharply right and our road, 'The String' alias the B880 turns sharp left and immediately begins the steepest section of the 780ft or so climb. Just at the point where I am sure we were both wondering when the energy giving properties of our breakfast were going to kick in, the gradient eased a little and settled into a long hard but eminently satisfying climb at a pretty even gradient for the 1.5 miles to the bealach (col).

The String runs from Brodick on the east side of Arran to Blackwaterfoot in the south-west. Our route led us to the ferry at Lochranza in the north of the island. The first half a mile or so was through a wooded area on the south side of Glen Shurig, then as we climbed out into open country we had grand views to our right down into the glen and across to the lower hills of the central mountainous part of Arran. It took us about 35 minutes to reach the bealach where we stopped for a drink and photos. The descent was a pure joy, a good road sweeping down the glen, we were soon under trees again but still with views to our right. After about

3 miles we took a turn to the right, leaving The String and continuing the descent to the little road that follows the coast all the way to Lochranza. The descent to the west is much longer and less steep than the climb from Brodick and as we lost height the view to Kintyre to the west began to open out. The mountain and river views being replaced by a stunning vista of blue skies above the blue/grey distant form of the Kintyre Peninsular with sparkling sea and all supported by the rocky shoreline that ran as far as we could see.

We stopped for a few minutes at the junction with the coast road, very little traffic, water lapping on to the stoney beach and the calls of oystercatchers all around us. The 11 or 12 miles north to Lochranza was just about the most perfect cycling you could imagine. For many miles the roads that wind around the island are immediately adjacent to the narrow rocky stoney beach and the ground to landward rising to quite dramatic cliffs for much of the way. We pedalled along at a steady pace but not too quickly as we both wanted to prolong the pleasure of the ride for as long as we could. Only in one place did the road leave the beach side where a sturdy shoulder projects into the sea and the road climbs sharply to overcome the obstruction. We eventually reached Lochranza about 12.45 hoping to find a cafe for lunch.

With all the many ferry crossings that Caledonian MacBrayne operate it is difficult to imagine that there could be a crossing where both points are so remote and sparsely populated. Lochranza boasts only a handful of dwellings whereas Claonaig boasts just a concrete slipway. As we cycled past the slipway towards the village we noticed the 'Sandwich Station' a rather solid looking shed no more than about 12feet x 10feet tucked at the side of the road opposite the slipway. Our search for a cafe proved fruitless and returning to the Sandwich Station we investigated more. If I had to rate all the lunch stops on the whole trip the Sandwich Station would come out the clear winner by a country mile. The young(ish) couple running it had been doing so for some years and I hope they will continue for as long as they want, dispensing their wondrous selection of doughy delicacies. A mouthwatering selection of fillings was offered with a choice of fresh homemade (I would guess that morning) walnut or focaccia bread. We both chose the smoked mackerel with salad filling, Mark went with the walnut bread while I opted for the focaccia bread. The portions amply matched our appetites and together with a shared cup of homemade soup and cups of tea, sat outside and watched the distant ferry approach while we ate and drank. The day just kept getting better!

Yet again we stood on the top deck and looked, this time at the receding profile of Arran, now there was no sleeping warrior just the shape of the unforgettable memory this morning's amazing ride had given us. Looking north-west, initially it was uncertain where we were heading, then small white blobs began to morph into the shapes of a slipway and a narrow road emerging from the dense deciduous canopy that seemed to cover most of the hillside in the vicinity of the slipway. We waited while our motorised travelling companions bumped off the ramp and drove away, to be quickly replaced by the 3 or 4 waiting vehicles. By the time we had cycled but a short way up the hill the ferry was already turning to commence its return journey to Arran. What struck us then was the utter tranquillity, we were alone on this peaceful sunny afternoon, no other noises broke the spell. We headed north-west across the peninsular to eventually join the A83 on the banks of West Loch Tarbert. This was a magical 5 mile ride, the road climbing gradually to about 350feet past conifer plantations some open ground but mainly deciduous woodland. I learnt later in the trip that Kintyre boasts one of the highest proportions of natural deciduous woodland in Europe.

When we turned right on to the main road the scenery was just as dramatic but more traffic made cycling less relaxed. The next 5 miles of more or less level cycling took us north-east to the head of the loch. The road was never far from the loch side winding in and out of the woods giving us an ever changing vista of trees, water, sky and all with the unbroken backdrop of imposing wooded hillsides that rose up on the far side of West Loch Tarbert. The final three quarters of a mile took us back across the peninsular to the villlage of Tarbert on the bank of Loch Fyne. Tarbert is very picturesque with an attractive waterside overlooking a small natural harbour. Loch Fyne is a majestic sea loch that extends north-eastwards from Arran only to find after many miles its way blocked by the mountains of the Cruachan Hills just south of Glencoe. We sat outside a waterfront cafe and enjoyed tea and cakes. While we were there a cyclist, who we had seen earlier pushing his bike into the village, approached us and enquired if we could help him with a chain splitter. We had earlier misinterpreted his wave as being a cheery greeting, whereas in fact he had tried to wave us down to help him in his mechanical predicament. Fortunately I did have the appropriate tool and he was able to repair his chain. His wife who had been riding separately arrived later and on discovering that the previous day they had cycled down the lower section of the Great Glen cycleway, which runs from Inverness to Fort William, I asked their opinion of it and whether they thought it suitable for a tandem. Their opinion was that we should have no problem. I was particularly interested as this route constituted the first part of our route north from Fort William. I have to say that 5 days later I rather questioned their judgement on that score.

We cycled out of Tarbert just before 4.00pm having spent well over an hour relaxing in the sunshine. For the first 3 miles the road has to negotiate its way over a lumpy hillside before it descends with relief to continue its loch side path northwards. For the next 8 or 9 miles to Ardrishaig the road valiantly clings on to the narrow strip of level ground between hillside and the loch. We made good progress but on some occasions the traffic did show us only grudging respect. At the mention of Ardrishaig any sailor familiar with the coastal waters of Great Britain is likely to get a bit misty eyed for it is the beginning (or end) of the Crinan Canal. This short but strategically very important waterway was built at the end of the 18th century and opened in 1801. It is only nine miles long and has 15 locks which raise the canal to a maximum height of 64 feet above sea level in its central section. A very significant matter is that there is no height restriction for vessels using the canal. The seven roads that cross the canal do so by means of six swing bridges and one retractable bridge. With the increase in sea borne trade during the 18th century the need for a safer route to the Inner Hebrides from the Clyde became apparent. Once opened it provided a sheltered short cut to the Sound of Jura thus eliminating the diversion of many miles around the Kintyre peninsular and more importantly the exposed route round the Mull of Kintyre.

Ardrishaig lies on Loch Gilp, a small afterthought of a loch situated at the point where Loch Fyne turns north-east. Its almost as if Loch Fyne could no longer be bothered with going north and thought it could have much more fun heading for the Cruachan Hills. We spent another half hour or so at the entry to the canal and chatted to the young woman in charge, who worked for Scottish Canals, the canal operators. There are towpaths on both sides of the canal all the way to Crinan at its western end, so we took advantage of that for the 3 miles to Cairnbaan where we turned off for the last 2 miles to Kilmichael Glassary. The Horseshoe Inn provided very comfortable accommodation and a splendid evening meal.

Day 17 Thursday June 1st
Kilmichael Glassary to Oban
46 miles
3535ft ascent

A strange day! A day of contrasts, a day of the best and worst, the most and the least! The best cycling, the worst rain, the most miles on minor roads, the least traffic, to mention but a few things. We had seen that the day's weather forecast was not too encouraging but I suspect we both felt that after such a glorious day the weather could not deteriorate that much! The local weather forecast predicted rain by 9.00am. The morning curtain opening routine revealed that the weather could deteriorate that much. Even the most cursory look at the sky showed very grey and weak looking clouds, weak in terms of not being strong enough to contain all the rain that they held.

There was never really much of a contest about which route we should take to Oban. The choice was either about 32 miles on main roads or 46 miles on NCR 78, but it was interesting at breakfast as we chatted to the chef who I think on the quiet was, or used to be, a cyclist. He extolled the virtues of the minor roads and we were keen to tell him that was the route we had chosen. We brought the Beast from its overnight quarters at 8.30am and even while we loaded up a fine drizzle was announcing the weather's intentions. The first couple of miles up the glen was pretty effortless cycling but we had barely reached the head of the glen before the rain began in earnest. The road then wound its way through the hills for about 5 miles arriving at Loch Ederline a tiny loch which lies not half a mile from the southern end of Loch Awe, all of its life it has suffered through the thoughtless action of the hills between which have prevented Loch Ederline from being part of the majestic, huge, deep and extremely beautiful Loch Awe.

Loch Ederline saw the end of level cycling for many miles. Our road roughly followed the north bank of Loch Awe for about 20 miles, but unlike the road along Loch Fyne which obediently stays by the waterside, our road rambled with gay abandon up and down the hillside. Never too far from the loch the switchback road ranged from the water side to at some points to well over 400feet above the loch. In spite of the inclement conditions this was an absolute gem of a ride, on a clear sunny day it would be unsurpassable. For the next 20 miles or so there was not more than the occasional short stretch of level road. It seemed to consist for a good part, of either steamy ascents when we both overheated massively in our waterproof gear, or adrenalin fuelled descents. Sometimes by means of variation we had long grinding ascents or lovely long more sedate descents, during which Mark would sometimes frighten me by steering one handed and taking photos on his smart phone with the other.

We had noticed that since Galloway and Arran there was very little wild blossom. The gorse, broom and may had more or less disappeared. Where there were farms or isolated houses and these were very few and far between, we did see some grand displays of azaleas and rhododendrons. This is such a sparsely populated area and it seemed that sometimes we would cycle for miles with hardly any evidence of man's intrusion in the landscape. Almost every ascent concluded with yet another stunning view, invariably featuring Loch Awe to a greater or lesser degree. We cycled past an ever changing composition of natural woodland, streams, meadows, rocky outcrops, conifer plantations and standalone trees that bravely displayed the scars of countless encounters with the elements. Although the rain was relentless at least it had the dignity to fall from a cloud base at a height that enabled views of most of the lower hills and enough of the more distant mountains to allow ones mind to fill in the gaps.

About 9 or 10 miles along Loch Awe we were lucky to find a small general store cum post office cum cafe at Dalavich, we much appreciated taking off waterproof coats for a short while. As often happened in this kind of instance, Mark would cause consternation by asking for Earl Grey tea, when the request was declined the matter was easily resolved by Mark changing his order to hot water only, to which he added tea bags from his own plentiful supply.

Warmed and refreshed we set off again and shortly crossed the River Avich, then a long climb of over 300ft up through a large wooded area, before dropping right down to the loch to cross the next river. Another 5 miles brought us to Annat where we turned left, away from Loch Awe, on to the B845 and shortly after came to Kilchrenan where to our surprise and delight we found a pub offering a good lunch menu. So in spite of a morning cycling through such a remote area we had fared very well with regard to refreshment.

After lunch we were not surprised that the rain still fell. A short spell of 2 or 3 miles took us north over some low hills before dropping down into the valley of the River Nant which offered us much easier cycling to Taynuilt. Here we turned left on to a main road for the briefest of 'hello goodbyes' before turning left again back on to NCR 78. Compared to the morning's exertions we were now cycling on easy street. Our road looped south and west for a few miles then we were back to a river side road, this time along Glen Lonan which took us to within a couple of miles of Oban. A last climb took us over some wooded hills before a final high speed descent brought us to a very soggy Oban. The next day's ride demanded an early start to catch a ferry, so we headed straight for the ferry terminal to check times and get our tickets. Similar to this day's ride the options for getting to Fort William, my next stopover and the end of Mark's section, were starkly different. Either a shorter direct route on main roads all along the east side of Loch Linnhe, or a rather challenging route through Ardgour which is the remote area immediately west of Loch Linnhe and south of Loch Eil, which merges into Loch Linnhe at Fort William. This option did demand an early morning ferry crossing from Oban!

Ferry tickets purchased we made our way to the backpackers hostel which was in a central location, so only a short pedal to the ferry. It was still raining, as it was when late we ventured out to find somewhere to eat. The rain was even heavier as we made our way back after a superb Indian meal.

Day 18 Friday June 2nd
Oban to Fort William
52 miles
3500ft ascent

When Mark and I had talked about routes the minor road option for this last leg to Fort William looked so attractive that it was difficult to countenance doing any other route. The task we had set ourselves by making this choice was a challenge and quite a high risk strategy. The challenge came not in respect to the cycling, which although quite a demanding day was similar to a lot of other days, 50+ miles and 3 or 4 thousand feet of climbing. The challenge was that the day involved 3 ferry crossings, 2 to get us on to Ardgour and one at the end to get us back across Loch Linnhe to Fort William harbour.

Ardgour is such a sparsely populated area that it does not warrant its own ferry connection from Oban and instead, potential visitors need to travel from Oban to Craigmure on Mull, then drive 5 miles or so up the coast to Fishnish for the short crossing of the Sound of Mull to Lochaline on Ardgour. Both these services are operated by Calmac and so would be pretty reliable and an early 7.30am service would give us a good start. At the end of the day the short, half a mile crossing to Fort William is a privately operated passenger only ferry, the last crossing being at 4.30pm, which gave us a deadline, for if we were to miss that we would be faced with a 20 mile detour to get to our destination.

Mark and I were quite happy that barring incident it was perfectly feasible especially if we caught the first ferry of the morning. A 6.00am alarm call, a quick cup of tea and a bowl of cereal, Mark even managed to have his porridge and we were all packed up by 6.35. We then had to extricate the Beast from the shed where it had spent the night. Freed from its uncomfortable overnight quarters we loaded up and at 6.45 were pedalling off to the ferry. Thankfully the rain had passed through and although there was still a lot of cloud the forecast was quite reasonable and the early morning sun fighting its way through the clouds gave cause for optimism.

At 7.30am prompt the ferry pulled away from the quay at Oban, yet again we stood on the upper deck in spite of the very chilly breeze forcing its way up the Firth of Lorn. Looking back, views of Oban were soon reduced to monochrome tones. The high cloud cover in the eastern sky was backlit by the strong early morning sun, so the hills and the town nestling beneath appeared only in silhouette. As a contrast the view westwards to Mull was slightly hazy but the island did stand out in tones of green and grey. There was still some low cloud flirting with the higher slopes, suggesting that the weather had not quite made up its mind about its conduct for the day.

The trip to Craignure on Mull took just under an hour so by the time we got back on the road we still had about 45 minutes to make our way to Fishnish for the second ferry of the morning. It seemed to be company policy to allow all the vehicles to disembark before the cycles, which was sensible as it meant the bicycles would not be harried by vehicles all eager to explore their new environment. The 5 miles to Fishnish were pretty unremarkable, level cycling with only the occasional view to our left up into the higher part of Mull. We had about 20 minutes to wait for the ferry, tranquility was certainly the name of the game, hardly a sound to break the peace. The sheltered water was not bothered by any breeze and sailors were eagerly awaiting their new socks as more small patches of blue sky were appearing. Ardgour was about 2 miles away but even at that distance we could see some pretty lumpy hills in the direction of our intended route. A small white shape on the far side of the Sound eventually took on the form of a Calmac ferry. On its final approach to the slipway the ramp was lowered and the ferry scrunched its way to a halt as the ramp made contact with the slipway. In calm conditions I noticed on the smaller ferry crossings I made that no lines were taken ashore, the boat being held in position by the weight and hydraulic pressure of the ramp. The new arrivals quickly vacated the ferry and ourselves together with the few cars that had collected made our way aboard. The boat was on its way again in not much more than 5 minutes.

It was clear to us that we were not likely to find any friendly cafes or pubs until we reached Corran, which was about 40 miles away. Apart from the little settlement at Lochaline we could see no other signs of habitation apart from a few isolated dwellings scattered along the road. So it was with relief that we parked up outside a very smart general store overlooking the ferry slip. Having purchased some tasty comestibles, we sat outside and enjoyed an alfresco breakfast.

Lochaline is situated at the narrow entrance to ... yes you have guessed correctly, Loch Aline. There was a steady climb of about 350ft over the large wooded hill that dominates the west side of the loch. After 3 miles we dropped down again into the glen where the road crosses the River Aline. The road passed by the southern end of Loch Arienas then turned sharply eastwards following the river. The terrain here was so different to Kintyre, we were now in real mountain country. Big hills or small mountains were all around us, in the immediate vicinity were summits ranging up to about 1500ft, further to the east towards Loch Linnhe were some peaks over 2000ft.

For the next 5 miles we had really steep slopes on our left rising from the roadside. For a way we followed the north side of the river but then the road left the river as it contoured gently northwards. The scenery was spectacular, with the weather steadily improving, most of the time bright sunshine showed everything with that clarity which only seems to occur at this time of year. Near the coast were quite extensive conifer stands but now only the occasional small pockets of trees generally in accessible places close to the road. As the road turned away from the river we began to climb, over 4 miles we gained about 600feet. At the top of the climb the road once again changed direction as it curved eastwards. We now had the higher ground on our right and to the left we looked down to another river. A short descent brought us to a junction, the A884 'main road' turned sharply to the north-west but we turned on to the B8043 which continued east. The following 15 miles or so were so beautiful, spectacular and consummately satisfying as a cycle ride that it ranks as one of the best parts of the whole adventure.

A mile of level cycling brought us to Loch Uisge and as we followed the north bank the road began to turn towards the south-east, all around us the open rock strewn mountainsides. The descent quickened and as we lost height in the road's anxiety to reach the coast we passed stands of mixed woodland. A final rush and a most picturesque, quiet, sheltered little bay demanded our further attention. It seemed a perfect place to stop for a picnic, we turned sharp right, back on ourselves, on to a track that lead past a little chapel, through some trees along the edge of a small beach to a handful of houses that constitutes the community of Camasnacroise.

We sat on a small patch of grass adjacent to the chapel and enjoyed our picnic lunch. The sun was warm, the views magnificent and the chilly breeze had been completely absorbed or deflected by the trees and hillside above us. We would have loved to linger longer but there were still miles to cover and although the time was not yet 1.00pm we did not have too much to spare. Across the little bay we could see the road winding round above the shoreline and disappearing from view. Within a couple of minutes of setting off we rounded that bluff and it is no exaggeration to say that nothing we had seen or looked at on the map quite prepared us for the spectacle of the next 3 miles. A narrow strip of the shoreline had been fashioned enough to accommodate the road. In places rocky shoulders had been hewn away to allow egress of the road. All along the vertiginous lower flank of Meall nan Each, in Scottish terms quite a modest mountain of just under 2000ft, rose from the roadside cliffs. The views were very reminiscent of many such views that could be seen in travelogs of remote Mediterranean islands, South American Pacific coast or other exotic locations.

Just when we thought the afternoon could get no better, our attention was drawn away from the view ahead which had completely captivated us since lunch. To our right was an uninterrupted panoramic view across Loch Linnhe to the mountains of Glen Etive. Since leaving the higher ground partial cloud cover had given way to less cloud and fairly unbroken sunshine, so the loch and hills beyond were in sharp relief. Far away to the south and absorbed into the bright sunlight lay Oban.

Then scanning right to left the hilly backdrop to the loch became more dominated by bigger hills. On one occasion when we had stopped to take in the view it was with great excitement that I realised we were now looking across to the bottom end of Glen Coe. The Pap of Glen Coe could be clearly seen, a little standalone hill about 2500ft high that overlooks Glencoe village and Loch Leven, proudly announcing to southward bound travellers the imminent appearance of its much more imposing cousins.

Our road then left the water's edge to head briefly into the hills again. Another climb and 2 or 3 miles passing lochans and streams with hills now close by to our right and for the first time since lunch, in places to our left vistas of crags and rocky slopes above. We descended to cross the River Tarbert and turned right on to the A861, within a mile we were back along the side of Loch Linnhe, although this time on a better, wider and busier road. We were now only 6 or 7 miles from Corran, where if so desired the adventurous Ardgour traveller can be introduced to the delights of the A82 trunk road which lies just a short ferry ride across Loch Linnhe. We stopped at the hotel opposite the ferry and enjoyed several pots of tea while watching the ferry unload and load, smug in the knowledge that we were to have a much more interesting crossing to the 'other side'.

On leaving Corran the poor A861 is immediately demoted to the status of a single track road with passing places, much better for cycling though. For most of the remaining 10 miles or so to Camusnagaul, where we were catch the little ferry to Fort William, the road closely followed the shoreline. In just two places it ventured briefly away from the water's edge where there was a river to cross. At the first of these we stopped on the narrow bridge to take a photo of the picturesque Inverscaddle Bay. While we stood on the bridge an empty logging lorry with trailer appeared round a bend ahead, there was something about its progress towards us that made us quickly lift the tandem on to the pathway, seconds later it thundered past using the whole width of the roadway and without any perceptible slackening of speed. To date our experiences of these logging lorry drivers bore out the rather dubious reputation that they enjoy.

The view across Loch Linnhe had changed again, we now looked up Glen Nevis with Fort William straddled along the water's edge below, and the massif of Ben Nevis looming above the town like a slightly malevolent warden. I found the last mile or two rather strange. Mark and I had in seven days come from North Yorkshire and now Fort

William, the end of Mark's section was getting ever closer, just the other side of the loch. All of a sudden we arrived at Camusnagaul where Mark quickly located the ferry jetty. We joined another cyclist and waited for about 20 minutes. More or less on time the little boat seemed to suddenly appear, we unloaded the panniers and wheeled The Beast down to the jetty. The boatman was very helpful and friendly, he lifted the tandem on board with the ease that I would have shown lifting a carbon fibre solo. He roped it to the outside of the cabin and then we were off for the sixth of my ferry crossings. In just a few minutes we were in Fort William cycling through the town I know so well having been the setting off point or final destination for many of my backpacking adventures. On this occasion it was to be a brief stopover before heading north again with Ian my last pilot.

It felt like a bit of an anti-climax, cycling along the main road south, looking for our respective B and B's. Such is the demand for accommodation in Fort William that when I booked in late January/early February all I found in a dozen or so calls was a guesthouse almost on the edge of town, about a 2 mile walk from the station. Mark had booked only a day or two before leaving for Yorkshire and had managed to find room less than half that distance out.

We arranged to meet later that evening to have a last meal together before meeting our wives, who were travelling by train from Devon and due to arrive about 10.00pm. All went to schedule and we made plans to meet the following morning. We spent a leisurely time with them, walking up to the visitor centre at the foot of Ben Nevis. Mark and Lesley finally left us about 4.00pm to find their rented cottage in Roy Bridge, which they had booked for the following week.

Ali and I spent the next 2 days combining walks and a train trip on the Mallaig line, with shopping for essential kit replacements. The weather forecast was not too encouraging, at least for the next week so I thought it prudent to replace my waterproof overshoes and cycling jacket.

Ian was flying up to Glasgow on Monday and providing there were no delays would arrive by coach from Glasgow airport by early evening. This bit of the planning had the potential to cause a problem, a flight delay of even a couple of hours would mean missing the last through coach to Fort William.

However the force was with him and he disembarked, on time, very tired but much relieved that our last leg could at least start as planned. A couple of beers, a good meal and nonstop conversation left us all needing an early night. A late evening check of the BBC weather website revealed a depressing prediction for the next day. Ali was due to leave on the 7.44am train, so as she travelled south we would be pedalling north for the final 12 day leg. Although Fort William is less than 200 miles from Cape Wrath and the north coast we estimated we would clock up over 500 miles before finishing at Inverness in 12 days' time.

Day 19 Tuesday June 6th
Fort William to Shiel Bridge
62 miles
3378ft ascent

The swish swish of the taxi's windscreen wipers only enhanced my low spirits. I had waved goodbye to Ali on the 07.44 train and was now heading back to have breakfast with Ian and to prepare for our journey. Curtains of rain were being ushered up Loch Linnhe by an impatient and grudging wind. The little waterside road Mark and I had cycled 4 days earlier was invisible, completely absorbed into the dark grey outline across the loch. Ian and I breakfasted together, both keen to get started although apprehension concerning the inclement weather was uppermost in our minds. Also Ian had not 'unwound' after a demanding 4 days of work followed by the journey.

The Beast had been stabled under a lean-to roof at the rear of the guesthouse, so we were sheltered while we checked everything. A slow puncture was dealt with by replacing the inner tube and we were soon ready to load up. The rain was now persistent but light, although all the signs were indicating that it was in for the long haul and that the current slight slackening of volume was most likely to be due to the rain saving its energy for later. A mile or so along the busy main road approach to the town we dived off on to a cycle path, which Ian easily followed as it wound through the housing estates on the north side of town . We turned on to the bottom end of the Great Glen Way at Banavie. This is a walking and cycle way along the Caledonian Canal, all the way to Inverness. The first 5 miles were on the canal tow path. I was familiar with this section from when I started my Cape Wrath Trail from Banavie station.

The Cape Wrath Trail is more a concept walk than an established walk as there is no defined route between Fort William and Cape Wrath. In the last 2 decades it has become acknowledged as being Britain's toughest long distance walk, with a direct route passing through some of the most remote and challenging areas of the UK. I completed the 200+ miles of my solo and unsupported CWT in 13 days of early May 2004.

The rain was no more than a drizzle now as we lingered by the flight of 3 locks. There was plenty to look at, some large and expensive looking yachts and 2 police launches occupied by large and expensive looking policemen supping mugs of tea, in their warm and dry cabins. Presumably they were involved in the low speed pursuit of some unfortunate miscreants. We did expect later to come across maybe a couple of canoes being paddled by false bearded, stripey jumper wearing desperados bearing lumpy sacks marked 'swag'.

This section of the canal has an elevated position. The wide towpath is on its east bank and the river that flows from Loch Lochy to Loch Linnhe on the east side of that but maybe 40 - 50 feet below. So from the path one has a fairly uninterrupted view of the mountains above Fort William, namely Ben Nevis, Carn Mor Dearg and The Grey Corries. To the left across the canal are a series of lower but still impressive hills which all enhance the impression that one is travelling back into the hills after the temporary civilising effect of Fort William and its environs.

Gairlochy at the southern end of Loch Lochy marked the end of the towpath and also the end of relaxed cycling for the day. We crossed the canal and turned right on to a little road that contoured north above the loch before descending to cross the River Arkaig. Shortly after that the road, having become utterly overwhelmed at the prospect of finding its way along the forest clad ,vertiginous slopes that tumble nearly 3000ft in to Loch Lochy, turns sharply west and proceeds along the level bank of Loch Arkaig. Little did it realise that in about 15 miles it would expire at the end of the loch, exhausted from the task of trying to find a way through the impenetrable mountain mass of Knoydart, that lay ahead.

At the point where the road turns west we carried on north-east on to the cycle way. Thus began an utterly miserable section through the dripping forest at the side of Loch Lochy. It is only about 6 or 7 miles but it felt like an eternity. The route is one that would be greatly enjoyed by mountain bikers. For anything less it is a pretty demanding ride and for a fully laden tandem, being much heavier and less manoeuvrable, it is not to be recommended. The track pitches and turns, seldom flat it undulates its way through the trees, with some really steep short sections. Ian did a magnificent job under exceedingly taxing circumstances. Somehow avoiding the large potholes and drifts of knobbly tyre wrecking stones. The steep parts were the worst, both going up or down, to steer around obstacles whether at low speed or while trying to reduce speed safely on a steep descent, needed great skill and strength. Conversation was in short supply and those 'bon mots' that did pass between us were generally accompanied by a liberal quantity of expletives. I didn't realise at the time that there was another issue colouring Ian's appreciation of the day and that was the matter of his waterproof cycling jacket. Just before he came north he had bought himself a new jacket, persuaded by a smooth talking assistant that it was definitely the best thing in waterproofing since the advent of gore-tex. As we proceeded that morning I could see the fabric darkening especially around his shoulders. I thought to myself 'that is not an auspicious sign' as it indicated water being absorbed and not repelled. Some time later while we stood in a puddle under dripping trees and consumed much needed energy bars, he voiced his concerns and also his opinion of the aforementioned silver tongued retail advisor. So that was another piece of grit in life's ointment as far as Ian was concerned.

We eventually reached some dwellings among the trees and it became clear that we had reached the top end of Loch Lochy. It was with a huge sense of relief that we had emerged unscathed from the embrace of the waterlogged forest. We paused for a moment at Laggan locks and we both agreed that we would ignore the minor road that continues on the west side for some way. We crossed the waterway at the locks and followed the towpath for a short distance, then there was no option but to put ourselves at the mercy of the A82. Within a couple of miles we reached Invergarry and turned left on to the A87.

Invergarry is not by any stretch of the imagination a bustling centre of the Highlands, but it does have an excellent hotel. We had a much needed break for refreshment involving several pots of tea and plates of corned beef hash. An hour or so later we felt more equipped to confront the remaining challenges of the day. Bearing in mind our slow progress that morning these were the majority of the climbing and probably about 50 miles of cycling. One of the drawbacks of cycling in this area is the shortage of roads. For the rest of the day our route was the A87. For the first 3 miles after lunch we climbed, following the river up to Loch Garry. Mostly through the conifer woods but we did get occasional views, mainly of misty mountains!. The road contours along the north bank of the loch and then begins a long climb gradually leaving the loch far below. From the hotel the road climbs about 1000ft to the high point of the day, high above Loch Loyne,. Much of the road is through woods and the higher we climbed the colder it became. The rain was heavier and any views much less rewarding. We were heading north-west and near the highest point the road turned to the north-east skirting around the west side of a large and barren mountainside. The road is quite open here and a blustery westerly wind made life a bit more uncomfortable. The descent to Glen Shiel was a relief, by the time we turned left in Glen Shiel we had lost about 600ft of elevation. This section of the A87 from Invergarry to Shiel Bridge must be one of the most spectacular in the Highlands. So it was a disappointment that we could not appreciate the views. Since 1990 I have walked in this area and climbed quite a few of the mountains so at least I knew what majestic mountains lurked behind the cloudy mantle that covered everything above about 2000ft. This is a seriously wild, lonely and hostile area of mountains. These are definitely in the Premier league of British hills, maybe not in contention for any silverware but still hills to be greatly respected.

From the T junction, where the A887 becomes the A87, to Shiel Bridge is about 20 miles. A really lean area for door to door salesmen as The Cluanie Inn is the only habitation. We were prepared for the headwind, but still somehow, when we turned left cycling did seem to get unexpectedly harder. Maybe it was the traffic just adding another level of discomfort to proceedings. The next 8 miles or so to the inn were hard work. A short climb for a mile and a half then an interminable 7 miles or so contouring along the north bank of Loch Cluanie. This is very bleak open terrain and the wind was unrelenting. We did stop briefly on one occasion to admire the lack of a view and to consume another energy bar. We joined other travellers seeking refuge in the Cluanie Inn. The management of this august establishment won, hands down, the award for most expensive tea. For the princely sum of £4.80 we were given enough tea for 2 large cups and a refusal for hot water. Our need for warmth and rehydration overcame our grudging resentment and we ordered a second pot.

As we set off on the last leg of the day, the rain was even heavier. We had a final climb of about 200ft, followed by the long descent to Shiel Bridge. We covered the 2 miles to the watershed of Glen Shiel in about 10 minutes. At this point the glen narrows significantly. Two of the most spectacular mountain ridges in the UK look down on this section of road. To the north lies the Five Sisters ridge and to the south the imaginatively named South Glen Shiel ridge. The latter is a fearsome line of seven 3000+ft peaks that form an effective barrier between Glen Loyne and Glen Shiel for everything bar ravens, eagles and stout hearted nimble footed hill walkers.

For this last adrenalin fuelled descent Ian was in no mood to take any prisoners. Having wound the Beast up to speed he positioned us well over towards the central white line(s) and any traffic behind just had to wait, but as we were travelling at speeds approaching 40mph that was no great hardship. Initially the road is following the river on its north side then switches to the south side for the final descent to sea level. We breezed through Shiel Bridge and in just a couple of minutes we found our digs and were stood on the forecourt of the Kintail Lodge, a hotel with bunkhouse.

After hot showers, several mugs of strong tea and handfuls of biscuits, we looked back through very slightly rose tinted glasses on what had been an exciting but very demanding day's cycling. Sharing the facilities of the bunkhouse with us were two guys from Bristol. It is fair to say they were in the autumn of their hill walking days and had clearly spent countless days on the hill together over many years. Their easy comfortable companionship was a joy to see. We spent a long time with them drinking tea and swapping stories of mountain experiences.

Day 20 Wednesday June 7th
Shiel Bridge to Portree (Isle of Skye)
52 miles
4006ft ascent

The obvious choice of route for this day was quite simple. Stay on the A87, a nice scenic route to Kyle of Lochalsh and the Skye bridge along the north bank of Loch Duich and then over the hills on the north side of Loch Alsh. In the process we could join the sightseers at the viewpoint near Dornie and gaze down with reverence on what is probably the most iconic view in the Scottish Highlands, that being Eilean Donan castle. Once on the Isle of Skye there is little choice of roads. Apart from one brief diversion it would be the main road all the way to Uig. However as I pondered the options, I recalled there was a vehicle ferry still operating even after the Skye bridge opened. For a lot of the initial route planning I used Mapometer a free mapping app. This was very useful allowing the plotting of route and giving details of distance, elevation etc. The system is based on Google type mapping which is not good for shewing hills and contours. Sure enough the ferry was still running, crossing the Kyle of Rhea, a narrow sliver of water whose sole purpose in life is to ensure the continuation of Skye's island status. I used Google Street View and saw that the location was about as idyllic as could be imagined and so, I was hooked. Next time I spoke to Ian I explained what I planned and he enthusiastically agreed that we should take that option. So it was decided, instead of the A87 we would back track to Shiel Bridge then on to a friendly looking little road that would take us to Glenelg. Then an old fashioned ferry trip, over the sea to Skye, another unassuming little road across the moor and we would join the main road 2 or 3 miles from the bridge.

It was some time later that I revisited the issue, this time looking on the 1:50,000 OS map. I did a double take and maybe even a triple take, even with my poor sight, my magnifier revealed black arrows and contours, lots of them all crossing the 'friendly' little yellow road. The road from Shiel Bridge runs for about half a mile round a bay just above the beach then climbs for 2.3 miles to the high point of 1120 feet above sea level. So even if the tide was in, still a good climb in anyone's book. Near the top the map showed a series of hairpin bends with black arrows. Then just to compound my discomfort, the 'unassuming little road' on Skye the other side of the ferry, was no cakewalk either. Over a similar distance it climbed 920feet but only had 2 black arrows. When I told Ian the reality of our decision, he very flatteringly said something to the effect of 'by the time you have cycled from Cape Cornwall to Shiel Bridge you will fly up that'.

The forecast was not so bad for the day. Although we were in an unsettled spell of weather with a series of fronts threatening to upset things for at least the next week or so. Often in these conditions the inland mountain areas fare less well than the coastal parts. Having breakfasted well we bade farewell to our Bristolian friends and loaded up the Beast. Before setting off we took time to look around, the hotel is in a beautiful position looking down Loch Doich and across to the hills we would soon be climbing. There was moisture in the air but the cloud base was certainly higher and the clouds more broken than the previous day. Indeed an optimist could have been forgiven for concluding that the rain clouds were quite happy now to move on and make other lives a misery. We pedalled back to Shiel Bridge just before 10.00am and were soon on the friendly little yellow road. For just a short way the road passes prettily and innocently under trees along the edge of the loch (oh no! The tide is out!). There was no messing with half measures, in under 50 yards the steep climb began. As a cyclist used to hills one accepts that on most long ascents the gradient varies, with steep sections then easing and allowing breath to be drawn. We both felt that this climb was constant, for the 2 miles or so up to the hairpins a lung busting 1:12. Then it got steeper! The road runs through trees for most of the way, so at least we did not have the distraction of a view to look at. I think by the time we had climbed the first half mile or so we knew we could keep going although the spectre of the black arrows still loomed over us. Ian piloted magnificently, no mean feat to steer a steady course at sometimes under 3mph.

There had been very little traffic, just a few cars and the inevitable clutch of German motorcyclists growling by on their fat motorbikes. The first and second hairpins were both right handed and even though the gradient steepened to justify black arrow status we managed alright with more huff, puff and push. Just a couple of hundred yards further on came the last bend a left handed 180degree hairpin. The road at this point was at least twice the width and the inside of the bend - our side of the road - was impossibly steep. Fortunately no sound of traffic so Ian pulled across to the extreme right and we powered round, at 1.5mph. Nothing could stop us now, not even the last steep section. The gradient quickly eased and just before the highest point we pulled in to the lay-by viewpoint. It was with a terrific sense of achievement that we hugged and high-fived, neither of us had been confronted with such a climb before. To have done it on a fully laden tandem was even better!

After a couple of minutes drawing deep breaths, back slapping and general self congratulating, we began to drink in the scenic splendour. The previous day's dearth of views just seemed to accentuate the magnificence of what lay before us. Immediately to our right and obscuring the northern end of the South Glenshiel Ridge were the lumpy lower slopes of a 2300+ft mountain that overlooks the southern end of Loch Duich, just beyond we could see the very bottom end of

Glen Shiel with the mouth of the river and the adjacent main road. Behind that and arcing away up the Glen Shiel was the flank of the Five Sisters ridge. The sisters themselves were not to be seen, obviously with their minds on greater things for their heads were in the clouds. Almost opposite was a bay where the road is forced to find a way across the deposits so thoughtlessly discarded on the edge of Loch Duich by one of the many substantial rivers that drain this part of the Kintail mountains. Loch Duich disappeared from view to our left behind the hill we had just conquered. In the 40 minutes since we left the hotel the weather had slowly improved. The cloud base was still over 2000ft but there were definite breaks now with small patches of blue sky occasionally peeping through.

We set off about 15 minutes later and had gone no more than 500 yards when we rounded a bend and there was another wonderful view. This time looking west to Skye. Our road ran along the base of a massive hillside to our right and in the distance inconsiderate clouds obscured the tops of two of Skye's lesser hills. Climbing the pass between these hills would be our second challenge of the morning.

The descent was superb, the first mile or so through a conifer plantation on the side of the hill, then the second mile across the open hillside before our road joined a low level road leading to an isolated little community at the head of the glen. This was Ian's first high speed descent of the trip and he greatly enjoyed the thrill. Any fast descent by bicycle demands fine judgement, on a tandem even more so. The Beast is very stable at high speed and predictable, never any twitchy moments. Throughout the ride there were many long descents and I found as 'stoker' that I needed to concentrate probably as much as the pilot. Maintaining perfect balance is essential, while still trying to react with the pilot's changes of body position especially negotiating bends or cornering. So generally there was no time for relaxed sightseeing. As often happened, the pilot would go into a tuck position to reduce wind resistance, then I would follow suit and see no more than the pilot's backend, my crossbar and the road racing beneath my feet.

The next 3 miles were on the level and we just relished looking round and chatting. We hoped there would be an opportunity to get a well deserved drink. Ian turned off the road to the ferry and we headed to the village of Glenelg. It is probably over egging the pudding somewhat to call it a village. Including the outlying isolated farms and crofts there may be 30 or so dwellings in this, what many would describe as an idyllic location. There was no sign of a cafe but eagle-eyed Ian spotted a hand written sign by the community hall advertising 'Coffee Morning Today'. The local ladies were only too keen to welcome us and for the princely sum of £2.50 each, we had several cups of tea and as much cake, biscuits and jam scones as we could eat.

By the time we were pedalling off to find the ferry the sun was shining and much of the early morning cloud had dispersed. The sun was filtering through the trees that spread down to the waterside. The last mile and a half to the ferry were along the edge of the shore. The steep slopes of Skye rising up from the water less than a mile away. We descended to the slip and joined a little group of one car and a camper van. We began chatting with our fellow travellers and noticed an attentive collie dog checking up on things. We both assumed it belonged to the camper van. Another car joined us as the ferry neared the slip. Several cars were ushered on their way by a second collie that disembarked with the cars, then the two dogs began rounding us up and pushing us on board. The two helpers on the ferry came round collecting fares, one bone and two dog biscuits per person per trip. We thought this a bit expensive but then its not often one has the privilege of using a ferry operated by two dogs.

The cars and camper van soon disappeared, the ferry retreated to the mainland; utter peace and quiet embraced us, save for the creaking crank of the Beast and gulping gasps from Ian and I as we began the climb. The reality was that with a slightly more favourable gradient and a residue of adrenalin from the first climb, this one seemed easier. Even the black arrows at the top could not deter us, the road was straighter and we could see the parking place ahead which denoted the top of the climb.

We pulled in to the viewing area carpark and joined a group of German bikers. As always the bright yellow fully laden Beast attracted attention. We were soon chatting to a friendly group of Germans. Then followed a rather surreal few minutes. One of the group started talking about the UK's decision to leave the EU. The other guys melted away and we were left being almost lectured on the insanity of the our current situation. I for one felt it was none of his business and the conversation was discontinued as quickly as decency allowed.

The views both ways were superb, behind us the road disappeared dramatically round a bend below the steep section far below the blue waters we had just crossed. Beyond, the rocky green of the hills above Shiel Bridge, contrasted with the blue grey of the mountainous panorama behind, framed between the hills on either side of the pass we had just traversed. Looking west and north across a short stretch of moorland were the waters of the Inner Sound and the islands of Scalpay and Raasay. Although at that distance it was very difficult to see detail. To the left, the scree clad flanks of the Red Cuillin mountains and to the right the hills of the Applecross peninsular, a remote and beautiful area of Wester Ross that lies to the west of the mighty mountains of Torridon. Centrally but in the far distance above the islands a rather compacted view of the Trotternish Ridge. This is a unique mountain feature, a ridge that starts just above Portree and undulates northwards for about 16 miles. The height ranging between 1000-2000ft. It is a classic escarpment, from the east appearing as an almost unbroken vertical cliff face hundreds of feet high, from the west as little more than a gently rising heather clad hillside. Just 6 or 7 miles north of Portree The Storr lies adjacent to the cliff face. It is a dramatic rock pinnacle called The Old Man of Storr surrounded by a fantastic array of lesser rock stacks. Further north just beyond the only road that crosses the ridge is The Quiraing. Similar to the Storr, eons of weathering and erosion have created an almost Alice in Wonderland landscape of multi-level stacks, tables and pinnacles, all set underneath and immediately adjacent to the cliff face of the main ridge.

The time was now nearly 1.00pm. We had spent all morning on the two climbs, drinking tea and generally enjoying ourselves. There was still a lot of miles to cover and we needed to eat. The descent was fast and on a reasonably straight well surfaced road. We covered the 5 miles to the junction with our old friend the A87 in double quick time. Another 4 miles of easy cycling brought us to Broadford. I remembered from 15-20 years ago that there were facilities here. As we approached the village we came alongside a lady cyclist who being a 'local' told us where the various cafes were. We took her recommendation and a few minutes later dismounted on the forecourt of a very promising establishment. We sat outside, away from the wind and in the sunshine enjoying a very good much needed lunch.

Over lunch we had a bit of a discussion on tactics (of riding). The last two days had necessitated more riding on main roads than any day since Mark and I rode from Dumfries to Ayr. As on that occasion we found ourselves being hassled by drivers anxious to overtake at any cost, often passing too close for comfort. All just for the sake of not having to reduce speed by even a few mph. Ian suggested that rather than positioning ourselves approximately 2 to 3 feet from the edge of the road, we should be bold and occupy a line 5 - 6 feet from the edge.

This would generally mean we were between a third and halfway across our carriageway.

Just before we went on our way a funny incident occurred. For me it was one of those laugh or cry moments. Ian went off to find the toilets, on his return I asked where they could be found. He directed me to the indoor seating section of the cafe telling me the door was over to the left. Following his instructions I went into the cafe, from bright sunlight into relatively subdued lighting and I was surprised to see how far back the room went. As I walked towards the rear a figure clad in a yellow jacket was walking directly towards me. We stopped when we were a few feet apart, I could see behind him on the left two doorways. I stood aside to let him pass and he moved the same way I moved the other way and he likewise. To counter this rather awkward 'shall we dance?' moments, I asked him which doorway lead to the Gents. It was then that I realised I was stood not more than eighteen inches from a floor to ceiling mirror that covered the entire back wall of the room and I could have cried. Back outside with Ian we had a real laugh about it.

The weather now seemed set fine, all the early morning uncertainty had dissipated. We set off well refreshed from our lunch, blue skies and clear views although the temperature was still hovering around the chilly mark, certainly no early summer balminess. Ian put our new riding strategy into immediate effect, which together with a move on my part, to look over my right shoulder as I heard traffic approach to indicate that we were aware of their presence. The result was most encouraging and we noticed a significant reduction in the number of vehicles that overtook with no noticeable decrease in speed. When vehicles did overtake they tended to give us much more room, even though we were taking more room anyway.

After a couple of miles the road dropped down again to the coast. We now looked across a narrow strip of water to the lumpy little island of Scalpay. A neat slightly oval shape no more than four miles by three miles but still managing to fill its restricted area with hills. The largest of which rises to a height of over 1300ft. This stretch of road skirts around the lower section of the Red Cuillin. So for much of our way, to the left were grand views of the light grey scree slopes of this much neglected group of hills. I have had four or five walking holidays on Skye and never set boot on them. Furthermore I suspect that the majority of walkers visiting Skye similarly ignore them. Situated where they are, with some peaks well over 2000ft I would expect that views from many parts of the Red Cuillin are spectacular. However the reason for their exclusion from the 'A list' of desirable mountains, is the existence of their close neighbour the Black Cuillin. An area of no more than 6 miles square contain some of the most challenging mountains in the UK. Twelve 'Munroes' (mountains over 3000ft), one stand alone mountain Blaven situated across the glen from the west side of the Red Cuillin. The other eleven arranged in a fearsome horseshoe ridge around the almost inaccessible Loch Coruisk. The Gaelic names of all eleven contain the prefix 'Sgurr' and as a hill walker, if your itinerary for the day has the challenge of a Sgurr you should know you are due to climb a pointed, steep and probably technically difficult peak. There are several sections of the ridge that are officially classified as climbs, rather than scrambles. The difference being that on a climb if you let go your handholds you fall off and on a scramble you just feel giddy.

After two miles of cycling with Scalpay just to our right, the road turns sharp left and staying along the edge of the water, heads up Loch Ainort. At the head of the loch the main road turns north and climbs the lower flank of the northerly part of the Red Cuillin. It returns again to the waterside after three miles and turns to head up the longer Loch Sligachan. We turned right on to a little yellow road that follows the coastline of a rather remote and picturesque promontory, rejoining the A87 after 6 or 7 miles. The surface of this little used road was not all that could have been desired but skilful manoeuvring on Ian's part allowed us to enjoy all the views without mishap. As we gradually turned westwards we lost the view to Scalpay and gained the view to Raasay, its larger northerly neighbour.

A couple of miles on we re-joined the main road and continued for a few miles up the loch. Just beyond the head of the loch the road bears north again past the Sligachan Hotel and the junction with a road leading to the west side of the island. We had now turned our back on the Red Cuillin and were seeing the most northerly part of the Cuillin ridge. Sgurr nan Gillean the most iconic and prominent peak stood out like a huge pointed tooth in a dental set of mighty mountainous molars.

We began the climb of about 330ft across the boggy moorland stopping once for a photo but then getting our heads down for the last ten miles to Portree. There was a long gradual descent through stands of conifers following the river, to reach the bay on which Portree sits. Ian easily found our digs, the SYHA hostel and by just after 5.00pm we were checking in. The hostel is situated in a splendid location, south facing with an uninterrupted view to the mountains. This is a really well appointed hostel with excellent facilities. A wonderful exciting day was rounded off in the town with a couple of beers and a good meal. After our dinner we wandered down to the little harbour. The view across the mirror like water with the evening sunlight playing on the little boats was achingly beautiful, though unfortunately ruined by midges.

Day 21 Thursday June 8th
Portree to Berneray (North Uist Outer Hebrides)
38 miles
1200ft ascent

The variable weather continued its 'now you see it- now you don't' pattern. Sullen grey skies leaked a fine drizzle as if a warning of what it could do if so inclined. Time was not of great consequence, with our plan of taking the 2.00pm ferry to North Uist giving us four or five hours to cover the 18 miles or so to Uig up on the north-west coast.

Ian's first intention was to buy a good warm base layer. The unseasonal chilly weather had caught him out and since Fort William he had suffered being cold. Indeed both of us were extremely glad of our long cycling pants. Even in the sunshine of the previous day we both wore longs and jackets all day. We had found an outdoor shop on our walk back from the midge-fest so after breakfast and packing up we visited it and Ian was duly kitted up with a suitable long-sleeve base layer. On our return to the hostel it was pressed into immediate service and Ian remained snug and warm for the rest of the trip.

We pedalled north out of Portree about 10.00am. The weather now was dry but still pretty cheerless and a favourable wind helped us on our way. Just outside the town we stopped at a supermarket to buy provisions for that evening and breakfast the next day. The scenery here is unremarkable, wide expanses of boggy moor punctuated by lochans and streams. There was one feature worth noting, the cotton grass made a great display, the little white tufty heads nodding and swaying in the breeze. In places buttercups made a half decent show but nothing like as spectacular as the buttercup meadows of the Peak District and Yorkshire. For the first few miles the bottom end of the Trotternish Ridge was fairly close to our right but there was no indication of its dramatic nature, just gently rising ground and heathery hilltops.

To our relief the traffic was considerably lighter than the previous day. Unsurprising as the only traffic enjoying the delights of our old friend the A87 would be local and that bound for the ferry at Uig. After nine or ten miles we came to the splendidly named Loch Snizort Beag, one of the large sea lochs that divides this part of Skye Like the lumpy, warty fingers on a deformed hand, the three regions of north Skye, Trotternish, Waternish and the most westerly Duirinish, are all separated by large bays and sea lochs. This section up the east side of the sea loch did afford some grand views to our left across the water, but the most spectacular parts of this area are way over to the west and not to be appreciated from Trotternish.

Without really trying we covered the 18 miles to Uig in about 70 minutes. We found the ferry port and parked up the Beast, then spent a couple of hours enjoying mid morning tea/coffee, an early lunch and a bit of wandering around. The weather was still far from summery, or even springy, but at least the rain was staying away.

When we planned the finer points of the route, the attraction of incorporating the Outer Hebrides was irresistible, even though we realised that we could not really do justice to them in the time we could afford. However, due to the magnificent ferry services operated by Caledonian MacBrayne we were able to plan two nights and a day and a half's cycling. A search for hostels on North Uist revealed a basic unmanned hostel on Berneray, a little pimple of an island now permanently attached to North Uist by a causeway. The hostel comprises two converted Hebridean black houses situated just above the beach, looking across to Harris. Although very small and offering only the most basic facilities and operating on a 'first come, first served' basis, we could not resist planning this for our first night's stay. The planning gods were certainly smiling on us, there is a regular ferry service to Leverburgh at the southern end of Harris, the departure port was only about 20 minutes cycle from the hostel and the first ferry of the day was 7.00am which meant that with an early call we would be on Harris well before 9.00am. The final piece of the planning jigsaw was that with spending the second night in Stornaway another early morning sailing on the longer crossing to Ullapool, would allow another full day's cycling from there. So our foray to the Outer Hebrides would entail three ferry crossings but no significant loss of cycling time.

The one and three quarter hour crossing to Lochmaddy on North Uist was calm and uneventful, Ian spotted a number of interesting seabirds and as we drew nearer the low outline of the island took on more detail. Away in the distance to the north, the island of Harris boastfully displayed its mountainous profile. The OS map of North Uist reveals a strange landscape that seems to comprise of more water than land, even for those bits which should be just land. Parts of north-west Scotland, Coigach, Assynt and Sutherland display similar formations but North Uist seemed to take the geological eccentricity to another level. A myriad of lochs and lochans that seemed in places to be held together by a fine tracery of land. From Lochmaddy we had a fairly leisurely ride to Berneray, with several stops for photos and general sightseeing.

In spite of the overall impression of flatness there are hills on North Uist, in fact quite a few, standing 400-600ft above sea level. Similar to other parts of north-west Scotland, hills are just rounded humps left in isolation in a plain of peat moorland and lochans. Such was the scale and the magnitude of the erosion during the Ice Age, that this whole area was transformed, as the ice sheet ground and scoured its way across the land. As it subsequently retreated after the Ice Age, glacial deposition further added to the massive change this area had undergone, to create the unique topography of today.

We headed north-west on an open road with more water than solid ground to our right, we passed round a couple of hills to our left. A right turn took us north-east past a couple more hills which mark the most northerly tip of North Uist. Then a short stretch of road brought us to the causeway, the low level diminutive form of Berneray just a few hundred yards away across the bay. A roadside sign here is a prompt that I can no longer avoid the subject of otters. Some months earlier I had said to Ian (in hindsight, rather foolishly) that in the remote parts we would be cycling through that the chance of seeing an otter were quite good. This comment came back to haunt me! We were still in the early days of otter spotting though and it was with some excitement and anticipation that we stopped by a sign just near the beginning of the causeway cautioning road users of 'Otters Crossing'. We must have just missed the event as we saw nothing, not even wet footprints on the tarmac.

At the far end of the causeway was a turning to the ferry slipway, a useful clarification for Ian, of where we needed to go the following morning. The road then wound round a couple of charming, sheltered south facing bays. Their quiet waters being gazed upon by the many houses that nestled into the shallow hill above the road. It was here that we saw the first of the 'black houses'. To me, these old Hebridean dwellings looked like the forerunner to the classic 'croft' design which is so common across western Scotland. We stopped by the first of the bays, to look at seals basking on the rocks some way offshore. Cycling on just a short way to the next bay there were even more seals and much closer to the road. Eventually we came to the end of the road, Ian spotted the hostel, another two hundred yards on, across the close cropped grass.

The hostel did not disappoint, the situation just a few feet from the shoreline must make it pretty unique among the elite family of remote hostels and bothies. The downside would be for anyone arriving here in the throes of an easterly gale or heavy rain. Then one could be forgiven for not immediately recognising the charms of its location. Ian and I wandered around in a bit of a daze, doing some unpacking then just stopping to try and absorb the atmosphere. We staked our claim on two bunks, there was no differentiating between male and female sleeping quarters which made things a bit easier. Both of the faithfully restored houses contained sleeping areas, with toilet and washroom. In one of the houses a communal room provided seating and cooking facilities.

There were probably about 12 to 15 people sharing the hostel that night, a few cyclists, a few backpackers and a couple of motor tourists. Some camped outside but most were indoor camping. After two mugs of tea we sat outside chatting to some of the others, later on Ian and I walked along the edge of the pure white sand beach until we reached a gathering of camper vans, lurking with intent. It is quite noticeable that these wilderness loving, solitude loving free spirit, mobile home dwellers seem to collect in drifts, usually somewhere remote offering a dramatic view. It is interesting to speculate on the mentality. Do they enjoy the company of their like-minded fellow van dwellers? Or is it a case that secretly they all try to find 'that particular secluded bit of heaven', but when they find it already occupied, they cut their losses and park up, rather than driving on and risk wasting hours searching in vain for a little corner of heaven. We pondered long and hard, for at least a minute on such weighty matters, then returned to prepare our supper.

We needed to be up with the lark the following morning, but later, before we turned in, we spent some time stood outside gazing across to Harris, wondering what the morrow would bring.

Day 22 Friday June 9th
Berneray to Stornaway, Lewis, Outer Hebrides
62 miles
4131ft ascent

The ride up to Stornaway promised to be quite a taxing day with a lot of climbing, so we had chosen to catch the early 7.00am ferry. The embryonic hold of our duvets reluctantly released us and shortly after 5.30 we staggered outside into the new day. Across the water Harris appeared sombre and somewhat threatening in the early morning light. A heavy pall of dark cloud hung over the mountains like a bad memory. Yet again it was really chilly in the brisk north-easterly wind. As the previous evening the wind was showing no inclination to turn itself into the forecast westerly, which would be more favourable to our cause. Although not actually raining the atmosphere felt damp, but the clouds were quite high so with a measure of optimism we anticipated a fine day.

We loaded the Beast then made ourselves a mug of tea and ate what we could at such an early hour. As we pedalled away over the grass, past the somnolent camper vans, we both felt almost that we had been cheated by time. The 12 hours spent on Berneray had only increased the desire to return and explore the islands more thoroughly. As we rode round the two little bays where we had seen the seals, Ian slowed as he scanned the waters, searching in vain for a sighting of an elusive otter. The ferry departed on time, plotting its course in a big loop across the Sound of Harris, threading its way through the maze of islands.

The island of Harris and Lewis is, as the raven flies, about 55 miles from tip to tip. Harris the bottom part of the island comprises a very dramatic range of mountains. It is almost a reduced version of the much respected highland areas on the mainland. Ranging up to 2500ft they still pose quite a challenge to communications. The one main road on Harris winds a serpentine course from the bottom tip, through the mountains and on northwards. As we approached the south-west facing coast, the hills seemed to tumble into the sea, except for a short section where a scattering of white painted buildings glittering in the early morning sunshine, indicated the location of Leverburgh our destination.

Adjacent to the jetty at Leverburgh a narrow break in the ridge of hills along that section of coast gives access to the almost fjord-like Loch Steisebhat. We cycled away from the jetty and turned left on to the main road, across a short causeway with the expanse of the loch to our right. For three miles the road finds its way north-west, squeezed between the coastal ridge and the bigger hills inland. The ridge then briefly withers to little more than a pimple before it bursts back into life in the form of an impressive 1100ft mountain that marks the south-western extremity of Harris. This pimple on the coast ridge was enough to create a constriction in the Sound of Taransay. There was just enough land above sea level to form a sheltered bay between the 'mainland' and the mountain. The road curved right, following the coastline north. Over to our left, behind the pimple and the shallow remnant of the coast ridge, were the results of deposition over the millennia which have created a marshy strip then a shallow lagoon that gradually morphs into the most beautiful almost white beach. For a couple of miles the road runs along the edge of the beach then climbs 100ft or so over a rocky promontory. At this point the view back is breathtaking, the beach sweeps across to the mountain about two miles away, in the most perfect arc. Looking straight out into the Sound the uninhabited island of Taransay an impressive sentinel standing over 800ft high.

The road continued curving north and east past another white sand beach. This time where rivers draining from the mountains have created a white delta in the narrow bay. The road crossed the river then began a slow steady climb of about 350ft. After the dazzling white beaches, blue sea and blue sky the landscape quickly became rather drab and colourless, no doubt bearing witness to the harsh northerly maritime climate. There were grand views, looking down to our right to the river and the hills beyond. Ahead the road stretched uninvitingly upwards. To our left the steep craggy slopes of the mountain. No vegetation here to relieve the severity of the grey rock. After 3 miles or so the road turned through 90 degrees and continued NNE, now affording us splendid views over to the east coast of the island. We undulated our way across the high barren moor for 3 or 4 miles, then a sharp descent brought us to Tarbert. Yet another member of that elite family of villages. There are I think at least 6 Tarberts scattered across Scotland. This one sits in a steep valley which is in effect a narrow neck in the island, less than a mile of land holds the two parts together.

As with the Tarbert on Kintyre, when Mark and I visited 8 days earlier, the sun shone. We coasted down the hill through the village and before we reached the harbour found an inviting cafe. Much refreshed by copious quantities of tea and scones, we continued on our way. After a short climb the road heads north-west across the 'neck' to emerge on the north side of a sea loch. We followed the waterside, again looking out on the west coast. After a couple of miles contouring around the base of a large mountain, the road, now heading roughly eastwards begins to climb. At this point we really felt that we were threading our way through the mountains. A truly spectacular ride up to the highest section, about 600ft above the very dramatic Loch Seaforth. This sea loch on the east coast is narrow and deep, running north then east for about 12 miles. At one point it widens to accommodate the Island of Seaforth, although of diminutive size it reaches an impressive elevation of over 700ft. The mid morning scones had done their work and we were now looking forward to lunch, although we had no clear idea where that could be obtained. We stopped at the view point high above Loch Seaforth and consumed consolation energy bars. All other thoughts were then dispelled as we made one of the most dramatic descents of the Scottish element of the ride. For 2 miles we sped down a wide, dry, well surfaced road free of any traffic and visibility ahead which enabled Ian to see a clear road for 2 or 3 miles. Ian was very keen to better the 51mph that Adrian and I achieved somewhere in the Peak District but contented himself with a creditable 46mph. Eventually the adrenalin levels dropped back to normal and the question of lunch returned. Having crossed the river, close to Loch Seaforth, the road contoured east then north around the base of the most northerly mountain on Harris. We were now through the maze of mountains and heading for the lower expanses of Lewis.

We looked in vain for a cafe or hotel, but to no avail. It was another 5 or 6 miles before a garage cum general store offered the prospect of some comestibles. We sat on a wall and made short work of crisps, sandwiches, fizzy drink and cake, uninspiring at least it served the purpose of keeping the wolf from the door! Interestingly as we sat there and reviewed the remnants of our very modest repast, we were horrified at the amount of waste plastic, cardboard and paper it had generated. A sorry reflection on the pre-packed society. We set off at 2.45pm, refreshed but chastened, knowing we had an easy couple of hours to Stornaway. The weather was almost perfect, some sun, high clouds and no wind to speak of, but still chilly. Even though any threat of rain had disappeared hours ago we were both glad to keep wearing our jackets. The combination of jacket and long tights did keep us reasonably warm. The ride presented no great challenges, we undulated our way northwards across similar terrain to that of N. Uist. I think we were both reliving the fabulous ride through the mountains, culminating with the superb high speed descent. The riding required no real effort and the miles sped by under our wheels. Some time after 4.00pm we rolled into Stornaway. There was always a real sense of excitement when finishing a days ride, arriving at the new destination and looking for the night's digs. Stornaway had a particular but vague connection for me. A child in the same year as me at primary school moved there in about 1956. I have long since been unable to remember anything about the child but whenever I heard mention of Stornaway, all sorts of far away images would come to mind.

Reality revealed a neat town looking south over a bay which is mainly given up to the dock and ferry terminal. We had decided that our first priority was to buy our ferry tickets. As we had come to expect the efficient Calmac staff gave us full instructions, stressing the need for us to be there 45 minutes before the 7.00am sailing time. We could see from the extent of the vehicle holding area by the embarkation point that this was a very busy service. Our guesthouse was another mile further on, overlooking the adjacent bay. It was a clean comfortable little hotel and the proprietor was friendly enough, helpfully arranging a place where we could park the Beast. However it just seemed completely soulless, the sort of establishment likely to be favoured by Russian spies or salesmen of dubious weekend leisurewear.

After the, by now, normal routine of tea, showers and 'phone calls, we walked back into town for a beer and dinner. On the walk back Ian optimistically looked out for otters in the harbour. He became excited on seeing a moving shape about 80 yards off the beach, but it turned out to be a seal doing backstroke. So, disconsolate he followed me back to the hotel.

Day 23 Saturday June 10th
Stornaway to Achmelvich via Ullapool
35 miles
3517ft ascent

Just after 6.00am we pedalled off to the ferry complete with the picnic breakfasts our host had kindly provided in lieu of the cooked variety that would have been available later had we stayed on. The weather would have given scant encouragement to sun worshippers. While not actually raining the skies were threatening and foreboding. Unlike the previous afternoon when the ferry terminal was just acres of empty tarmac, now it comprised acres of cars, caravans, camper vans, coaches and lorries. By 6.20 we had duly positioned ourselves at the bicycle holding area, a particularly draughty and exposed place. For over half an hour an unbroken procession of vehicles rumbled past us. At 6.55 when the last dribble of motorised transport had been consumed, we and the other cyclists, like the last morsels of dessert were fed into the gaping jaws of the ferry.

This was by far the largest of all the 11 ferries we used, there was a choice of saloon areas and we duly found ourselves a table and prepared for the 2 and a half hour trip. By the time we were out on the open sea, rain streaked the windows and one could hardly distinguish leaden grey sea from leaden grey sky. No question of bird watching on this crossing! Having nothing better to do, we opened the breakfast bags, that did nothing to lift our spirits. A bacon sandwich, of sorts, stringy undercooked bacon lurking between thin slices of pappy poor quality bread. A small can of own brand 'fruit juice' that neither of us could face opening, because we knew that would only lead to more disappointment, a tasteless E.U. apple that owed its existence more to durability and resistance to travel damage than any consideration of taste or texture. I think there may have been a packet of biscuits as well but my memory has erased the detail. The queues at the cafeteria seemed endless so we decided to seek a decent breakfast in Ullapool.

Around 9.30 and on time we slid into Loch Broom and the ferry terminal at Ullapool, through sheets of rain and blankets of low cloud obscuring most of the mountains. It was a real disappointment, with good weather and clear visibility, the views coming in from the sea must be beautiful. The Summer Isles away to the north and the dramatic mountainous ridges extending S.E. for over 10 miles on either side of Loch Broom.

We extricated the Beast from the bowels of the ship and found a shelter on the quayside where we waited along with a couple of the other cyclists, looking out despondently on the rain. Then, surprise, surprise the rain, that five minutes earlier had looked as though it could have lasted all day, eased. The clouds were higher and it was with lighter hearts that we set off in search of breakfast. So far in the trip both Ian and I had resisted the temptation of full Scottish breakfast, as the high levels of protein do take a lot of energy to digest, however on this occasion we compromised and went for the fried veggie option.

Similar to Fort William, Ullapool has played a memorable part in several of my backpacking adventures over the last 12 years. Also Ali and I stayed there for 3 days in 2015. Years earlier we had come to Torridon, Skye and Wester Ross on a camping, walking holiday. We had intended to go further north, but Ullapool became a town too far. We ran out of time and had to turn south on to the A835, rather than turning left and heading up Loch Broom to Ullapool. So for years it remained a bit of an enigma with me and I must say that in 2004 when I finally walked in to the town en route to Cape Wrath, I was not disappointed. To me Ullapool marks the distinct change in geology in the northerly transition of Scotland. To the south lie the big mountain ranges linked together by spectacular majestic glens. Walking north from Fort William, for over 100 miles, one is confronted with a succession of glens and mountain ridges. To the north, travelling into Assynt and Sutherland, isolated mountains that even have different sounding names, Cul Mor, Stac Pollaidh, Suilven, Quinag, Canisp, Arkle, Foinavon and Ben Hope. These protrude from the glaciated landscape, surrounded by a myriad of lochans and stretch all the way to Cape Wrath and the north coast.

Well before 11.00am we were ready to face the day. The weather looked definitely more promising and we cycled out of town on the A835 to the accompaniment of the last dribbles of drizzle. By the time we had crossed the Ullapool River and begun the ensuing climb, the clouds were breaking and shafts of sunlight picked out the isolated patches of gorse that punctuated the hillside. We stopped partway up the hill to remove leggings and waterproofs. What a difference from 2 hours earlier, for once the temperature was quite comfortable. From Ullapool we had about 10 or 12 miles of the A835, but although this is the main westerly route to the north coast, the volume of traffic was nothing like as bad as we had experienced further south. This was a grand ride over the hills overlooking the entrance to Loch Broom. After a couple of climbs and descents the road turned N.E. and we dropped down to cycle along the edge of a sheltered bay before another up and down brought us to Strath Canaird. It is at this point that the view north begins to open out and we could see some of the mountains of Assynt. The nearest, Cul Mor and Cul Beag stand dramatically centre stage in the view north.

We turned left on to a minor road that begins its journey westwards by contouring round the lower slopes of Cul Beag. Ali and I had driven along this road in 2015 and were hugely impressed by the scenery. Travelling the road again in the slow motion of cycling was an incredible experience. I cannot recall a more spectacular road trip, not just in parts but the whole of the 10 or 12 miles to where we turned right to Lochinver. Within a few hundred yards from leaving the main road the view west unfolds as the road bears right around a wooded hill. A couple of miles ahead Loch Lurgainn, with our little road hugging its northern bank. In the distance to the right Stac Pollaidh a unique mountain, shaped like a Neolithic chisel head, protruding from the landscape to the west of the two Culs. But completely dominating the views are the mountains of Coigach, the area bounded by the roads we had just travelled and the sea to the west. These are an impressive range of hills some up to 2500ft that form an effective and forbidding barrier for communications between the main road through Strath Canaird and the ribbon of coastal communities that lie along the western edge of this peninsular. Indeed as the eagle flies it is less than 5 miles between the nearest of these isolated settlements and Strath Canaird but to travel by road would probably be at least 25 miles. The road is a single track with passing places. There seems to be a particular technique to driving this type of road, a sort of 'see who blinks first' attitude. When one of the participants in this game is a bicycle a lot of drivers seem unsure of what technique to adopt and end up not adopting any, just keep going! It was not a serious problem, we were enjoying ourselves so much that the occasional idiot driver did not upset us too much.

The road does twist and turn with some blind bends and sharp little ups and downs. It was at one of these bends before reaching the loch that we came, not quite screeching to a halt. Apparently, although I was unable to see it at any point, a red deer stag was standing in the road. I did enjoy Ian's whispered commentary which lasted for at least 5 minutes, during which no other vehicles disturbed us. After eyeballing Ian for a while the stag ambled off the road down into the thicket of greenery immediately to the edge. We gently moved forward 15 yards or so until we were directly above where the stag stood camouflaged in the undergrowth. All that was visible was his head and antlers, he changed position and still I could not see him. Eventually he just melted away, without a sound. Ian had taken some photos so I did see him digitally though not actually. The day just continued to get better! We proceeded along in a rather stop, start fashion because almost every turn in the road presented a different conjunction of loch, mountains, trees, distant hills and sky.

For the first 7 or 8 miles where the Coigach hills are closest they do so dominate the views. The north facing slopes of dark rock and scant vegetation, together with the cloudy conditions did present the hills in a rather sombre and ominous light. Further west the view seems to open out over the lower hills at the northern end of the peninsular. We turned right through quite an acute angle and immediately were faced with a steep climb of about 350ft. Near the top as views opened out we had a stunning panorama eastwards, now looking at the other sides of Stac Pollaidh and the two Culs, then further round to the left we could now see Suilven and Canisp. This next section of the ride could not have been more different to the road we had just cycled. After this brief elevated and open stretch the road plunged down through a series of S bends to cross a river. After that the road followed a real serpentine path, being neither level nor straight for more than a handful of yards. Hairpin bends, streams, rivers, steep ups and downs, wooded little valleys, lochans, stone bridges, thickets of birch and sheltered bays all vied with each other for attention. It was like nature's kaleidoscope in front of our wheels. Miniature roadside waterfalls discharged sparkling water into hidden culverts, small streams joined forces with bigger streams to become rivers, rushing down narrow defiles or wider valleys. Lochans of all shapes and sizes, ranging from little more than puddles to large expanses of open water, overflowed into one another, creating an endless source of sustenance for the streams. It was an utterly magical ride, the memories of which will remain in our mental filing cabinets forever.

All this excitement was making us thirsty and hungry. A steep descent brought us to a river. Immediately across the bridge the road turned sharp left to follow the river downstream. However eagle-eyed Ian had seen a sign! Crossing the bridge we hung a right, up an impossibly (but not for us) steep drive to a cafe. Once again copious quantities of tea and cake were consumed, fortifying the inner men. Not only that but while this fortification took place we dodged a very sharp heavy rain shower.

We followed the river for less than a mile, then the road turned sharp right and along the edge of a picturesque bay. The tiny village of Inverkirkaig nestles around Loch Kirkaig, a small sea loch, sheltered to the north, south and east by substantial hills. Turning right at the end of the beach we were faced with a sharp climb. For another 2 or 3 miles the road rose and fell crossing 3 more streams before a descent with a lochan on one side and a wood on the other brought us to Lochinver.

The west coast of Scotland has had a long history of fishing. Even this remote part of the north-west coast owes a great deal to the fishing industry which has long provided some level of relative prosperity and security to its inhabitants. In the 1990's the harbour at Lochinver was rebuilt and the fish handling facilities improved. In the late 19th century plans were developed for a rail connection to Invershin and also an alternative plan of an improved road to Ullapool. In the event both plans withered on the vine through lack of investment. This probably bore more relation to the difficulties of civil engineering, than the viability of the fishing industry.

One of the current attractions of Lochinver is the Pie Shop. In 2015 Ali and I sampled their fare although timing made it impractical to stay for a full meal. When I arranged accommodation for this trip I very much had in mind that we could feed here. The pies come in a selection of about 12 different fillings, the pastry being as fine as I have ever tasted with none of the indigestible qualities so common with a lot of commercially produced pastry. After checking out the Pie Shop we wandered along the edge of the loch. The village has certainly created an attractive impression. The tourism industry has recognised the importance of a 'quality product' and so many of the food and accommodation providers in this remote area have risen to the challenge and there seems to be no shortage of really good restaurants and guesthouses.

We just had another 4 or 5 miles to our digs. A search of hostels in this area had revealed an SYHA hostel at Achmelvich beach, just to the north-west of Lochinver. The description, like that of Berneray hostel, sold it to me. Being so close to Lochinver I had thought we could cycle back to the Pie Shop after sorting out at the hostel. The next 30 or 40 minutes cycling highlighted one of the problems of poor sight, being unable to see how many contours cross the road. There were several stiff climbs of 100 to 200 feet before we were finally rolling down to the hostel, positioned just behind the beach car park. We both agreed, there was no way we wanted to repeat that ride from the Pie Shop, in the evening after consuming a large meal.

The hostel did not disappoint, the warden, a very capable young woman was extremely friendly and helpful. Our twin room was very comfortable and we soon sorted ourselves out, showered and brewed a pot of tea. We sat outside to drink our tea and chatted with one of the other guests, however that episode was rather short lived. Looking seawards we saw a big squall gradually approaching. As the rain began to obscure the beach we made our move and just in time gained the sanctuary of the common room.

In view of both the weather and the distance to Lochinver we decided to talk to the warden about options for an evening meal. She offered to provide us with a cooked meal, but also suggested that the local taxi might be worth contacting, to see the possibility of travelling in style back to the Pie Shop. For a fee considerably less than we expected, the taxi lady from Lochinver made the double journey, allowing us the real treat of a great meal with no extra effort.

Day 24 Sunday June 11th
Achmelvich Beach to Durness
57 miles
4753ft ascent

A more leisurely start than the previous two days meant we had time to enjoy a good hostel breakfast. The pile of washing willingly taken in by the warden after our arrival, was returned to us clean and dry. The crowning kindness by the warden was to re-thread a drawcord in my cycling tights, a task that had defeated Ian and I the night before. We loaded up the Beast and prepared for what we knew would be quite a hard day. Expecting over 50 miles and a lot of climbing, it turned out to be my second hardest day in respect of altitude gain. The weather looked promising, not sunny but high cloud and the chance of showers. The temperature was not quite as unseasonal as it had been and we both braved shorts, although coats were worn and appreciated on occasions during the day.

We bade farewell to Achmelvich about 10.00am, excited at the prospect of the day's ride, but as with our departure from Berneray, sad that we had not been able to explore this lovely remote corner. The first few miles were retracing our wheel marks to just north of Lochinver. Although the evening before we had been reluctant to cycle back for our dinner, this 5 miles or so is a beautiful ride. With fresh legs we soon were back to the 'main' road and turned left to pastures new. The woods and rushing rivers that had accompanied us from Achmelvich soon gave way to a much more open vista of hills and lochs. Our road headed east, passing to the south of Quinag, one of Assynt's larger hills. To the S.E. we could see the more diminutive, but none the less dramatic forms of Canisp and Suilven. The road runs along the north bank of Loch Assynt, a large loch that arcs eastwards for about 6 miles. A stunning ride, with the loch on our right and to our left, the slopes of Quinag rising majestically over 2000feet to the ridge which links all 5 of its summits. Almost at the end of Loch Assynt we turned left on to the A894 at Skiag Bridge. Then came the first spell of hard work. A long strenuous climb of over 650ft in the next 2 and a half miles, took us up to an altitude of about 850ft. In spite of the expenditure of energy the views were incredible. To our left we now looked over to the other side of Quinag, so different to the south elevation. To our right although being too close to see much of it, the N.W. edge of Assynt's mightiest mountain, Ben More. A fearsome massif that extends for about 12 miles south to north and 4 miles east to west. The access to which is only really feasible from the west side. For the mountain is protected on all other sides by large lochs and extensive tracts of extremely inhospitable wild terrain. At the top of the climb a reprise of a mile as the road ambled to its summit and grand views opened to the north. Then the most exhilarating descent to sea level at Kylesku. Yet again we were blessed with a clear road and Ian was able to give the Beast its head and pick his own line through a scintillating series of sweeping bends and corners. We both tucked as low as we could and like motorcycle riders thrust out knees at the appropriate times. Reaching speeds up to 45mph during the 5 mile descent, we were yet again unable to break Adrian's Peak District record.

Still overflowing with adrenalin we turned off the main road and glided down the bottom end of the old main road to the hotel and ferry slip. Up until 1984 the only route northwards for this most westerly road was to cross, by ferry, the confluence of Lochs Glendhu and Glencoul. The small communities of Kylesku and Kylestrome on the north bank developed as a consequence of this. It was a similar situation to the old Ballachulish ferry, where the A82 Glencoe to Fort William road crossed

Loch Leven. However in both cases the 1980's saw the construction of bridges across these natural barriers, much to the relief of many travellers of the day. At Kylesku a group of small islands separate Lochs Glendhu and Glencoul from Loch a Chairn Bhain, the seaward section of this great sea loch. Now the road sweeps imperiously over the islands and water by means of two bridges, which are both impressive and aesthetically beautiful. In 2004 I walked across these bridges and thence eastwards over the considerable hills that lie to the north of Loch Glendhu. The view from high up looking down on the loch, bridges and road, demonstrated to me that with the right design, modern building and nature can be in harmony.

After the excitement of the morning an early lunch or late tea break was called for. The hotel served that purpose admirably and we enjoyed tea with egg and bacon rolls, while looking out over the loch. Just about 12.00 we set off, back up to the road then right, to take us over the bridges. At sea level there is only one way to go, upwards! A steady climb brought us to a memorial positioned in a view point lay-by above Loch a Chairn Bhain. This is to commemorate the WW2 top secret group that trained in these remote Scottish sea lochs, for their operations with the X craft and human torpedoes. We stopped for a short time to ponder the facts of this lesser known element of the last war. I did have a rudimentary knowledge of this episode of our history, but was very pleased for Ian to fill me in with more detail.

The 9 or 10 miles to Scourie, our next port of call, were comfortable riding. While never too far from the coast any height gain was modest. Nevertheless there was little level road, but no leg straining climbs. Mostly the road undulated between elevations of 100ft and 350ft. Progress could have been quicker but there were several stops, just to enjoy the views. The weather was still kind to us, no rain but 100% cloud cover. Out to the west the sky was a bit lighter but inland, to the east skies were exceedingly grumpy and threatened more than a passing springtime shower. This was my fourth visit to Sutherland and I have yet to see it in any conditions other than those that now prevailed. In a way though it seems almost fitting that this grey, wild, remote and severe landscape should be encased in cloud and not sullied by warmth and blue skies.

Scourie is quite a notable community for this part of Scotland, indeed it is the only village of any size in the 50 miles or so between Ullapool and Durness. Even so, this modest scattering of houses does boast a shop, church, hotel, petrol station, a village hall, public conveniences and even a charging point for electric vehicles. We didn't stop! The road curves clockwise through 270 degrees, following the line of least resistance around a hill and along the edge of a loch. It then leaves the village behind heading N.E. across the rocky watery moors again. Just a few miles out of Scourie we were swooping down a long straight section of road with the kindly S.W. wind helping us on our way, when Ian spotted a cyclist pushing towards us. We stopped and even I could see the poor guy was not in the most chipper state. Ian enquired whether we could help in any way. He answered in the negative and to be brutal, it appeared to us that the only effective help would have been a lift home, followed by two weeks of rest and TLC. He was a guy probably in mid or late 40's, although at the time he looked a lot older than his years. On a cycle camping holiday he had clearly felt it necessary to encumber himself with every gadget of modern camping, together with six complete changes of clothes. Neither Ian nor I had ever seen a cycle so ridiculously overloaded. There were front panniers, rear panniers complete with add-on exterior pockets, a huge bag and tent on top of the rear carrier. As if that was not enough he had a bulging 40 litre rucksack on his back. We politely enquired whether he thought he was a tad overloaded, and he agreed! It was not yet 1.00pm and he complained that his 'legs were gone' such a shame that he had ruined his holiday by not following the absolute basic rule of backpacking/cycle camping and that is to check and check and check again that there is nothing in your bag/s you can do without. After a few minutes of desultory conversation he literally pushed on muttering about getting to Ullapool that evening. We hoped he made it.

Soon after this we pulled off the road into a sheltered lay-by, it was lunchtime! The previous evening before we left the Pie Shop we each chose a pie for the next day's lunch. These were kindly cut in half and the separate halves wrapped in cling film. They were superb and briefly we re-lived the delights of Lochinver pies. Suitably refreshed we carried on and in just a few miles we came to Laxford Bridge, which it is probably fair to say is notable for very little other than being the site of a road junction. Road junctions are a bit like hen's teeth in this part of the country. Here the A894 joins the A838 which comes south from Durness then turns S.E. to Lairg and the east coast. A long route through glens past lochs and hills but still the preferred route from the north-west to the great metropolis of Inverness.

It was on this section that we began to get views to the east of Ben Stack, Arkle and Foinaven, three of Sutherland's more northerly mountains. Although shaded by the shrouds of heavy cloud hanging over them they were still clearly identifiable. The landscape was getting noticeably more wild and rugged now. In the space of about a mile and a half we passed four little roads on our left that all lead for short distances to a number of isolated properties on the edge of an uninhabited peninsular approximately 5 miles by 3 miles, surrounded for the most part by sea or sea loch. Just beyond the head of the sea loch at the tiny community of Rhiconich another road turns off to the left. This leads for about 12 miles along the north bank of Loch Inchard, connecting a string of little communities, the largest of which Kinlochbervie, like Lochinver, still has the remnants of a fishing industry. The road finally runs out of steam some miles further on at Balchrick and Sheigra.

Even though this is a no through road in a remote corner of north-west Scotland it is no stranger to visitors, for Balchrick is the nearest access to Sandwood Bay. A three mile walk across the moor brings the intrepid walker to this jewel in the crown of north-west Scotland. It is a wild, lonely, beautiful place, made even more attractive by the absence of any indication of human intrusion. Leaving Rhiconich we began a long climb of about 500ft. The landscape much more bleak and treeless. This last section of road from Laxford Bridge to the north coast, gradually leads further away from the coast and its moderating climatic influences. Whenever I hear on the weather forecast of severe conditions in the N.W. of Scotland I picture this stretch of road and the desolate moorland below the big hills. A mile or two to our right we passed the northern end of Foinaven beyond which lies Strath Dionard, a dramatic, straight boggy glen that extends south for 5 or 6 miles. On its west side the ridges and corries of Foinaven, to the east a spectacular unbroken ridge issuing from Cranstackie a 2500ft peak in the north and gradually descending to about 1500ft at the southerly end. For the first couple of miles from Rhiconich we looked down to our left on to a river, but as we gained height on to the high moorland, the road gained the security of the big hill to the north and we then looked down to our right on to the river flowing out of Strath Dionard and thence northwards, beyond which was Cranstackie and its associated hills which extended all the way to the north coast. We did stop a couple of times to take in these magnificent views and we did notice that behind us skies were looking very ominous with rain falling back towards Rhiconich. At the high point of the road we had the prospect of a 500+ft descent to the Kyle of Durness. Unlike the other fabulous descents over the last few days this road was dead straight, single track and about 5 miles long. The traffic gods were with us again, a couple of vehicles behind but they could be satisfied to follow us. Ian took up a line in the middle of the road and we were off. A superb ride with the river and estuary central in our field of vision. More or less at the bottom of the descent the road swings across the river to the right side of the glen. The road along the Kyle is quite open and we looked across towards Cape Wrath, all very grey with mist hanging around the tops of the hills. A final short climb brought us into Durness and I do admit to being a bit emotional with the realisation I had pedalled from one end of the UK to the other.

Looking south the rain appeared to be even nearer and we felt we had no time to loose in finding our digs. As it happened the rain never did arrive, which was fortunate because a rather farcical episode was about to start. Durness is not a large village by any stretch of the imagination and they do not go in for street names. Mainly because there are only two roads, the main road and a short-cut across a loop in the main road. Its scattered houses extend for about 3 miles along the main road. We stopped when the navigation app we were using told Ian we had reached the desired postcode. We had pulled up on the forecourt of a rather dilapidated WW2 pre-fabricated single storey building. One end of which looked as though in another life it had been a cafe and there was a wooden structure in front that could at one time have held a sign. We both agreed that we should cycle on a bit further, although I was having a premonition that Ian's locker of leg-pulling ammunition was about to be filled to overflowing. Having got nowhere in our search we stopped by the public hall and Ian 'phoned the B & B. Thence ensued a really strange conversation at the end of which he was little wiser. A bit more pedalling round and another slightly less confusing call later and it was established that the WW2 pre-fab was indeed our abode for the next two nights. The lady of the house was extremely kindly if somewhat distracted and we were duly shown to our room. Unsurprisingly we found we were the only guests! Our two night stay was memorable for not always the most desirable reasons. We were provided with two hearty breakfasts and the bedding appeared to be fresh and clean, but Ian did say as we walked off to find an evening meal, "Bob consider yourself lucky that you cannot see the state of the shower and toilet". Ali did admit later that when she made the booking for us she had experienced a really strange conversation with the lady, and suspected things might be a bit odd.

Already Ian has on occasions raised the subject of 'the Durness B&B', to my discomfort, but in the great scheme of things it has provided us with something to laugh and josh about and is all part of life's rich tapestry.

Durness does hold particularly bitter sweet memories for me. My first visit in 2004 happened because it was the finishing point of my Cape Wrath Trail. Cape Wrath and that corner of Sutherland, most of the land north and west of the A838, is under the control of the MoD. When not in use as a firing range it is open to public access. Between May and October a minibus service does take tourists from the Kyle of Durness to Cape Wrath. This is not as straightforward as it may appear because the whole area is inaccessible. The only possible access is by ferry across the Kyle and then a 10 - 12 mile route on what is now a very rutty and pot-holed military road to the Cape. That sounds all good and dandy, until it is revealed that even at the time of writing, the 'ferry' is a small RIB powered by outboard motor. The minibuses are taken over in the spring and stay there all summer.

In 2004 my carefully arranged plan was to approach from Rhiconich, Balchrick and Sandwood Bay then the last few miles up the coast to Cape Wrath. If I spent the last night just above Sandwood Bay I would be able reach the Cape by mid morning, thus giving enough time for the minibus and walk up into Durness to catch the coach to Inverness at 3.15pm.

The last few days of my backpacking trip had been rather stormy, especially the last night which fortunately I had spent in a bothy. When I reached Cape Wrath, about mid morning as planned, there was no sight of either mini-bus or tourists. Somewhat perplexed, after having a look round and taken photos I started to walk along the road, hoping before too long to meet the minibus.

There was no mobile signal so I had no means of ascertaining the problem. About halfway back to the ferry I was able to ring Donny the minibus man. To my dismay he told me that the conditions in the Kyle made it impossible for the ferryman to operate, not only that but because of the forecast it was uncertain when he would resume operations.

This was a real blow and for a while I struggled to take in all the implications. After having endured some pretty bad weather for the last three days, I then had the euphoria of reaching my goal, only then to have my 'escape plan' shot down in flames. My remaining food stock consisted of two squares of chocolate and a very small handful of nuts and dried fruit. A study of the map showed that it may be possible to gain access to the A838 some way south of the head of the Kyle, but the terrain between there and the ferry point could well prove challenging and I reckoned could take at least 3 hours. A couple of hours later I looked down to the estuary and saw that the tide was fairly low. As I neared the ferry slip I could see the whole of the estuary and the wide expanses of golden sand. Perhaps I could walk across!

About an hour later I was stood in a lay-by on the main road, drying my feet and chatting to an elderly local who I had noticed during my crossing, sat in his van watching my progress. He sagely told me I was lucky because 'there are quick sands out there!'

....

The following morning Ian and I cycled down to the little ferry slip at the mouth of the Kyle and joined the throng of tourists waiting for the ferryman. Ali and I made the trip to Cape Wrath in 2015 so I knew what to expect. We bumped our way over the moors for an hour or so and listened to the very informative and amusing commentary by the driver. The Cape is a lonely and exposed place and it is not difficult to appreciate why many sailors especially yachtsmen will wait for favourable weather before sailing around the north coast. For such a remote place there are a surprising number of buildings here. The lighthouse with its mighty foghorn, now fully automated required a considerable staff at one time. There is also another large deserted building some distance away which was (and still may be!) used by the MoD.

So that was the 'cape to cape' element of my adventure completed, although we still had 5 days and 200+ miles to go. The rest of the day was spent eating, drinking and exploring the Smoo caves, just on the edge of the village.

No mention of otters has been made for the last few days. Whenever we came across a suitably 'otter friendly' place we would search in vain for signs of these elusive mammals. Ian kept muttering darkly about how I had promised that we would see some. I probably did not help matters by suggesting that after these fruitless observations I expected a whole family of otters would emerge, waving at our receding backs.

Day 25 Tuesday June 13th
Durness to Armadale
49 miles
3637ft ascent

Ever since Mark and I set wheels on Scottish soil two weeks earlier, the weather had not really been consistent from one day to the next. When Ian arrived at Fort William, armed with the best forecast money could buy, he confirmed the likelihood of the unsettled spell continuing for possibly a couple of weeks, as a series of low pressure systems rolled over us from the Atlantic. Certainly when Ian and I checked the forecast on the evening before leaving Durness there was very little from which to draw any comfort, predicting rain till early afternoon. This was confirmed this morning when we opened the curtains of our south facing bedroom, which looked out across the road to the moors and distant hills. There were no hills, very little moor and the road contained puddles, the surfaces of which were being disturbed by the light rain.

For the umpteenth time since my trip began the morning sorting and loading of the Beast was done in the wet. We posed for a photo outside and noticed that the previously missing sign had been refitted, proudly advertising Cafe and B & B. We set off in a drizzle but both of us keen to make a start on the second half of the north of Scotland section. Ali and I had driven along the north coast in 2015 so I was prepared for the very hilly road that lay ahead. Soon after leaving Durness we cycled past two beautiful white sand beaches. We were helped on our way by quite a brisk south-westerly wind. After 3 miles or so the road began bearing to the right as we approached Loch Eriboll, a large sea loch which extends for 7 or 8 miles SSW. By now the road was at an elevation of only about 150ft but the surrounding moorland was exceedingly bleak and cheerless. It is certainly a noticeable feature in these northern parts that at low level in a sheltered situation, some trees and shrubs can live quite happily. However even a modest gain of altitude generally means that due to the exposure to strong cold winds, very little in the way of half hardy vegetation can exist. There are dramatic views up the loch and to the hills beyond. We were encouraged that we could see them and also the drizzle had stopped. We contoured along above the loch, but the downside of our elevated position and grand view was that the prevailing wind now had us fully in its sights. Although the clouds were higher we were disturbed to see that the head of the loch and beyond was obscured by a big rain shower. The next few miles were really hard work and we struggled at times to make 9 or 10 mph. When at last we descended to cross the head of the loch the rain had moved on. Not for the last time during this day, showers that sometimes were quite close, very graciously passed us by. Progress improved markedly as we turned north. With the wind behind us on occasions we were rolling along at over 20mph without too much effort. The road on the east side of Loch Eriboll takes a course at low level along the base of a rather spectacular ridge that for most of the way to the north coast rises to between 800ft and 1000+ft. Some way along we pulled in to a lay-by where there is an information board which details the part Loch Eriboll played at the end of WW2. Being a wide, deep and relatively sheltered expanse of water it became the location of one of the strangest episodes towards the end of WW2. During the space of two weeks from May 10th to 25th 1945, German U boats began to gather here prior to surrender. In all, 33 vessels, the largest gathering of the German submarine fleet at any time, anywhere in the world. Following the surrender the submarines were sailed out into the Atlantic and scuttled.

Towards the seaward end of the loch the road begins bearing east again and in a sequence of 4 short steep climbs and a number of longer leg strainers, rises from sea-level to over 700ft. By now we had been cycling for over 2 hours, so once over the high point stopped for a short break. Visibility now was better than it had been for two days, with a fair amount of blue sky. The weather was clearly still very unpredictable but at least for a short time we enjoyed the southerly panorama of moor and mountains. Duly refreshed we wheeled away on the 3 or 4 mile descent to the Kyle of Tongue. Here the road crosses the Kyle on a mile long causeway. Then immediately up a steep hill past the village of Tongue and thence onwards to contour at about 250ft around Ben Tongue a substantial hill nearly 1000ft high whose twin peaks must make quite an imposing sight when viewed from the sea. Part way up the hill we stopped at The Ben Lomond Hotel for lunch and the first pot of tea.

We continued east across another section of high moor interspersed with several lochans. Then a descent to Borge Bridge and another long hard climb and a couple of miles across the moor to yet another high speed descent to the River Naver. Here the road turns sharply north to descend the escarpment into the river valley. Just a mile beyond the bridge over the River Naver we came to Betty Hill, one of the few communities in this long north coast road. In spite of the many climbs of the day we had made good time, so we had decided that should the opportunity present itself we would stop for another break. True to form

Ian spotted the Tourist Information Centre which also served as a cafe. Here we enjoyed our second pot of tea, scones, cream and jam. The scones were superb, real fresh baked delicacies and we had no hesitation in honouring the cafe our prestigious 'best scones of the trip' award.

Betty Hill is a seaside village but there is only a distant view of the bay and little to suggest that it attracts many holiday makers. We set off on the last leg of the day's ride with only 5 or 6 miles to our next B&B. It was though a fairly demanding ride. Heading east out of the village the road quickly climbs 400ft up on to the moor once again. Just a couple of miles over the moor then a final descent. Ian found the guest house and we pulled up on the drive of Armadale House. After the experience of the Durness accommodation we were perhaps rather on the defence and alarmed at the first impression. The house was a rather grand 19th century country house the exterior of which was in need of some attention. Closer inspection revealed scaffolding on one elevation indicating that attention was already in hand. The interior of the house had been beautifully and tastefully restored by the Dutch lady who had bought the property.

When I booked the room she told me there was no hotel or restaurant in the vicinity but she would be pleased to provide an evening meal. She did us proud with just the sort of food cyclists need after a day of hills. Mince and tatties, a really tasty beef mince stew, sliced gherkins (a Dutch delicacy apparently) and a huge bowl of boiled Scottish potatoes. A bottle of good red wine and a tasty sweet dish made the meal perfect. Had the evening been warm sunny and June-like we may have been tempted to walk the half mile or so to Armadale Bay, but a chilly breeze and cloud made it a more appealing option to just sit there, chat and finish the wine!

Day 26 Wednesday 14th
Armadale to Thurso
53 miles
2972ft ascent

We bade farewell to our lovely Dutch hostess at 9.50 and headed east again on the A836. The weather looked more promising than it had the previous morning. Clouds were high and broken, revealing a rather hesitant sun on occasions. The stiffish southerly breeze was still with us, which would not be welcome if it persisted for our run south to Inverness. At least it was a warm wind, unlike that which had accompanied us for most of the time. The day's ride was to be a day of bays, six in all, although we did not always get particularly good views of them. Armadale Bay adjacent to our B&B was the first, to be followed by Strathy Bay, Melvich Bay, Sandside Bay, Thurso Bay and Dunnet Bay.

We cycled across the two rivers that flow north into Armadale Bay then the first climb of the day, 300ft up on to the moor for 2 or 3 miles then down again to Strathy. The up and down process repeated itself to our third bay and the village of Melvich. As we climbed out of Strathy we both noticed that although we were still ascending to about 300ft the climbs were less steep and a much more favourable gradient. The third climb from Melvich confirmed this observation and proved to be the final large climb on our trip eastwards. As we headed further east the big hills were losing their influence. The Sutherland hills that had been so much in evidence to the south on our ride from Durness, had given way to the great expanses of the Flow Country of Sutherland and Caithness. The descent to Sandside Bay and the village of Reay brought us to a choice of routes for the next 10 miles or so to Thurso. For only the second time since leaving Ullapool we could choose to either stay on the main road or take a 'yellow road' alternative.

Ian and I had been slightly apprehensive about the amount of "A" road cycling but since the Isle of Skye we had encountered no real problems on the roads. The road surfaces were good and apart from the single track section up to Durness roads were of an adequate width, allowing traffic to pass comfortably. Nevertheless we did enjoy the yellow road to Thurso. The countryside now was much less spectacular. Moors were giving way to farmland and within the space of just a few miles, west of Thurso the transition was complete. I suspect this is due to a change in geology as well as a slightly less harsh climate.

For hundreds of miles of Scottish roads with first Mark then Ian we had got used to a seemingly endless, ever changing panorama of visual delights. Mountains, hills, lochs and rivers, stoney foreshores and white sand beaches, headlands, cliffs and rocky islands, banks of gorse and wilderness woodland, rushy streams and splashing waterfalls, had all regaled us for mile after breathtaking mile. Now a gentler, more down to earth landscape similar to that of Galloway prevailed. It was like a gourmet on a diet of nourishing wholefood after feasting on rich exotic delicacies for days on end.

The ride to Thurso was easy and relaxed, unsettlingly flat, we kept worrying about where the next hill would be. A rather unusual feature in this area is the way of separating fields. Instead of dry stone walls or hedges, huge flakes of slate like stone are set side by side vertically in the ground, creating a barrier resembling what is done in some graveyards now when all the headstones are removed from the graves and leant against a boundary bank. Another feature of the latter part of the morning's ride were the wind turbines along the coast. Like an army of skeletal sentinels, continuously conducting a semaphore conversation with each other.

We had made good time and arrived in Thurso shortly after midday. Our plan was to carry on to Dunnet Head for our most northerly photocall. Then we would be all set to head south the next morning. Ian soon found the Backpackers Hostel and although the advertised time for check-in was 5.00pm a very accommodating member of staff signed us in and gave us access to our room. Having lightened our load to the tune of two panniers we set off for Castletown where we hoped to find some lunch. We hove to outside a rather smart hotel and unabashed entered and enquired regarding lunch. We were amused by their reaction, as they ushered us as far away as possible from the prying eyes in the restaurant and showed us to a backwater of the bar area. Later some adjoining tables were occupied by very smart looking businessmen, but we didn't really mind! Their obvious reservations about our lack of sartorial elegance was not reflected in their service and we enjoyed a splendid lunch.

Dunnet Head is the true most northerly point of the UK mainland, being a couple of miles further north than John O' Groats and about 10 miles further to the west. It protrudes from the north coast rather like a crooked thumb and enclosed on the western side is Dunnet Bay the last of the six. Cycling from Castletown we soon came to the beach. The road follows the beach for two miles then begins the gradual climb on to the headland. Dunnet Bay is about 2 miles wide and 3 miles deep, going from the beach to the point where it starts to widen. It faces north-west, so for millenia has acted like a giant trawl net, trapping the sand and sediment driven eastwards by sea and prevailing wind. Huge sand dunes have resulted fringing the beach for the whole of its length. The afternoon weather had closed in, no more sunny spells. Visibility was still good but the cloud was heavier and the wind had a bit more urgency about it, as if to say 'if you don't seek shelter soon I can't be held responsible for the consequences'.

The headland rises to about 400ft above sea level and the last few hundred yards were quite a steep climb before its wide grassy windswept extremity with the lighthouse and car park. We stopped and parked the Beast leaning against a rather smart monolith which advised visitors that they were on Dunnet Head etc.. We posed there, adopting our best 'we have cycled from one end of the kingdom to the other' pose and a kind German lady did the honours. Nearby is a viewing point overlooking a section of cliff face where a large number of Dunnet Head's huge sea bird colony could be seen. We saw guillemots, razorbills, fulmars, kittiwakes, puffins, several species of sea gull, skuas and gannets patrolling out to sea. Walking a few hundred yards across the headland to the east side we found another far superior vantage point. Here we looked on to a much wider and closer section of cliff. Thousands of sea birds nest here and being the height of the nesting season the air was full of birds either returning to their nest sites with food or just off for a spot of fishing. When we were able to divert our attention from the cliffs and the birds we had the Orkney Isles to look at. Of the larger islands South Ronaldsay and Hoy are the nearest, being only a few miles from Dunnet Head. When we first looked over to The Orkneys before lunch we could plainly see The Old Man of Hoy just off its west side. We spent well over an hour sightseeing but for a while had been aware of a band of rain to the west. It seemed to be gradually heading our way so we decided to head back to Thurso. We had a fabulous descent to the beach then in spite of the headwind made very good time back to the hostel. Once again we escaped the rain and with the Beast happily stabled enjoyed tea and biscuits in the hostel common room.

Day 27 Thursday 15th
Thurso to Helmsdale
54 miles
2079ft ascent

All the hostels in Scotland that we used operated a system that included a DIY breakfast in the cost of the room. Up until Thurso the other hostels whether SYHA or private concerns had provided the wherewithal for a decent basic meal, in the form of cereal, fruit, bread, cheese, marmalade, jam, tea and coffee. Although the accommodation was good at Thurso the necessary comestibles were limited in both choice and quantity. Our ability to find a half decent breakfast was further hampered by the arrival in the kitchen shortly after us, of a family, who on finding no sun loungers and towels to commandeer proceeded to monopolise use of all kettles and toasters.

Before we could load up the Beast Ian did a bit of maintenance on the bike. He had noticed that both front and rear brake blocks were pretty worn, so these were duly replaced. The weather was its normal grumpy noncommital self, with full cloud cover that was reasonably high but gave no confidence that it would stay that way. The wind if anything had strengthened into a pretty brisk south-westerly. The first 15 miles or so were retracing our wheel marks to Melvich, where we would turn left to head south on the A897, which would take us all the way to Helmsdale. We cycled out of Thurso on the B874, the little yellow road. In spite of the wind on our port side with fresh legs we made good time to Reay where we joined the A836 for the last few miles to Melvich. We waved goodbye to the wind turbines but they were too busy frantically signalling to each other to notice us. As soon as we turned south we felt the full impact of the wind and we realised that we were in for a bit of a slog. The A897 is a good indicator of the remote nature of this very sparsely populated extremity of the UK. It extends about 40 miles from Melvich on the north coast to Helmsdale on the east coast, where it joins the A9. Apart from isolated farms and houses there are only two communities along this road, Forsinard and Kinbrace. Both of these are close to the Inverness to Wick railway, which helps to keep them in touch with civilisation. Anyone employed to maintain 'give way' signs and repaint white lines at road junctions would have a pretty easy job, for there is only one road junction. That is at Kinbrace where the B871 leaves the safety of the A897 to wander for many miles west and north across the Flow Country, until with great relief it eventually joins another 'B' road in the middle of nowhere. From there the intrepid traveller can either scuttle north to Betty Hill or turn south for a long and scenic route to Lairg and ultimately Inverness.

The gradient of the road is very gentle, rising from about 100ft above sea level at Melvich to about 650ft at the watershed just south of Forsinard. Climbing 550ft in over 12 miles is not too much of a challenge. The wind while not gale force by any means, was an energy sapping wind and we really began to feel its effect after a short distance. The road follows the Halladale River on its east bank for 8 or 9 miles then crosses to the west side for the last 3 or 4 miles to Forsinard. Initially the valley is almost pastoral in appearance with farms and fields but gradually fields give way to moorland and although there are farms all the way, they become more widespread and the countryside more exposed and bleak. Ali and I had driven down to Helmsdale in 2015 and I was struck then by the transition in the landscape. I can remember thinking what a splendid road to cycle, easy to say from the sheltered comfort of a car! Indeed had it not been for the headwind we would both have enjoyed the ride far more. Although this area cannot compete with the dramatic scenery of mountains and coast the Flow Country has a wild beauty that is relatively unspoilt. Unfortunately human activity in the form of inappropriate use of the land as an investment opportunity has resulted in large areas having been used for timber production.

The RSPB has a large field station at Forsinard and we were hoping to meet up with the brother of a friend of mine who had worked for the RSPB for many years. For the last few years he had spent a good deal of his time at Forsinard working on a scientific project to restore previously drained forestry land to the original peat bogs. Earlier that morning we had arranged to meet him at lunchtime but were not quite sure what prospects there would be for lunch. The last few calories of our rather meagre breakfast had long since burned off. We were running on empty and it was telling on both our strength and humour. We found the last few miles really hard as the gradient was steeper and the headwind had became more bothersome the higher we climbed. To our great relief we found a little cafe adjacent to the railway station. It was just a wooden summer house in the garden of a house, large enough to seat about a dozen people. We 'phoned Trevor to let him know we had arrived and he said that he and a couple of colleagues would join us for lunch. There being no other lunch seekers, the five of us sat in the little tearoom and talked about their work and also our ride. It was a most illuminating conversation with the three of them explaining the scientific background, practical implications and funding issues of this most fascinating project. They reckoned that it would be at least 30 years before a realistic assessment could be made on its success or otherwise. All too soon they had to get back to work and we needed to put feet to pedals. We decided to have a quick look at the RSPB field centre which was set up in the station building. Lucky we did so because only a few minutes later the heavens opened and not for the first time we avoided a drenching. Just a short distance beyond the station the RSPB have built a large hide out on the boggy moorland about quarter of a mile from the road. It is accessed by a wooden boardwalk and had the weather been more favourable we would have happily spent some time there.

The high point on the road from Melvich to Helmsdale is only about a mile and a half from Forsinard, so by rights shortly after setting off again we should have felt the benefit of cycling downhill. For a good half an hour it seemed as though we were still going uphill. By the time we reached Kinbrace we had lost about 200ft of elevation and the wind was not quite such an impedance and at last we were rolling. We passed Loch an Ruathair on our right from which flows the Bannock Burn, the other one! Just below Kinbrace it loses its identity as it teams up with the River Helmsdale. We followed the river and railway all the way to the coast. The terrain below Forsinard is not so wild as the northern section, there is more woodland and noticeably more farms and dwellings, which suggests that the climate is more moderate away from the north coast. The surrounding country is more hilly than the moorland further north. The valley becomes gradually more defined as it begins to turn to the east, with steeper sides rising to the hills above. Cycling was easy now, downhill and even getting a bit of a push from the wind we made really good progress.

The last 3 miles are quite dramatic, where the river has forced its way through the substantial hills. The valley turns to the south again and then a final kink eastwards, which means that the view does not open out to the sea until the last few hundred yards before reaching Helmsdale. The village is restricted to the level ground to either side of the mouth of the river, here also the A9 pushes its way northwards. Our accommodation for the night was at the Bannockburn Inn, a comfortable old pub in the centre of the village.

The subject of otters was back on the agenda, after Ian was told in the pub that they could sometimes be seen at dusk in the mouth of the river. After our meal we did walk down to the sea and then back along a riverside path. It was a chilly evening so I left Ian to his otter spotting and returned to our room. Yet again he was to be disappointed, clearly the Scottish otters had not read the bit in the script where it said 'enter otters, stage left, waving and dancing'.

Day 28 Friday 16th
Helmsdale to Cromarty
53 miles
2062ft ascent

Apart from being yet another otter-free zone, Helmsdale proved to be a very satisfactory stop-over. We were on the road by 9.20 to start the one section that neither of us were looking forward to. The downside of the route we had followed thus far was that there was no alternative to the A9 for part of the ride to Cromarty. At least the weather was dry when we started. Similar to so many other days, 100% cloud cover, high but not without the threat of rain.

The A9 follows the east coast pretty closely from further north down to Inverness. The coastal strip is quite narrow but wide enough for the road to avoid climbing over the big hills which sometimes rise up from immediately next to the road. With only fairly gentle undulations most of the time we made swift progress and covered the 22 miles to Loch Fleet in under 2 hours. Although traffic was not too heavy it still sped past at an alarming speed on occasions. Very bravely Ian maintained our riding technique of positioning ourselves further in to the carriageway. As before we sensed that it did make drivers slow down a bit and at least gave us more thought than they probably would have done if we had been on the extreme outside. Nevertheless it was not a pleasant start to the day and it was with great relief that we turned left on to a minor road by Loch Fleet.

The main road runs close to the water around the head of the loch, then just at the point where it begins a 300ft climb over a wooded hill, a tempting little yellow road diverges to continue along the loch side. Within just a couple of hundred yards Ian spotted some seals out on a sandbank. We stopped and the first thing we noticed was the silence. It was as though we had passed through a portal into a parallel universe. We drank in the peace and quiet, gradually relaxing from the tensions of the A9. Just a short way further on we stopped again, this time a much larger group of seals spread over two sandbanks the nearest being less than 50 yards away. This time Ian found his binoculars and counted well over 100 seals including pups: the only sounds to break the silence were the occasional grunts and barks of the contented seals. Once again Ian's ottery expectations were raised as it did seem to be an ideal environment for these elusive mammals.

Having dallied for about half an hour, but feeling much more at peace with the world we continued on our way. After about two and a half miles the road leaves the loch side to cross a flat and unmemorable peninsular for about 3 miles to Dornoch.

We parked up in the middle of town, it was midday so an early lunch was not out of the question. Dornoch is certainly an interesting looking place with many old buildings which clearly had quite an historical story to tell, but it is very touristy. After twenty minutes or so of wandering we decided to ride on to Tain for lunch. After 3 miles cycling west fairly close to the sands of Dornoch Firth, we were forced to briefly re-establish our rather strained relationship with the A9. Four miles on the A9 took us across the bridge over Dornoch Firth to the turning left to Tain, in no time at all we had found a cafe and were all set for lunch. What a splendid lunch it was! Ham omelette with a large quantity of cheesy garlic bread on the side and the inevitable pots of tea. Just after 2.00pm we emerged from the cafe warm and replete, but even before we had put foot to pedal, it started to rain! This last section of the great tandem adventure had proved a bit of a challenge. Although this run in to Inverness did present a few options other than the A9, nothing really seemed a fitting conclusion to the ride. Until we established there was a little summer only vehicle ferry across the narrow mouth of the Cromarty Firth. Moreover it had the wonderful name of the Nig ferry, how on earth could we not use this as the eleventh and final ferry of the trip. Everything was right about this. It would give us a 50+ mile run from Helmsdale, we could stay the night in the village of Cromarty and then have just about a 30mile ride to Inverness on the final day. This would allow ample time to check the Beast in to the cycle shop who were to pack it prior to despatching it home.

From Tain our yellow road headed east then south across a rather flat and unspectacular peninsular that protrudes into the Moray Firth, made even less appealing by the grey lowering skies and the chilly rain. We arrived at the ferry slip just after 3.00pm. As we approached we were mystified by the sight of narrow steel towers in close formation reaching heavenwards. Once we were out on the water we could see that they were the retracted legs of drilling platforms and there were quite a number of them laid up along the foreshore of the Firth.

Our B&B was only a few wheel turns from the ferry and before 4.00pm we checked in to a very comfortable little guesthouse, where we received a warm welcome, complete with tea and homemade cake. Later, a walk around the village and waterfront revealed some of the history of this small settlement at the northern tip of the Black Isle. In earlier times when the Cromarty Firth had been of great significance to the Home Fleet Cromarty had been an important administration centre accommodating a considerable number of naval personnel. There are many very interesting old buildings and both Ian and I agreed that Cromarty warranted another visit to learn more of its fascinating history.

Day 29 Saturday 17th
Cromarty to Inverness
32 miles
2111ft ascent

We set off on our final ride at 10.00am, the weather was sunny, chilly and very windy. The wind gods that had smiled benevolently upon us for most of the trip had certainly forsaken us over the last few days. The south-westerlies that had been favourable to us were now stronger than at any time and really 'in our face'. Not far out of the village we began the last big climb, 700+ft over the ridge that forms the spine of the Black Isle. It was a steady climb and maybe because we were in fairly good trim, an extremely enjoyable one. As we climbed, on the north side of the ridge, the view to the north gradually opened up, so as we ascended we kept getting tantalising views through field gates and from open stretches of road. At the top we were rewarded with the full majesty of the views, not quite panoramic, but good enough. To the south and east the sparkling waters of the Moray Firth, beyond which lay Aberdeenshire. To the north Cromarty Firth and stretching into the distance the hills and moors of the Flow country.

The Black Isle is rather a misnomer, it is in fact firmly attached to the mainland. Apparently the derivation of 'Black Isle' refers to the nature of the very dark and extremely fertile soil. On the ride from Cromarty to Inverness evidence of this was all around us with field after field of amazingly verdant potato plants and other crops. Although on the ride from Helmsdale we passed many farms and gardens the Black Isle appeared to be so much more fertile. We had not seen such productive farmland and colourful gardens since leaving England.

At breakfast we had talked to the couple who ran the B&B about our singular lack of success in the otter-spotting department. The conversation then moved sideways and they told us of the delights that could be seen at Cromarty Point. Probably no otters but a very good chance of seeing dolphins. As it would be only a short diversion Ian suggested we take the opportunity as at least it may ameliorate the disappointment caused by the non-appearance of the otters. From the ridge we had a great descent to Rosemarkie on the south-east coast from where it was only a couple of miles along the narrow spit of land to Cromarty Point. The Moray Firth is an extensive area of water. The outer part washes the coasts of Caithness and Aberdeenshire, it then narrows at Cromarty Point for another 8 miles or so to Inverness. Almost opposite Cromarty Point on the other bank is Fort George, on another spit of land. Together the two points form a pair of sandy mandibles in the mouth of the Moray Firth, constricting the width from 3 miles to no more than half a mile.

From Rosemarkie we found the minor road that goes south-east to the point. A dispiriting two mile cycle with the fierce crosswind. Beating our way past the golf course and a wide selection of holiday retreats we eventually hove to in the car park. This is clearly a location favoured by fresh air lovers and dog walkers, as well as dolphin lovers and lapsed otter watchers. In Winnie The Poo there is a wonderful description of Piglet in a storm, 'his ears blowing behind him like banners in the wind'. As we joined the many people enjoying the salty there were indeed many banners in the form of ears, hair and scarves. Armed with binoculars Ian soon spotted a pod of 5 or 6 dolphins swimming and breaching as they headed seawards less than 50 yards from the shore.

We cycled back up towards Rosemarkie but turned left to its twin village Fortrose. The ride to and from the point was a clear demonstration of the effects of a side wind. Going north-west was just as hard work as the outward leg. Its a phenomena that any cyclist will confirm and most sailors of sail vessels will probably be able to explain. We climbed back towards the ridge but then turned south-west to contour along before turning south-east for a brief and final re-acquaintance with the A9. For the last few miles to Inverness we had the luxury of a dedicated cycle-way alongside the main road, which was just as well as the volume of traffic on this section was pretty intimidating.

The Kessock Bridge is a splendid, handsome piece of engineering, taking the A9 across the narrow gap where the Moray Firth squeezes through to become the Beauly Firth. The northern end is higher than the Inverness end so we had a downhill cycle not that we could enjoy that aspect of the crossing. The crosswind was ferocious and quite scary nevertheless it was an exhilarating experience with magnificent views. Later in the day Ian established through the wonders of the internet, that at the time we crossed the bridge sea-level winds of 30mph were recorded at Inverness airport about 6 miles away.

That was to be the last bit of excitement at the end of an incredible 1500 mile cycle ride. Ian navigated us straight to Bikes of Inverness and in no time at all the Beast was unloaded and wheeled in to a storage shed behind the shop, where in due course it would be packed up ready for the journey south. It was a very poignant moment walking outside and leaving my wheeled companion in its solitude.

....

None of this would have been possible without the help of 5 remarkable people. Firstly and most importantly my wife Ali, who for many years has supported and encouraged me before and during numerous adventures, most of which were solo trips to remote parts of the Scottish Highlands.

Then there are the 4 people that made my last trip possible. My particular heartfelt thanks go to the pilots 4. Their cycling and navigating skills took us safely from one end of the UK to the other, by a very demanding circuitous and wonderful route, averaging 55 miles and 3000ft ascent every day.

The Beast returned home 6 days after leaving it at Inverness and Adrian kindly helped in re-attaching all the various bits and pieces that had been removed to facilitate its safe transportation.

8. Appendix

After the first short trip to The Cairngorms I drew up a list of kit and food that remained more or less the same for subsequent trips

Clothes
- 2 pairs Smart wool socks
- 2 pairs Smart wool extra thick socks
- 2 pairs Smart wool liner socks
- Zip-off trousers
- 2 Merino wool short sleeved vests
- 2 pairs Lowe Alpine pants
- Thin Pertex windproof jacket
- Paramo Viento jacket
- Paramo Alta jacket
- Paramo waterproof trousers
- Teva slip-on shoes – designed for use in water
- Brasher boots (leather) + spare laces
- Lowe Alpine hat – with fold down ear flaps
- Gore-tex gloves and liners
- Gore-tex gaiters
- Baseball cap

Equipment
- Sleeping Bag – Softie 12 Osprey + silk liner
- Tent – 1 man Single hoop (£50)
- Thermarest mat full length medium weight
- MSR Dragonfly stove + fuel bottle + 2 x 500ml Coleman fuel
- 3 boxes matches + 2 lighters
- Whisky flask + malt whisky
- Plastic mug + teaspoon + desert spoon
- 2 x compasses Silva
- 2 x whistles
- ½ litre stainless steel billy
- 35mm Nikon idiot proof camera
- Karrimor 100L Independence rucksack + 2L hydration system
- Large waterproof liner
- 2L Platypus water bladder
- Aqua Mira water purifier
- Foil emergency blanket
- Mobile phone
- Note book + pencil + pen

- O.S. 1:50000 maps – 33,25,19,15,9, + photocopies of bits from 41,34,20
- Torch/emergency beacon light
- Tissues + toilet paper
- Mountain Suds liquid soap
- Leki pole (knob type which doubles as camera stand)
- Antiseptic handrub
- P60 sun cream
- E45 sunblock
- Lip salve
- Ortleib bowl + Paramo towel
- First-aid kit :- tick twister, antiseptic wipes, antistan cream, compeed blister plasters, savlon, plasters and lint, nailclippers, file.
- Swiss Army knife + nylon cord + approx 1 metre gaffer tape (wound round soap bottle)
- Sundry different size sealable poly bags

Food

approximate daily ration
- 60/70grams Oatsosimple with muscavado sugar and milk powder
- 100grams soluble energy powder
- 1 x 500gram Real freeze dried meal
- 2 x tea bags + powder milk
- 80grams 70% chocolate
- 40/50grams cous-cous
- Mueslibar / sesame seed snap / energy bar
- 1 portion dried tomato soup powder
- 100grams mixed nuts and dried fruit
- 100grams dry roasted pumpkin seeds

....

Five Men on a Bike - Spoke Story

Day 3 - late- 1st broken spoke discovered in rear wheel while the Beast was being washed

Day 4 - early- phoned Thorn, OK to call in later and get spoke replaced. Reached Thorn in Bridgwater at lunchtime waited for them to do the necessary. They gave us 6 extra spare spokes.

Day 8 - 2nd broken spoke discovered at Worcester before setting off in the morning. Adrian bought spoke key from cycle shop next door and replaced spoke, without spending time checking wheel.

3rd broken spoke discovered when we stopped for lunch. Adrian spent an hour or so sat in a pub garden replacing and trueing wheel.

Day 9 - morning, we phoned Thorn while having a break at Stone, Adrian had long discussion with them over possible courses of action. They agreed to post a complete set of new spokes to our friends in Settle, where we would arrive on Day 11.

Day 10 - 4th broken spoke discovered midday, in the Peak District. We found a nice wide verge in the shade and Adrian spent nearly 2 hours on the repair.

Day 11 - arrived in Settle late afternoon to find parcel of spokes had been delivered that morning, thank you Thorn.

Day 12 - (day off) Adrian spent all day rebuilding the wheel.

No further problems.

....

Grand Total stats for the tandem ride - according to Strava

1492 Miles
86439 feet of ascent

This represents 58 feet of climbing for every mile covered.

Lightning Source UK Ltd.
Milton Keynes UK
UKHW010108180820
368392UK00001B/33

9 781839 451942